BEYOND
IMAGE
AND
CONVENTION

Southern
Women

A series of books developed from the Southern Conference on Women's History sponsored by the Southern Association for Women Historians.

edited by

Virginia Bernhard

Betty Brandon

Elizabeth Fox-Genovese

Theda Perdue

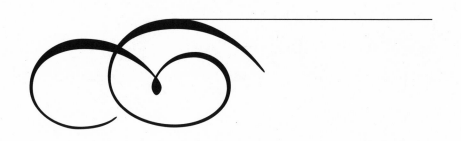

BEYOND IMAGE AND CONVENTION

Explorations in Southern Women's History

edited by

Janet L. Coryell

Martha H. Swain

Sandra Gioia Treadway

Elizabeth Hayes Turner

UNIVERSITY OF MISSOURI PRESS

COLUMBIA AND LONDON

Library of Congress Cataloging-in-Publication Data

Beyond image and convention : explorations in southern women's history
    / edited by Janet Lee Coryell . . . [et al.].
        p.   cm.—(Southern women)
    Includes index.
    ISBN 0-8262-1172-0 (alk. paper).—ISBN 0-8262-1173-9 (pbk. :
alk. paper)
    1. Women—Southern States—History.   2. Afro-American women—
Southern States—History.   I. Coryell, Janet L., 1955–   .
II. Series.
HQ1438.S63B48   1998
305.4'0975—dc21   98-6206
                                                                          CIP

Designer: Stephanie Foley
Typesetter: BookComp, Inc.
Printer and Binder: Thomson-Shore, Inc.
Typeface: Giovanni

DEDICATED TO WOMEN
WHO SURVIVE LIFE CHANGES
AND STRIVE TO CONTINUE
AND SUCCEED

Contents

Editors' Introduction 1

"Common Disturbers of the Peace": The Politics of
    White Women's Sexual Misconduct in Colonial
    North Carolina
    KIRSTEN FISCHER 10

Between Mistress and Slave: Elizabeth Wirt's White
    Housekeepers, 1808–1825
    ANYA JABOUR 28

Enthusiasm, Possession, and Madness: Gender and the
    Opposition to Methodism in the South, 1770–1810
    CYNTHIA LYNN LYERLY 53

Making the Most of Life's Opportunities: A Slave
    Woman and Her Family in Abingdon, Virginia
    NORMA TAYLOR MITCHELL 74

Her Will against Theirs: Eda Hickam and the Ambiguity
    of Freedom in Postbellum Missouri
    KIMBERLY SCHRECK 99

Half My Heart in Dixie: Southern Identity and the Civil
    War in the Writings of Mary Virginia Terhune
    KAREN MANNERS SMITH 119

Making the Connection: Public Health Policy and Black
 Women's Volunteer Work
 SUSAN L. SMITH 138

Sarah Patton Boyle's Desegregated Heart
 JOANNA BOWEN GILLESPIE 158

Alice Norwood Spearman Wright: Civil Rights Apostle to
 South Carolinians
 MARCIA G. SYNNOTT 184

About the Authors and the Editors 209

Index 213

BEYOND
IMAGE
AND
CONVENTION

Editors' Introduction

"There is nothing in the whole world so unbecoming to a woman," wrote Oscar Wilde, "as a Nonconformist conscience." Conformity to standards of conventional feminine behavior, including passivity, agreeableness, and the acceptance of male dominance, hierarchy, and the conventions of the mainstream, has been used to define, control, and judge women through the centuries. Perhaps nowhere in American life has the importance of preserving the conventions been more firmly enshrined than in the American South. The image of the Southern Lady, promoted in pulpit and press in the last century, and personified in Technicolor by Melanie Wilkes in *Gone with the Wind*, has long been the norm by which southern women's lives were measured. The Southern Lady was genteel, self-controlled, and never went beyond her God-given, male-defined boundaries. Her behavior was not only impeccable, it was thoroughly and absolutely conventional.

But it was not reality. And with the advent of women's history and the publication of works on southern women (as opposed to ladies), the paragon of ladyhood began to tumble off her pedestal.[1]

---

1. Julia Cherry Spruill, *Women's Life and Work in the Southern Colonies* (Chapel Hill: University of North Carolina Press, 1938) gave the first push by pointing out the myriad activities in which southern women were engaged that went far beyond the image of ladyhood where ladies directed the slaves and did little else. Anne Firor Scott, *The Southern Lady: From Pedestal to Politics, 1830–1930* (Chicago: University of Chicago Press, 1970) destroyed the mythic creature through modern scholarship. Catherine Clinton, *The Plantation Mistress: Woman's World in the Old South* (New York: Pantheon Books, 1982) and Elizabeth Fox-Genovese, *Within the Plantation Household: Black and White Women of the Old South* (Chapel Hill: University of North Carolina Press, 1988) led the vanguard for more radical interpretations. Now historians have widened the field considerably with works such as Kent Anderson Leslie, *Woman of Color, Daughter of Privilege: Amanda America Dickson, 1849–1893* (Athens: University of Georgia Press, 1995);

1

Scholars today are more aware of those women whose lives could not be defined as conventional based on the old model. Two volumes of published essays, stemming from two earlier conferences on women's history sponsored by the Southern Association for Women Historians, advanced certain themes apparent in all women's history but especially applicable to the history of southern women. Essays based upon papers presented at the First Southern Conference on Women's History in 1988 at Converse College illuminated the "histories and identities" of women whose individual or collective experiences were little known. From the Second Southern Conference on Women's History at the University of North Carolina at Chapel Hill held in 1991, a volume appeared that told the "hidden histories" of women in the New South era. Like its earlier companion, this second collection portrayed southern women in circumstances not usually described in mainline studies of the South.[2]

The following collection of essays is from the Third Southern Conference on Women's History, this one held at Rice University in June 1994. From the myriad papers delivered there, the editors have selected nine essays to develop the theme that southern women have gone "beyond convention" throughout time. Their failures to conform to expected standards of behavior have given historians unique opportunities to explore how southern women chose to contradict convention and to measure the degree of their rebellion. The essays presented here also show us how historians continue to go beyond convention in expanding the concept of what constitutes history. A new cadre of scholars has used previously untapped sources to craft provocative and exciting essays that range over more than three hundred years of southern history.

Margaret Ripley Wolfe, *Daughters of Canaan: A Sage of Southern Women* (Lexington: University Press of Kentucky, 1995); and Marjorie Spruill Wheeler, *New Women of the New South: The Leaders of the Woman Suffrage Movement in the Southern States* (New York: Oxford University Press, 1993). The list of historians working on southern women's history is immense and impressive.

2. Virginia Bernhard et al., eds., *Southern Women: Histories and Identities* (Columbia: University of Missouri Press, 1991); Virginia Bernhard et al., eds., *Hidden Histories of Women in the New South, Southern Women* (Columbia: University of Missouri Press, 1994).

The first three essays illustrate episodes in the lives of eighteenth- and early-nineteenth-century southern women who lived beyond the pale in their own time. Kirsten Fischer's description of white women's sexual misconduct in colonial North Carolina and Anya Jabour's account of a Virginia matron's vexatious white housekeepers suggest that women who were at the bottom of the social ladder had little to lose in defying convention, despite penalties for their obstreperous behavior and defiance of propriety.

Fischer documents a number of cases where renegade couples engaged in illicit sex, interracial relationships, skinny-dipping or other forms of "naked co-mingling." Some women overstepped the bounds of the law by operating "bawdy houses" or working as prostitutes. Although these outcasts were eventually caught and punished, usually by lashings or extended terms of servitude, Fischer finds in their defiance more than a manifestation of alternative social and sexual mores. She sees their aberrant behavior as a challenge to moral authorities and the conventional relations of gender, race, and class; this mischievous subculture defied political control by colonial North Carolina elites. Mining court records, Fischer has developed an aspect of the social history of a colonial underclass.[3]

On a smaller scale, the housekeepers of Elizabeth Wirt, of Richmond and Washington, also defied elite authority. Anya Jabour details the manner in which white housekeepers in the Wirt household set themselves apart from the slaves they were expected to supervise, while enduring restrictions and conditions that mimicked those of women bound in slavery. While Wirt was determined to command the lives and duties of her white servants, they were bent on resisting the ill-defined and incessant demands of a shrewish employer. The hierarchies of race and class did battle inside the home where, in Jabour's words, "the mixed-labor system of the urban upper South maximized the potential for confrontation over the issue of household status." This essay defines the domestics' hierarchy within the confines of a family whose mistress felt compelled to defend her own position

3. This approach is similar to Mary Beth Norton's in her history of the "gossipy women" of Maryland, "Gender and Defamation in Seventeenth-Century Maryland," *William and Mary Quarterly*, 3d ser., 44 (January 1987): 3–39.

of authority and superiority. In addition, analyses of architectural barriers, which appear both here and in subsequent essays, begin to suggest the importance of physical household structure in preserving class distinctions. Jabour's essay is also instructive for what it tells us about economic deprivation, which forced white women—widowed, abandoned, or never married—into domestic employment. Based extensively upon the William Wirt Papers, this study is further proof that the papers of prominent men are rich in family and women's history.

Cynthia Lynn Lyerly writes about episodes in the history of Methodism in four southern states. By focusing on the religious enthusiasm of women and the reaction to it, Lyerly delineates the intersection between race, emotional expression, and dementia. Male critics reacted to these episodes by declaring religiously rebellious women licentious, mad, or possessed. The real basis for opposition by male parishioners to what women proclaimed to be their "deep impression of religion" was a fear that women were trying to assume moral leadership within both church and community. As Lyerly argues, "gender was just as pivotal a factor as class in the contest for religious authority" in the years 1770 to 1810 and even afterward. Preachers and congregations learned early the basis for women's claim to authority and the right to share in church governance: their time, money, and labor were essential for the church's survival. Nonetheless, church fathers sought to deny women their expressions of religious fervor to diminish one of the "only avenues white southern women had to public moral authority and uncensored self-expression."

The enthusiasm of young Methodist women plays a role in Norma Taylor Mitchell's essay as well. Virginia Campbell, niece of David and Mary Campbell, a prominent Abingdon, Virginia, couple, was prompted by her Methodist faith to educate the extended slave family belonging to her aunt and uncle. Mitchell's focus, however, is not on Virginia but on one of the slaves, known only as Hannah, who lived in close quarters, literally, with her owners for almost forty years. Virginia's tutoring, the slaves' own Methodist teachings, and paternalistic treatment by the Campbells all combined to embolden Hannah and three generations of slaves living in this impressive household. Often away at Richmond, David Campbell instructed his slaves so that they could manage in his absence. Gradually, Hannah and her progeny developed a degree of autonomy and power that surpassed that of the vast majority of bondsmen and women. Indeed, through long periods of Campbell family absences and illnesses, Hannah pushed so hard to win that autonomy for herself and her family that her master became anxious. After his death, Hannah did not live to see freedom, but, thanks to her, the skilled younger members of her family were better prepared than were most freedmen and women for their new lives after 1865.

Kimberly Shreck relates the sad account of a slave that differs greatly from Taylor's portrait of Hannah and her family. Life after emancipation was highly circumscribed for the unfortunate Eda Hickam of Cooper County, Missouri. Hickam argued before a state court in 1890 that she had never been told of emancipation and was thus due back pay for twenty-five years of unpaid service. From 1865 to 1889, she had lived in isolation, working as a domestic for the white Hickam family. In court her oppressors argued that she was "family," yet she was given no share of inheritance at her master's death. Shreck's examination of the case from both sides reveals the thin line that existed between slavery and freedom. It raises a question, likely to remain unanswered, about how many slaves, lacking kinship networks, lived in a state of virtual peonage. Hickam, even if freed, would have had few employment options other than domestic service. Although Eda Hickam's four trips to court availed her nothing in the end, her decision to bring suit, at a time when Cooper County was caught in the grip of virulent racism, was an act of bravery.

Best-selling author Mary Virginia Terhune, who wrote under the pseudonym Marion Harland, left her native Virginia when she married. She moved to New Jersey, where she lived in comfort and without distraction, writing in traditional genres: cookbooks, domestic manuals, and antebellum southern novels. She promulgated republican motherhood, respected prewar southern gender traditions, and never supported women's rights, yet she proved that a woman could have a highly profitable career outside her home and family. Conceding to the literary marketplace, she altered her views about the South, abandoned the Lost Cause, and chose not to pen propagandistic romances about errant Yankees and pious Confederates. Some of her works were plainly attacks on perceived flaws in southern culture, defying literary conventions set by other southern writers of her day.

Karen Manners Smith sees in Terhune's postbellum work an "eagerness to participate in the reconciliation process," though she herself remained "unreconstructed" in her attitudes about race. Although Terhune sought a literary breakaway from her contemporaries, she could never tear herself away completely from her southern past. Smith's serious consideration of this popular novelist exemplifies the continued need for historians of women to examine the lives and works of those writers whom literary critics might dismiss as "scribbling women," as Nathaniel Hawthorne did. Those "scribblers" tell us much about the social history of women readers in the nineteenth century.

The last group of essays in this volume describes ways in which southern women confronted white discrimination against blacks. Susan L. Smith examines the efforts of middle-class black women to set up public health programs to provide care for their citizens when their communities were neglected by both the federal government under New Deal programs and state public health departments. She examines a health project that Alpha Kappa Alpha operated in the Mississippi Delta from 1935 to 1942 as the epitome of both social welfare and political activism. Without grassroots black women's voluntary organizations, public health services would not have made it to the black community. As Smith demonstrates, "the story of black women's health activism helps to expand our understanding of the public political meaning of women's private volunteer work." Although AKA's leader Dorothy Boulding Ferebee promoted the project from her Washington office, two women on the scene were crucial to the Delta project's success. Ida Louise Jackson, a Mississippi-born AKA president, and Dr. Arenia C. Mallory, a Lexington, Mississippi, educator, were the driving forces behind creating the clinics and maintaining ongoing research on socioeconomic conditions among black sharecroppers who had long been neglected by the white power structure. Smith's essay shows that the "neighborhood union" work conducted in urban centers by black women activists had rural counterparts.

Sarah Patton Boyle first took her stand against segregation and discrimination in 1950 and thus preceded the civil rights movement of the 1960s. Boyle, a white, mainline, Virginia Episcopalian, considered her conversion to desegregation the only course any true Christian could take. In her essay, Joanna Bowen Gillespie provides an explication of Boyle's book, *The Desegregated Heart* (1962), within the historical context of the times. This included the resistance by white Virginians to racial advancement and their retaliation against Boyle in the form of threats from the White Citizens' Council and a cross-burning by the Ku Klux Klan. Through extensive writing in secular magazines and church journals, Boyle fought against what she found to be the true religion, even among more liberal southern Episcopalians: a devotion to the nobility of the Southern Cause rather than to Christianity. In denouncing her church's paternalism toward the Negro, Boyle joined a small band of dissenters that included Lillian Smith and Virginia Durr. Gillespie terms Boyle's denouement of misguided church views "an earthquake." Always a "true Southern lady," she went beyond the conventions of her era in daring to challenge religion and church.

Marcia G. Synott writes of another white apostle of civil rights, Alice Norwood Spearman Wright. Rather than work for interracial understanding through the church, Spearman sought the support of South Carolina's white clubwomen and their allies to promote the cause of desegregation through interracial dialogue. In more effective ways, she worked as the executive secretary of the South Carolina Council on Human Relations from 1954 to 1967. Synott's portrait of Alice Spearman during these years reveals much about the position of white clubwomen on racial matters and the response of black leaders to her overtures. As a "bridge" between the generation of white women activists of the 1910s and 1920s and those of the civil rights movement of the 1960s, Spearman is a worthy subject of this sensitively written essay. She is a useful example for those who contend that "Men Led, but Women Organized" the movement for racial justice in the South. Synott adds to the growing number of studies on women active at the grassroots level in the civil rights movement—studies that have changed the history of the movement in significant ways.

There are discernible gaps in this collection, as should be admitted for any volume of only nine essays. Readers are invited to return to the two earlier publications from the Southern Conferences on Women's History to find accounts of individuals, organizations, and topics that complement those here. In earlier collections more twentieth-century studies describe the intersection of race and gender from the Progressive Era to at least 1940. The women's club movement and suffrage received fresh treatments as did those women who were both rewarded and punished for flouting convention in their push for social reform. Like the "unruly" women, described in this third volume, who parted company with "the better element," there were outspoken women whose hidden histories reveal intense suffering during incarceration in prison or asylum for offenses against society, real or perceived.[4]

This latest collection continues an emphasis upon women crusaders for racial justice: white women of conscience and privilege, the black professional class, and leaders of grassroots movements. Perhaps more than any other effort, the civil rights movement has brought southern women to a common ground. And it seems likely that it will be the history of this cadre that is integrated into mainstream monographs and texts more than that of any other group of southern women. Such are the rewards for those who struggle beyond the bounds of convention.

There are similarities among the women whose histories appear under the rubrics of "identities," "hidden histories," or "beyond convention." These women challenged the prevailing hierarchical structure, the conservatism toward gender and race and, where possible, acted to change that structure. They represent the less-well-known side of southern women's history, giving us all a fuller, truer picture of the complexities of life in the South. No longer will we be able to stereotype the southern woman as white, middle-class, conforming, and docile. Just as the benign image of moonlight and magnolias has gone with the wind, so must the concept that southern women were incapable of challenging traditions. They were indeed capable—and courageous—to defy the norm.

4. See Kathleen C. Hilton, " 'Both in the Field, Each with a Plow': Race and Gender in USDA Policy, 1907–1929," and Lynne A. Rieff, " 'Go Ahead and Do All You Can': Southern Progressives and Alabama Home Demonstration Clubs, 1914–1940," in *Hidden Histories,* ed. Virginia Bernhard et al., 114–33; 134–49; Mary Martha Thomas, "The Ideology of the Alabama Woman Suffrage Movement, 1890–1920," and Elizabeth Hayes Turner, " 'White Gloved Ladies' and 'New Women' in the Texas Woman Suffrage Movement," in *Histories and Identities,* ed. Virginia Bernhard et al., 109–28, 129–56; Mary Ellen Curtin, "The 'Human World' of Black Women in Alabama Prisons, 1870–1900," and Steven Noll, " 'A Far Greater Menace': Feebleminded Females in the South, 1900–1940," in *Hidden Histories,* ed. Virginia Bernhard et al., 11–30; 31–51.

Future collections of scholarship emerging from the triennial South-ern Conference on Women's History may bear titles that are variations on this theme: that the unexplored or underexplored history of south-ern women is essentially that of women who have not led traditional lives nor remained within expected boundaries. Such is the growing legacy to the history of the South of the Southern Association for Women Historians.

"Common Disturbers of the Peace"

The Politics of White Women's Sexual Misconduct in Colonial North Carolina

KIRSTEN FISCHER

In early June 1697, a white woman named Dorothy Steel ran away from her husband, William, near Albemarle Sound in northeastern North Carolina. Seeking refuge further south, Steel hired William Lee and John Spellman "to goe with her to Ashley River." Three other men also joined the expedition, and together the runaways stole what they could from William Steel, including "One Bed, one Rug . . . a pott," three firelock guns, a trunk, and their mode of transport: "a Canoe and Sailes." On June 24, approximately forty miles from Cape Fear, the hungry fugitives encountered "sum Indians" and gladly "bought sum venson of them." Soon thereafter, however, Indians shot at them, and the travelers returned fire and reversed their direction, planning now to go north to Virginia. Halting briefly in her old neighborhood, Dorothy persuaded thirty-year-old Elizabeth Vina to join them. Roger Snell, a neighbor, spied the runaways and asked "whi thay stayed and lurked about thare," advising them to "begon spedyly or he would go and fetch the Constable and sese [seize] them." Vowing that "thay would dey before they would be taken," the runaways set off again.[1]

For their helpful comments on the various drafts of this essay I thank William Chafe, Janet Coryell, Laura Edwards, Christina Greene, Nancy Hewitt, and Marjoleine Kars. The research for this paper was funded in part by a dissertation grant from the National Endowment for the Humanities.

1. *Crown v Lee and Spelman,* Jury's Presentment, (n.d.), Miscellaneous Court Papers, 1689–1770, Raleigh: Division of Archives and History, North Carolina State Archives (hereinafter NCSA). William Lee, John Spellman, James Seserson,

For two days they rowed along the shore toward Thomas Pollock's plantation on Salmon Creek. There they disembarked and enjoyed "sum tobaco and Rosting yeares of Corn of Colonel Pollickes negro Manuell," a slave who, together with his wife, managed the plantation without supervision. The fugitives then "gave a gunn" of William Steel's to Tom Andover, a free black man who agreed to "pilaite [pilot] them to south Key." In August, the fugitives' luck ran out: they were apprehended and brought to court. Elizabeth Vina and another traveler testified that "William Lee and Dorothy Stell did Ly together upon one bed all the voige [voyage]." Lee admitted as much in court, and John Spelman, though he did not make a confession, was also convicted of having sexual relations with Dorothy. On October 9, the court ordered that Lee and Spellman each receive thirty-nine lashes for "ravishing" Dorothy Steel and that Steel herself suffer thirty stripes for "Unlawfull Departing from her husband and going away with an adulteror."[2]

Illicit liaisons like Dorothy Steel's presented a challenge to authority in the early South. Political tracts and sermons routinely extolled the virtues of female modesty, deference, and submission to the male head of household. Steel eschewed these prescriptions for appropriate female behavior when she ran away from her husband and engaged in extramarital sex. Certainly not all acts of unlawful sex defied social norms or challenged the status quo, but some illicit liaisons did display irreverence, even scorn, for mainstream mores. Steel's flight, her sexual liaisons, and her declaration that she would rather "dey" than return to her husband, demonstrate a deliberate rejection of the social and sexual restrictions imposed by the colonial government and the Anglican church.

But even when the surviving documents do not reveal an ideology of resistance, illicit behavior could entail a symbolic disruption of

---

and Elizabeth Vina, depositions, August 24, 1697, Colonial Court Papers—Civil and Criminal, NCSA.

2. Lee, Spellman, Seserson, and Vina, depositions; Jury's Presentments, October 9, 1697, in *North Carolina Higher-Court Records, 1670–1696*, ed. Mattie Erma Edwards Parker, vol. 3 of *The Colonial Records of North Carolina* [Second Series], ed. Mattie Erma Edwards Parker et al., Raleigh: Division of Archives and History, 1963– , 90. Walter Clark, ed. *Laws of North Carolina*, vol. 23 of *The State Records of North Carolina*, ed. Walter Clark, 16 vols. numbered 11 through 26 (Winston and Goldsboro: State of North Carolina, 1895–1906).

the social order, whether or not it was intended as such. The private and public realms were inseparable in the eighteenth century: the church, the state, and the traditional household represented different aspects of a patriarchal society grounded in dependents' obedience to their masters and women's submission to their fathers and husbands. When Dorothy abandoned her marriage and had sex with another man, her circumvention of sexual and marital norms represented a considerable challenge to the social hierarchy. Dorothy's flight and adulterous activity broke the domestic rules that lay at the heart of the social order.

In addition to the breach of her nuptial vows, Steel's adventure included theft, aid to other runaways, and unlicensed trade with Tom Andover and Manuell—multiple transgressions in which whites and free and enslaved blacks interacted with one another in clandestine and unlawful ways. Such misconduct thwarted the regulatory statutes designed to control interactions among the lower orders and suggests a shared acceptance of certain activities that did not accord with official standards of propriety. These three aspects of Dorothy Steel's case— resistance to mainstream sexual norms by individuals and groups, the symbolically subversive potential inherent in some acts of sexual trans- gression, and the appearance of sexual misconduct in conjunction with other illegal acts—gave one white woman's sexual misconduct a political dimension that prompted magistrates to respond with a display of state power.[3]

The impact of sexual misconduct depended in part on the social context in which it took place. In North Carolina, the transition from a frontier outpost to an established colonial settlement occurred slowly. Geographic obstacles hindered the rapid growth of the settlement just south of the Virginia border along the Albemarle Sound: the shift- ing sands of the Outer Banks defeated settlers' attempts to establish permanent harbors, and the many swamps and rivers made travel by land an arduous enterprise. Early North Carolina remained relatively isolated from the rest of the colonies, and the immigrant population

3. North Carolina's 1715 law prohibited harboring or trading with runaway servants or slaves without permission from masters and mistresses. Susan H. Brinn, "Blacks in Colonial North Carolina, 1660–1723" (M.A. thesis, University of North Carolina, 1978), 33–35, 44–45.

stayed comparatively small. In 1715, for example, there were approximately 14,800 Euro-American and 1,800 African American settlers in North Carolina, compared to Virginia's 74,100 white and 20,900 black inhabitants.[4]

Before speculators could survey North Carolina's fertile lands, less wealthy immigrants arrived, hoping to make a living by raising corn, wheat, and tobacco and by harvesting timber. Many of the newcomers were former indentured servants who had completed their terms of service in Virginia and found themselves unable to buy land there. In 1708 the Virginia Council reported that "many of our poorer sort of inhabitants daily remove into our neighboring Colonies, especially to North Carolina." The colony soon developed a reputation as backward and unruly. Frustrated Anglican ministers decried the lack of an established church in early North Carolina, while ineffective government officials bemoaned the settlers' unprincipled behavior. For decades the colonial upper crust in North Carolina and elsewhere echoed Virginia Governor Thomas Culpeper, who warned in 1681 that "Carolina (I meane the North part of it) alwayes was and is the Sinke of America, the Refuge of our Renegadoes, and Till in better order, Dangerous To us."[5]

The delayed colonial settlement in North Carolina was reflected in the stratification of wealth. In 1732 Governor Burrington complained that "there are not a sufficient number of Gentlemen" in the colony and that "there is no difference to be perceived in Dress and Carriage" between the common people on the one hand and court justices and government officials on the other. As late as 1765 a Frenchman traveling through the southern colonies commented that "very few if any rich people" lived in North Carolina. He described the colony as an "azilum" for indentured servants who had served their time in Virginia

4. Peter H. Wood, "The Changing Population of the Colonial South: An Overview by Race and Region, 1685–1790," in *Powhatan's Mantle: Indians in the Colonial Southeast,* ed. Peter H. Wood, Gregory A. Waselkov, and M. Thomas Hatley (Lincoln: University of Nebraska Press, 1989), 38; Harry Roy Merrens, *Colonial North Carolina in the Eighteenth Century: A Study in Historical Geography* (Chapel Hill: University of North Carolina Press, 1964), chap. 2.

5. Colonel E. Jenings, president of the Virginia Council, to the Lords of Trade, November 27, 1708, in *Colonial Records of North Carolina,* ed. William L. Saunders (Raleigh: State of North Carolina, 1886–1890), 1:692; Lord Culpeper to the Board of Trade, December 12, 1681, British Public Record Office, class 1, piece 47, folio 261, photocopy filed as 70.507.1–4, NCSA.

and Maryland: "[W]hen at liberty they all (or great part) Come to this part where they are not Known and setle here. [I]t is a fine Country for poor people, but not for the rich." Under these conditions elites found it difficult to emulate the lifestyle of their peers in Williamsburg. In particular, they discovered that it was nearly impossible to impose an orderly and effective government on North Carolina's recalcitrant inhabitants. In this context, illicit sexual acts further flaunted settlers' disrespect for norms of propriety and highlighted the limits of elite control.[6]

While North Carolina had a reputation as a hotbed of illicit activity, court magistrates in other British colonies also wrestled with cases of sexual misconduct. In New England's county courts, by far the largest category of criminal cases prosecuted between the 1690s and the Revolution involved extramarital sex, most commonly fornication or adultery. In Virginia as well, sexual offenses were the most commonly prosecuted crimes in the county courts, and the Virginia assembly passed more laws pertaining to public morality (sexuality, blasphemy, and drunkenness) than statutes protecting the state, persons, or property. In North Carolina, at least one in ten criminal charges concerned immoral behavior of some kind, and the range of sex-related offenses included fornication, adultery, bigamy, interracial sex, homosexuality, prostitution, bestiality, rape, abortion, and infanticide. The fact that North Carolina's newer and less efficient court system did not prosecute moral offenses to the degree that courts in other colonies did only exacerbated critics' concern about lawlessness in the colony.[7]

6. Letter from Captain Burrington, Governor of North Carolina, February 20, 1731/2, in *Colonial Records of North Carolina*, ed. William L. Saunders, 3:332–33; "Journal of a French Traveller in the Colonies, 1765," *American Historical Review* 26 (July 1921), 738; see also A. Roger Ekirch, *"Poor Carolina": Politics and Society in Colonial North Carolina, 1729–1776* (Chapel Hill: University of North Carolina Press, 1981), chap. 2.

7. Cornelia Hughes Dayton, *Women before the Bar: Gender, Law, and Society in Connecticut, 1639–1789* (Chapel Hill: University of North Carolina Press, 1995), 160; David H. Flaherty, *Law and the Enforcement of Morals in Early America*, *Perspectives in American History* (Cambridge, Mass.: Harvard University Press, 1971), 5:203–53; Arthur P. Scott, *Criminal Law in Colonial Virginia* (Chicago: University of Chicago Press, 1930), 281, 291; Donna J. Spindel and Stuart W. Thomas, "Crime and Society in North Carolina, 1663–1740," *Journal of Southern History* 49 (May 1983): 223–44.

In fact, it is difficult to know what percentage of North Carolina's population engaged in illicit sexual relations. Many, perhaps most, white residents shared lawmakers' notions of morality and conformed to widely held expectations of appropriate behavior. Critics often exaggerated their reports of misconduct. In 1711, for example, the notoriously bitter Reverend Urmston described the North Carolina settlement as "a nest of the most notorious profligates upon earth. . . . Women forsake their husbands come in here and live with other men." But even if some accounts of misconduct were overblown and the majority of whites upheld mainstream sexual norms, the continuous complaints about misconduct in the colony and the appearance of repeat offenders in court indicates that defiant subcultures formed a distinct and persistent presence within the larger colonial culture of North Carolina. Legislators perceived, for example, that "to the great Scandall of this Government, many persons" who lived together "as man and wife" were actually "unmarried to each other." To crack down on such couples, North Carolina lawmakers imposed fines of fifty shillings for fornication and twice that amount (five pounds) for adultery. Any culprit who could not pay received a public whipping of up to twenty-one lashes.[8]

Despite these penalties, many couples endured repeated prosecution rather than give up their unlawful bedfellows. Some couples probably considered themselves as good as married but never bothered with the legal formalities; for them, long-term relationships constituted common-law marriages. Others chose to put off official marriages for economic reasons. Widows, especially those with property, stood to lose their wealth to new husbands if they remarried. This may explain why widow Elizabeth Braizer shared her house with planter William Barker but did not marry him even though they had two children together. Similarly, widow Martha Godwin did not marry until she was prosecuted in April 1757 for having lived in adultery with Samuel Hollamon since the previous December. Godwin's reluctance to marry her lover may have been due to her superior wealth and status. When her former husband died in 1753, Godwin inherited a four hundred–acre plantation and two slaves. Hollamon, by contrast,

8. Mr. Urmston's Letter, July 7, 1711, in *Colonial Records of North Carolina*, ed. William L. Saunders, 1:767; Clark, *Laws of North Carolina*, 5.

was described as a "laborer" in a suit accusing him of assaulting Isaac Middleton, a servant. In her decision to marry Hollamon, Godwin must have weighed the costs of further prosecution against the transference of her property to a new husband.[9]

Often various members of a single family engaged in similar kinds of misconduct. The Sikes family of Edgecombe County, for example, displayed a penchant for unlawful behavior: William Sikes lived "in baudry" with Mary Clenny and kept her "as a Concubine"; Joseph Sikes did the same with a woman named Lurany Rose, and Ben Sikes was arrested for adultery as well. In Pasquotank County, Alexander Jack and Ann Cartwright, Thomas Cartwright and Mary Roads, Daniel Roads and Elizabeth Burnham, John Burnham and Sarah Sawyer, and Joseph Sawyer and Dorothy Hastings were among the couples whose family ties linked them in a mesh of unlawful relationships. These cases suggest that long-term liaisons could attain social legitimacy outside the aegis of legal authority. Clearly not everyone imbued unlawful relations, be they casual or committed, with the shame that ecclesiastical and civil authorities ascribed to extramarital sex.[10]

9. *Crown v Barker and Braizer*, Arrest warrant for Barker and Braizer, October 17, 1739; Jury's Presentment, [October] Court, 1739, Perquimans County Civil Action Papers, NCSA; Weynette Parks Haun, *Perquimans County North Carolina County Court Minutes (Court of Pleas and Quarter Sessions), 1738–1754, Book II* (Durham: the author, 1988), 63–65, 72; *Crown v Hollamon and Godwin*, Arrest warrant for Hollamon and Godwin, April 28, 1757; Jury's Presentment, April Court Session, 1757, Bertie County Criminal Action Papers, NCSA; Will of William Godwin, Secretary of State Papers, May 4, 1752, NCSA; *Crown v Hollyman*, Jury's Presentment, August Court, 1753, Bertie County Criminal Action Papers, NCSA.

10. *Crown v [William] Sikes*, Jury's Presentment, February Court, 1758, Edgecombe County Criminal Action Papers, 1758, NCSA; *Crown v [Joseph] Sikes*, Jury's Presentment, February Court, 1758, Edgecombe County Criminal Action Papers, NCSA; *Crown v Benjamin Sikes*, Arrest warrant for Sikes, October 24, 1764, Edgecombe County Criminal Action Papers, NCSA; *Crown v Alexander Jack*, Jury's Presentment, April Court, 1751, Pasquotank County Civil Action Papers, NCSA; Arrest warrant for Roads, June 28, 1743, Pasquotank County Civil Action Papers, NCSA. Ten years later, Mary Roads had another illegitimate child with shipwright John Smith. *Crown v John Smith*, Arrest warrant for Smith, August 15, 1753, Hyde County Civil and Criminal Action Papers, NCSA; Arrest warrant for Daniel Roads, December 3, 1746, Pasquotank County Bastardy Bonds, NCSA; Arrest warrant for John Burnham, November 4, 1746, Pasquotank County Bastardy Bonds, NCSA; Summons for Joseph Sawyer, July 25, 1748, Pasquotank County Bastardy Bonds, NCSA.

For some people, having lovers and children out of wedlock despite injunctions to the contrary may have been conscious acts of resistance to authority, a specialized form of nose-thumbing.[11] But even for those who did not perceive their own intimate behavior as overtly political, feelings of humiliation and shame did not necessarily accompany unlawful relationships to the degree hoped for by government officials. It was not that misbehaving Carolinians cared nothing for the opinions of others, or that they were completely free from the social restraints that existed in the larger colonial society. Rather, those people carved out spaces for alternative standards of acceptable conduct within the larger culture. These co-existing moral codes found some of their most concrete expressions in intimate relationships that clearly disregarded state and church definitions of appropriate unions.

White women who engaged in extramarital liaisons already posed a significant challenge to norms of female deference, but this challenge was exacerbated when a woman's partner was black. As slavery spread in eighteenth-century North Carolina, lawmakers wrote increasingly detailed statutes that adjudicated race relations and prohibited inter-racial interactions of all kinds, including sex and, more especially, marriage. Virginia first outlawed interracial unions in 1691, and by 1715, the North Carolina legislature had followed suit, prohibiting the marriage of a white person to "any Negro, Mulatto or indyan Man or Woman," with the penalty for violation of the law set at fifty pounds. Any "White woman whether Bond or Free" who had a mixed-race child had to pay a fine of six pounds or work two years without pay, and those mothers who were already servants had two years added to their indentures. Over time, the law became more specific in its definition of race: in 1741 no white person could legally marry "an Indian, Negro, Mustee [a person of African and Native American descent], or Mulatto man or Woman or any Person of Mixed Blood, to *the Third Generation*, bond or free." This prohibition of mixed-race marriages prevented whites from establishing legal families with non-Europeans and defined as illegitimate all mixed-race children of

11. This phenomenon has been noted elsewhere; see Rosalind Mitchison and Leah Leneman, *Sexuality and Social Control: Scotland, 1660–1780* (Oxford: Basil Blackwell, 1989), 219–24, 242–43. Daniel Scott Smith and Michael S. Hindus, "Premarital pregnancy in America, 1640–1971: An Overview and Interpretation," *Journal of Interdisciplinary History* 5 (spring 1975): 537–70.

white women, thereby safeguarding the transference of property from one generation of white males to the next. This legislation dovetailed with the remarkable stipulation, first passed in Virginia in 1662 and then adopted by other colonies, that a child's status as slave or free followed that of the mother. This extraordinary departure from English customs of patrilineage ensured that the children of enslaved women would be slaves even if their fathers were free, making the fertility of slave women a means by which slaveowners increased their human property. But this legal innovation also meant that the mixed-race children born to white women were free, adding to the free black population at a time when legislators wanted to reserve free status for whites only.[12]

Despite the legal prohibitions, white women continued to have sexual relations with African American men, and mulatto children provided evidence of those relations. Sarah Williamson, for example, a white woman from Currituck, appeared before the general court in July 1716 after the birth of her mulatto son. Amy Demsey, the free black daughter of a white woman, was born in Bertie County in 1723. In 1725, Margaret MacCarty, a white woman, married Ed Burkitt, a free black man. In July 1727, "Severall persons" in Edenton knew that Elizabeth Puckett, a white woman, had "left her husband and hath for Some Years cohabited with a Negro Man of Capt. Simon Jeffries." In 1746, two-year-old Delaney Bright, the daughter of a white woman, was apprenticed for thirty-one years with the stipulation that she receive "Meat Drink Washing Lodging and Apperrele fitting for Mallatoe's." Around the same time Ruth Tillet, a "freeborn coloured woman," was "born of a Free Woman named Ann Tillet . . . supposed by a black man." In 1749 the Women's Meeting of the Pasquotank Society of Friends publicly denounced Damaris Symons for "Lewdness in whoredom with a negro man." Five years later, Jemima Griffin, a white woman, named her newborn "Mulato daughter" Patience. Clearly, Anglo-American women who continued to engage in relationships

12. Clark, *Laws of North Carolina*, 65, 160 (my emphasis); A. Leon Higginbotham and Barbara K. Kopytoff, "Racial Purity and Interracial Sex in the Law of Colonial and Antebellum Virginia," *Georgetown Law Journal* 77 (August 1989): 1967–2029; Kathleen M. Brown, *Good Wives, "Nasty Wenches," and Anxious Patriarchs: Gender, Race and Power in Colonial Virginia* (Chapel Hill: University of North Carolina Press, 1996), chaps. 4, 6.

with African American men ignored, perhaps even scorned, the legal prohibition of interracial sex.[13]

While some women from prominent families, like Damaris Symons, engaged in illicit sex, unsanctioned unions were most common among servants. At least half of all the European immigrants to arrive in the British colonies before 1776 worked as servants. Some were convicts, involuntarily transported to the New World. Others came willingly, pushed to choose the uncertainty of servitude abroad over the hardships created by overpopulation and high unemployment at home. These colonists received their passage to America by entering into contracts called indentures that obligated them to work for a master or mistress for a certain number of years, usually between four and seven, in exchange for room and board. During these years, servants performed a wide variety of work: women cared for the garden, dairy, and poultry yard; cured meat and pickled fruits and vegetables; cleaned house, spun thread, washed and mended clothes, and prepared meals. Men worked in the fields, cut and stocked firewood, transported goods to market, and tended the large farm animals.[14]

Although servants remained legally free, they nonetheless experienced considerable restrictions. Servants could not, for example, switch to different masters at will, nor could they prevent the trade of their labor to others. Significantly, masters also controlled the matrimony of servants: servants who married without permission from their masters paid for their unsanctioned unions with an extra year of servitude. By preventing marriages, masters kept indentured women

13. Parker, *North Carolina Higher-Court Records,* 5:114; Petition of Amy Dempsey, no date, Colonial Court Records, Miscellaneous Papers, 1677–1775, CCR 192, Folder: "Freedom of Slaves," NCSA; *Crown v John Cotton,* July Court, 1725, General Court Criminal Papers, NCSA; Cain, *North Carolina Higher-Court Minutes* 6:425; Indenture of Delaney Bright, July 10, 1746, Pasquotank Apprentice Bonds, Folder: "B," NCSA; Petition of Ruth Tillett, Pasquotank County Pleas and Quarter Session, March 1783, NCSA; Eastern Quarter Symons Creek Monthly Meeting (in Pasquotank), reel 1: Women's Minutes, 1715–1768, Friends Historical Collection, Guilford College, Greensboro, North Carolina; Indenture of Patience Griffin, March 30, 1759, Pasquotank County Apprentice Bonds, Folder: "Name Unknown," NCSA.

14. Richard S. Dunn, "Servants and Slaves: The Recruitment and Employment of Labor," in *Colonial British America: Essays in the New History of the Early Modern Era,* ed. Jack P. Greene and J. R. Pole (Baltimore: Johns Hopkins University Press, 1984), 157–94.

and men in the position of dependents and denied male servants the option of becoming heads of households themselves. Masters apparently preferred unmarried servants, since they obliged most servants to remain legally single even when long-term relationships among servants resulted in children. Legal unions and legitimate families thus became privileges of class.[15]

Servants' inability to marry legally did not keep them from creating meaningful partnerships, however. When indentured women and men developed long-term relationships with each other, they effectively established what the marriage laws proscribed. Jane Warren and carpenter Jacob Tice, for example, both lived on Aaron Blancherd's plantation for several years in the 1730s. Warren and Tice had a child together and lived as a family, the laws against fornication notwithstanding. Such couples may have wanted to marry but, denied legal sanction, chose to carry on their relationship and establish families without formal acknowledgment. These long-term relationships suggest that people adapted their moral standards to the economic and legal constraints that shaped their lives. People in lower social classes may have expanded their notions of acceptable sexual behavior to accommodate the legal restrictions on their personal relationships. Thus, while alternative notions of morality did not exist in isolation from the colony's normative rules of behavior, morality was also not simply imposed by the upper strata of society.[16]

The particular restrictions placed on servants may explain why indentured women's sexual transgressions were sometimes overlooked or simply forgiven. Servant women's sexual vulnerability to their masters and other men was a known fact. Because servant women convicted of fornication had two extra years added to their indentures, masters had an economic incentive to impregnate their servants. In recognition of this incentive (and the many resulting cases of pregnancy), a law of 1715 stipulated that when the master was the father of a servant's child, the servant would be sold to someone else for the remainder of her term and the money donated to the church parish. Nonethless, many masters still considered sexual access to servant women their prerogative, and sexual vulnerability continued

15. Clark, *Laws of North Carolina*, 159.
16. Arrest warrant for Jacob Tice, July 24, 1739, Chowan County Miscellaneous Papers, NCSA.

to complicate the daily lives of many servant women. Perhaps for this reason a woman's previous sexual experience and childbirth did not necessarily hinder a later marriage. Elizabeth Odum, for example, was pregnant by planter Thomas Ward when she married Otho Holland in early 1744. In October of 1745, when Elizabeth's son was a year old, Otho Holland sued Ward for forty pounds for child support. Had Elizabeth Odum been the daughter of a wealthy planter intent upon making a financially sound match, her premarital pregnancy might have harmed her marriage prospects. But servants understood that the coercive circumstances of their working conditions sometimes resulted in pregnancy, and an unwed servant mother may have received more understanding from her peers.[17]

Some servants responded to the ban on marriage with outright defiance. This was the case with Hanah Davis, who in January 1724 ran away from her master, Dr. George Allen, a man who violently abused his servants. For a whole year Hanah Davis avoided recapture, during which time Allen invested the considerable sum of thirty pounds in a search for her. In autumn 1724 Davis persuaded Bartholomew McGowan, an Irish servant, to join her. Together with an accomplice named John McCormack, the outlaws stole goods valued at over fifty-four pounds from McGowan's mistress, the widow Ann Metcalf. Davis and McGowan then got married (or pretended they had been officially married), and Hanah took on the alias "Susanah McGowan." When they were caught in January 1725, the court sentenced the couple to thirty-nine lashes each for theft. For running away Hanah received two extra years of labor to Allen, twice the length of time of her absence, and "four Years more for his Extraordinary Expences & Charges" in getting her back. Her one year of freedom therefore cost Hanah Davis six added years of servitude to George Allen.[18]

Hanah's rebellion demonstrates that the meaning of marriage depended on one's status in early America. Marriage certainly brought

17. Clark, *Laws of North Carolina*, 65; *Holland v Ward*, July Court, 1747, Chowan County Civil Action Papers, NCSA.

18. Hue and Cry for Bartholomew and Susanah MacGowan, January 15, 1725, General Court Criminal Papers, NCSA; Jury's Presentment, January 11, 1725, General Court Criminal Papers, NCSA; *Allen v Davis alias McGreen* and *Metcalf v Macgreen*, March 1725, in Robert J. Cain, ed., *North Carolina Higher-Court Records, 1724–1730*, vol. 6 of *The Colonial Records of North Carolina* [Second Series], ed. Mattie Erma Edwards Parker et al., (Raleigh, N.C.: Division of Archives and History, 1963–), 88.

constraints to upper-class women: married women lost their rights to own property, make contracts, and represent themselves in court.[19] But women without property faced different circumstances, and for female servants who were denied the right to a legally sanctioned and protected relationship, matrimony attained more positive meanings. When Hanah and Bartholomew established their new life as a married couple, their marriage served as camouflage in their new community, as a marker of freedom and self-determination for themselves, and as a challenge to the moral authority of a legislature and judiciary that did not recognize their union. Although their illegal behavior challenged the constraints placed upon them as servants, it did so in ways that did not contest the patriarchal institution of marriage. The prohibition of marriage did function as a point of resistance among servants, but it left intact the hierarchy of dependents in the colonial household.

Other forms of disorderly conduct were less explicitly tied to unlawful sex, but they also challenged notions of propriety. On a steamy day in July 1737, for example, an indignant Edenton resident saw Hannah Nugent, Frances Tool, Jeremiah Vail, and William Bailey "striping themselves Naked and going into the water togather in the face of the Town." The affronted citizen informed a magistrate of the impromptu swim, and he, in turn, ordered the sheriff to summon the four culprits to court. Having heard the case, the presiding judges ordered that the men give bond for good behavior in the future, and that the two women, Hannah and Frances, receive ten lashes each on their bare backs at the "publick Whiping post." The women suffered whippings because they could not afford to pay bond for good behavior; access to cash could have staved off the pain and humiliation of the public thrashing. But the outraged informer and other like-minded spectators may have felt that the public humiliation was an appropriate reprimand for the transgression of female modesty. If women who were properly meek, submissive, and, above all, chaste began to strip shamelessly "in the face of the town," who could answer for the consequences? Men and women who socialized together in such openly physical and "promiscuous" ways showed a disregard for

19. Marylynn Salmon, *Women and the Law of Property in Early America* (Chapel Hill: University of North Carolina, 1986), chap. 3.

propriety that demanded punishment lest such irreverence spread and weaken the constraints placed on other forms of conduct.[20]

Taverns, also called tippling houses or "ordinaries," were especially rife with illicit activity. A plethora of misconduct transpired in such gathering places, including drinking, gambling, prostitution, interracial socializing, brawling, and thieving. In 1715 an exasperated North Carolina assembly declared that the "loathsome Sin of Drunkeness is of late grown into common Use within this Province & [is] the Root & Foundation of many Enormous Sins." Henceforth, the lawmakers decreed, "for the Better prevention of Riots and disorders in Ordinarys," innkeepers would have to obtain a license, renew it annually, and post a bond "for the due Observance" of the law.[21]

Single or widowed women were likely petitioners for a tavern license, and between 1741 and 1753, eight women received licenses to keep ordinaries in Edenton. In Chowan and Pasquotank Counties, for example, 20 percent of all tavern licenses were issued to women, some of whom were innkeepers of long-standing: Dorothy Sherwin, Mary Wallace, and Elizabeth Wallace each kept a tavern in Edenton for over twelve years. In addition to providing "good Wholesome, and cleanly Lodging and Dyet for Travellers," innkeepers were not to permit unlawful gaming nor "on the Sabbath Day, suffer any Person to Tipple and drink more than is necessary." Just as importantly, the legislature sought to prevent lower-class people from congregating without permission from their superiors. Innkeepers who harbored any sailor, servant, or slave without his or her master's consent could lose their license, and anyone operating an unlicensed tavern had to pay a five-pound fine or suffer "at the Public Whipping Post, on his or her bare back, Thirty lashes, well laid on."[22]

To a society with increasingly rigid categories of race, one of the most unsettling aspects of ordinaries was that they provided a meeting place for blacks and whites. Elites suspected that the lower classes, sharing grievances and emboldened by rum, might make common cause.

20. Weynette Parks Haun, *Chowan County North Carolina County Court Minutes (Court of Pleas and Quarter Sessions), 1735–1738; 1746–1748, Book II* (Durham, N.C.: the author, 1983), 45.

21. Clark, *Laws of North Carolina*, 4, 80.

22. Ibid., 182–85; Alan D. Watson, "Ordinaries in Colonial Eastern North Carolina," *North Carolina Historical Review* 45 (January 1968): 71, 73.

Certainly everyone knew that interracial networks of theft and illegal exchange persisted despite the injunction that trade with any servant or slave required the master's written consent. In 1706, for example, a white woman named Rebekah Baily was arrested for "unlegally receiving Six pair of Buttons" belonging to Mr. Thomas Peterson. The buttons had been delivered to her by a "Negroe Woman belonging to William Glover Esquire." Taverns provided a place where schemers could plan ventures of trade or theft, and some taverns became centers of routine and perhaps organized robbery. In the 1720s and 1730s, Margaret and Robert Kingham, who ran an unlicensed tippling house in Bertie County, were tried for theft, assault, murder, and helping three prisoners escape from jail. In 1736 the general court indicted Mary and William Waltham for theft, harboring burglars at their ordinary, and using foul language repeatedly.[23]

Some illicit exchanges involved sex; arrangements ranged from sexual barter for goods or favors to the outright sale of sexual services. While the colonies did not have the equivalent of London's long-standing neighborhoods of ill repute, "lewd and disorderly houses" probably existed in every larger town. Prostitutes were especially available in places like New York, Boston, Philadelphia, and Williamsburg, but women sold sexual services in smaller communities as well. Colonial women worked as prostitutes on their own or in brothels for a number of reasons. Some women were forced into the trade by the loss of a husband's financial support or because they were orphaned at a young age and left vulnerable to male seduction and violence. Girls who had been kidnapped, or "spirited," from England sometimes became prostitutes. Others continued the trade they had begun in England, where they had been imprisoned and then transported to the colonies as convicted felons. Sometimes these women were not banished from England so much as bribed to go to the colonies: ships'

23. Perquimans Precinct Court Records, January 6, 1706, in *Colonial Records of North Carolina*, ed. William L. Saunders, 1:650; Saunders, *Colonial Records of North Carolina*, 2:553–55; *Crown v Kinghams*, Jury's Presentment, July Court, 1736, General Court Criminal Papers, NCSA; *Crown v Robert Kingham*, Jury's Presentment, March Court, 1733, General Court Criminal Papers, NCSA; *Crown v Walthams*, Jury's Presentment, March Court, 1736, General Court Criminal Papers, NCSA. Haun, *Chowan County North Carolina County Court Minutes . . . Book II*, 53–54. *Crown v Mary Waltham*, Jury's Presentment, October Court, 1738, General Court—Criminal and Assize, NCSA.

captains on their way to southern plantations stopped by houses of correction, handed out liquor to the women there, and then cajoled them into moving overseas.[24]

Prostitution had long been considered a moral debasement of women, but in the context of England's colonial wars, prostitutes received heightened attention. Reformers feared that the spread of immorality and disease would cause soldiers and sailors to lose their stamina and vitality. "If this Lustful Fire be not quench'd, or else be timely restrained," one forecaster wrote, " 'twill soon emasculate the Age, consume the Strength, and melt down the Courage of the Nation. . . . If we design to maintain our Martial Vigour, for which we are now renown'd thr' the World, we must keep at a Distance from Venus' tents." To combat the negative effects associated with prostitution, eighteenth-century English reformers launched sustained efforts to regulate and control sexual commerce.[25]

In the southern colonies, efforts to curb prostitution were fueled by concerns about illicit lower-class behavior and interracial socializing. Widow Elizabeth Marston, for example, a tavernkeeper in Edenton in the 1720s, was allegedly "a common Bawd" who allowed "the persons that frequent her house" to commit "great disorders to the disturbance and annoyance . . . of the neighbourhood." James Trotter accused Marston in 1728 of being "a Bawd to Your own Daughters," claiming she had "putt two of [her] own daughters to Bed with two Men in Virginia and received a pistole of the Sayd Men" in return. Trotter added, "One of Your Daughters had a Mollatta Bastard in Virginia and he would prove it." Trotter's words may have been spurious slander, as Marston claimed, but if she did indeed run a "disorderly house," chances were that it was not an establishment for whites only.[26]

24. A. Roger Ekirch, *Bound for America: The Transportation of British Convicts to the Colonies, 1718–1775* (Oxford: Clarendon Press, 1987), 172–73; Abbot Emerson Smith, *Colonists in Bondage: White Servitude and Convict Labor in America, 1607–1776* (Chapel Hill: University of North Carolina Press, 1947; repr., New York: W. W. Norton & Co., 1971), 141.

25. *An Essay on Conjugal Infidelity, Shewing the Great Mischief that Attend Those that Defile the Marriage Bed* (London: T. Warner, 1727), 12–13, quoted in Donna Andrew, *Philanthropy and Police: London Charity in the Eighteenth Century* (Princeton: Princeton University Press, 1989), 57.

26. *Marston v Trotter*, Elizabeth Marston, deposition, March Court, 1729, in Cain, *North Carolina Higher-Court Records*, 6:554–55.

Illicit social and sexual exchanges among the laboring classes un-
nerved wealthier Carolinians because such liaisons bridged the gap of
race and status and challenged the efforts of the elite to divide and
rule a diverse colonial population. Clandestine interracial activity,
be it theft, aid to runaways, or sex, took on the aspect of politically
subversive behavior and portended more widespread forms of lower-
class collaboration. Indeed, these multiple and often simultaneous
forms of social and sexual misconduct posed a threat precisely because
they were perpetrated by the "poorer sort." Court magistrates could
more easily tolerate fornication, adultery, and prostitution as lapses
of the elite, but they vigorously prosecuted the same infractions if the
offenders came from the lower ranks of society. In other words, the
political impact of any given transgression hinged more on who was
breaking the law than on what actually transpired.

Yet if "disorderly houses" caused concern among the elite, prostitution hardly represented a moment of female insurgency. Based
on the exploitation of women's sexuality under conditions of limited
economic opportunities, prostitution demonstrates how gender could
create particular vulnerabilities for lower-class women. In addition to
the general social stigma and physical vulnerability that prostitutes
endured, there were disastrous moments when the courts cracked
down on brothels, sometimes with lasting impact. Edmund Gale,
for example, one of the wealthiest men in Edenton, hounded Elizabeth Abell in July 1737 for keeping a "disorderly house without any
Lycense" and entertaining other people's servants. He complained to
the court, and Abell gave bond for good behavior and promised that
in the future she would not "sell any more Liquor as a tipling house,"
but the trade in liquor, while offensive to Gale, was not foremost
on his mind. He appeared again before the bench later that month
and this time "duly proved to this Court" that Abell not only kept a
"Tippleing house" without a license, but that her house was "Lew'd
and disorderly" and contrary to law. If she was not a prostitute herself,
Gale implied, Abell was the keeper of a brothel, or at the very least
she countenanced unlawful activities in her house. For her "Lewd
and Vile actions," Abell was permanently banished from Edenton. She
was kept in close confinement until the designated day when she was
"tyed to a Carts tayl and . . . whipt out of the Town by receiving Thirty
Lashes on her bare Back well laid on." The court-ordered spectacle of

pain, humiliation, and banishment suggests the extent to which the activities in Abell's household were perceived as threatening; Abell's "Lew'd and disorderly" house prompted a theatrical reassertion of government authority.[27]

Cases like Abell's illustrate the degree to which sexual and social misconduct served as a testing ground for power in which the symbolic importance of the event often eclipsed the impact or intent of the original misdeed. When fornication, adultery, and skinny-dipping defied norms of appropriate conduct, the responses to these infractions could be a display of state power that retraced the limits of personal autonomy. In a variety of ways, misbehaving white women posed significant challenges to the social order in colonial North Carolina. Runaways like Dorothy Steel and Hanah Davis spurned their prescribed role as women subservient to husbands and masters, servant women established extralegal quasi-marriages in the face of nuptial restrictions, and some white women continued to have sexual relations with African American men. Widespread misconduct among neighbors indicates that subcultures sustained alternative sexual and social mores. Even when misconduct was not necessarily intended as a self-conscious display of resistance to sexual norms, women's illicit behavior could represent a symbolic challenge to the ability of lawmakers and court judges to enforce their notions of order and good government. In a world where the personal and political realms overlapped, sexually misbehaving women became "common disturbers of the peace" whose actions undermined norms of female deference and highlighted the limits of state authority.

27. Haun, *Chowan County North Carolina County Court Minutes . . . Book II*, 46–47; Clara Ann Bowler, "Carted Whores and White Shrouded Apologies: Slander in the County Courts of Seventeenth-Century Virginia," *Virginia Magazine of History and Biography* 85 (October 1977): 411–26.

Between Mistress and Slave

Elizabeth Wirt's White Housekeepers, 1808–1825

ANYA JABOUR

In 1808 Ann Perry, an unmarried white woman, accepted a position as housekeeper for Elizabeth and William Wirt in Richmond, Virginia. Perry's new post as the Wirts' housekeeper required her to share a dwelling with Elizabeth Wirt and her lawyer-husband, William, their two young children, a white male legal apprentice, five adult slaves, and several slave children. Initially Perry must have hoped to occupy a position of high status in the Wirt household; when William described his household in 1808, he classed the housekeeper as one of the "whites," separate from the "servants," a term he used only to denote enslaved blacks.[1]

Elizabeth Wirt hired Perry to assist her in keeping house while she nursed what her husband called her "delicate" health, which had been brought on by bearing four children in five years and watching two of them die in infancy. As Elizabeth's second-in-command, Perry was responsible for such skilled tasks as spinning, weaving, and dairying,

I would like to thank David M. Katzman of the University of Kansas for his helpful comments and suggestions on an earlier draft of this essay.

1. William Wirt to Benjamin Edwards, July 2, 1808, William Wirt Papers, Maryland Historical Society, Baltimore (hereinafter MHS). Although the Wirts used the word *servants* as a euphemism for slaves, I use the term to refer collectively to all the members of their household who were not members of their family: white hired help, free blacks, hired slaves, and the Wirts' own slaves. I use the word *domestic* or the phrase *domestic servant* in the same way, *mistress* to express the mistress-servant relationship that Elizabeth Wirt expected, and the term *employer* is used in the general sense to refer to all individuals who purchase the labor of another person.

as well as supervising the Wirts' slaves at their work in the house and garden. The housekeeper's supervisory role and personal responsibility for highly skilled labor set her apart from the Wirts' slaves, as did the use of an honorific in the title the Wirts gave her, "Miss Ann."[2]

Perry initially was successful in her new work, producing "right smart pots of butter" and causing Elizabeth Wirt to "rejoice at such good accounts of the spinning." But "Miss Ann" soon lost favor with her mistress. During the summer and fall of 1809, which Elizabeth spent at her sister's plantation in the Virginia countryside, William hinted at the first signs of trouble. While he said that "Miss Ann seems attentive to her duties and obliging," he noted that the housekeeper had trouble managing the slaves. "She is anxious for your return—I suspect the servants vex her," he remarked to Elizabeth. The following summer William informed Elizabeth that Miss Ann had "had a great quarrel" with a slave woman named Marinda, who apparently was stealing the cotton she was set to spin.[3]

Elizabeth was certain she knew the reason for Miss Ann's lack of success: the housekeeper attempted to set herself apart from the slaves she supervised. "Miss Ann is highly censurable for [stirring] up this sce[ne of] confusion & complaint," she charged, "when nothing would be easier than to put a stop to it by setting with her work in the room with Marinda." Rather than working side by side with the slaves she supervised, Elizabeth complained, "Miss Ann" preferred to maintain physical distance between herself and the slaves. "I should like to know if it is not the business of a housekeeper to see work executed," Elizabeth demanded, "and not like a Princess to issue her orders and expect to be obeyed while she withdraws to her closet, or elsewhere."[4]

Elizabeth retaliated by moving the housekeeper from her "closet" to another room and installing curtains and carpets in Perry's former room for use as "a family eating room." Elizabeth's action was a sharp reminder that although "Miss Ann" counted as one of the Wirt

2. William Wirt to Benjamin Edwards, July 2, 1808, William Wirt to Elizabeth Wirt, September 8, 11, 1809, June 27, July 16, 22, September 9, 1810, Elizabeth Wirt to William Wirt, September 26, 1809, MHS. (Hereinafter, William Wirt is designated WW, and Elizabeth Wirt, EW.)

3. WW to EW, July 16, 1810, EW to WW, September 26, 1809, WW to EW, September 17, 1809, June 27, July 16, 1810, MHS.

4. EW to WW, July 18, 1810, MHS.

household's "whites," she was not a member of the Wirt family. The Wirts never referred to their housekeepers as servants, reserving that term for their slaves, but Elizabeth Wirt made it clear to Perry that she was, in fact, a servant, a subordinate whose privileges depended, as did those of the Wirts' slaves, on her mistress's pleasure. Perry's claim to superiority already threatened, she must have been prepared for any further assaults on her status. When William rebuked her harshly for giving the wrong orders to one of the slaves, "Miss Ann drew" her lips into "a green persimmon pucker," he wrote his wife. William's challenge to Perry's authority in the presence of the slave she was overseeing must have been the final straw. Apparently the housekeeper soon exercised the remaining right she had as a free white servant—the right to quit—and left the Wirts' employ.[5]

The Wirts' struggle with Ann Perry set the tone for housekeeping in the Wirts' Richmond and Washington, D.C. households between 1808 and 1825. The Wirts were members of the emerging urban professional class in the nineteenth-century United States. Elizabeth Wirt was the second daughter of Robert Gamble, a successful Richmond merchant; William Wirt was a prominent Virginia lawyer and served as the United States attorney general from 1817 to 1829. The Wirts, like other well-to-do white southerners, owned slaves to perform routine household tasks, including large-scale textile production and meat preservation. Like city dwellers throughout the nation, they also hired white domestics for certain tasks. Only the presence of slaves and servants allowed the Wirts to maintain a high level of household production while they adopted a new ideal of a private family in which the mother assumed primary responsibility for affectionate child rearing. While hiring housekeepers resolved certain contradictions for the Wirts, it created new problems as well. Chief among these difficulties was the ambiguous status of housekeepers in the Wirt household. The unclear rank of housekeepers created confusion and resentment among the women who mediated between the white family and its black slaves. Housekeepers had their own goals, and as free workers, they used

5. EW to WW, July 18, 1810, WW to EW, July 22, 1810, MHS. William's letter is the last mention of Ann Perry as the Wirt's housekeeper. In September the Wirts were forced to rely on day labor to do the laundry. See WW to EW, September 9, 25, 1810, MHS.

the labor market to forward their struggle for autonomy and status. As Elizabeth Wirt and Ann Perry's repeated disagreements suggest, "Miss Ann" and the white women who succeeded her occupied an uncomfortable niche between mistress and slave.

Throughout the nation, household servants were accorded low status. In the nineteenth-century United States, while other working-class whites expressed their independence by withdrawing from the homes of their employers to form their own communities, a new class of domestic servants continued to live with their employers, or, in the case of slaves, with their owners. The parallel between slavery and domestic service was evident to both employers and the women and men who labored in their households. As one historian of domestic service has written, "household work was . . . rooted in servitude and not far removed from slavery."[6] Like slaves, domestics remained in highly personalistic mistress-servant rather than employer-employee relationships regulated by the market economy. Although they were not set apart from their employers by skin color, white domestics were reminded of their inferior status in a variety of ways. Household servants were required to wear livery, stay in certain parts of the house, and exhibit deference to their masters and mistresses. Small wonder that, as domestic maven Catharine Beecher expressed it in 1841, "the term servant, and the duties it involves, are, in the minds of many persons, nearly the same as those of the slave. And there are few minds, entirely free from associations which make servitude a degradation."[7]

6. David M. Katzman, *Seven Days a Week: Women and Domestic Service in Industrializing America* (New York: Oxford University Press, 1978), 146; Douglas T. Miller, *Jacksonian Aristocracy: Class and Democracy in New York, 1830–1860* (New York: Oxford University Press, 1967), 5–7, 53; Daniel E. Sutherland, *Americans and Their Servants: Domestic Service in the United States from 1800 to 1920* (Baton Rouge: Louisiana State University Press, 1981), xi–xii, 3–6, and chap. 7; Faye E. Dudden, *Serving Women: Household Service in Nineteenth-Century America* (Middletown, Conn.: Wesleyan University Press, 1983), chaps. 1–3; Elizabeth Clark-Lewis, *"This Work Had a' End": The Transition from Live-In to Day Work* (Memphis: Center for Research on Women, Memphis State University, 1985), 3. Useful contemporary work includes Susan Tucker, *Telling Memories among Southern Women: Domestic Workers and Their Employers in the Segregated South* (Baton Rouge: Louisiana State University Press, 1988); Judith Rollins, *Between Women: Domestics and Their Employers* (Philadelphia: Temple University Press, 1985).

7. Catharine E. Beecher, *A Treatise on Domestic Economy, for the Use of Young Ladies at Home, and at School* (1841; reprint, New York: Source Book Press, 1970), 200.

Domestics throughout the nation struggled to assert their autonomy and gain respect, but white servants in slaveholding households had an additional reason to demand symbolic recognition. Frederick Law Olmsted made several astute comments on the debasing of labor, especially household work, in the slaveholding South. Some women, he noted, would prefer death or prostitution (Olmsted apparently considered the latter alternative the more terrible of the two) to domestic service, believing "that the position of servant, or of those who sell their labor and skill by measure of time and not by measure of amount, is worse than that of slaves." In the South, where domestic service was most closely associated with the degradation of slavery, many white domestics refused to work with blacks. Those who did often focused their demands on changes that would allow them to remain aloof from their black coworkers, such as separate dining and living arrangements.[8]

The mixed-labor system of the urban upper South maximized the potential for confrontation over the issue of household status. Mistresses in border cities like Richmond and Washington, D.C., could choose from a variety of servants, ranging from free whites to enslaved blacks, with a mixed group of free, escaped, hired, or self-hired "quasi-free" blacks, muting the distinctions among the different types of household workers. Although they always owned slaves, Elizabeth and William Wirt were on the cutting edge of a trend to hire white women for household work, primarily as housekeepers. Often the only whites in the household other than the Wirts, Elizabeth Wirt's housekeepers were assigned the task of mediating between mistress and slave.[9]

8. Frederick Law Olmsted, *A Journey in the Seaboard Slave States, with Remarks on Their Economy* (New York: 1863), 202. See also Katzman, *Seven Days a Week*, 185.
9. WW to EW, September 18, 1818, EW to WW, December 13, 1812, May 9, 1824, Laura and EW to WW, November 20, 1818, MHS. On mixed labor and the growing preference for white domestics, see Stephanie Cole, " 'Because His Mistress Cannot Manage Him': African-American Men as Domestic Servants in Antebellum Cities" (paper presented at the Third Southern Conference on Women's History, Houston, Tex., June 1994); and Stephanie Cole, " 'A Middle-aged White Woman Would Be Preferred': Defining Domestic Roles in the Urban Upper South, 1800–1850" (paper presented at the Berkshire Conference on the History of Women, Poughkeepsie, N.Y., June 1993). On "quasi-free" slaves, see Loren Schweninger, "The Underside of Slavery: The Internal Economy, Self-Hire, and Quasi-Freedom in Virginia, 1780–1865," *Slavery and Abolition* 12 (September 1991): 1–22.

William Wirt sent word to Elizabeth to direct one housekeeper to "order all the servants, in my name and at their peril, to respect her commands as those of a second mistress." As "a second mistress," a housekeeper was responsible for a wide range of tasks. Elizabeth Wirt once defined a housekeeper as a woman "to keep House for me & help to sew." In addition to sewing and keeping house, a task that included supervising the Wirts' variable force of five to ten adult slaves, the Wirts' housekeepers were also expected to care for the Wirt children's clothes and to sleep with the younger children. By 1818, the Wirt family included ten children, ranging in age from infancy to fifteen years old. As the older Wirt daughters came of marriageable age, housekeepers occasionally served as chaperones.[10]

Job descriptions for housekeepers required that they be distinct from black "servants." In the South, white household servants, including nurses, governesses, and housekeepers, were assigned tasks that slaves were not trusted to do properly: supervision and childcare. Racial hierarchy dictated that supervisory tasks be assigned to whites. Southern household mistresses apparently hired white women as housekeepers because they assumed that supervision could only be done competently by other whites. Popular notions of domesticity and family also encouraged nineteenth-century parents to hire white female housekeepers. Contemporary childcare literature warned against leaving impressionable young children with corrupt (read immigrant or black) servants. Elizabeth Wirt clearly distrusted the slaves where childcare was concerned. While she visited her sister in the Virginia countryside in 1812, she urged her husband, who remained at home in Richmond, to take an active role in childcare. "Oh! that I could take a peep at my dear Laura, Robert, and Elizabeth, this morning—God bless, & protect them! My dear Husband, let me intreat of you—to devote yourself to them—be a Father & Mother to them—until I can take a part of the burthen off you. Deny yourself the pleasure of dining *out* with your friends—for then, you know they must be necessarily left entirely with the servants, and exposed to accidents—and that my imagination is continually teeming with." Hiring white servants, many

10. Between 1807 and 1817, WW owned from two to nine slaves. Richmond City Personal Property Books, 1806–1807, 1809–1817, Virginia State Library and Archives, Richmond (hereinafter VSLA).

southerners believed, would give them more leisure to care for their own children and, in addition, would provide back-up caregivers in their own image. For southerners like the Wirts, who did not consider slaves to be members of their extended family, white servants may have served as a buffer between the white family and its black slaves.[11]

The presence of white and black servants in the same household could just as easily blur the boundary between servants and family members, however, by eliminating race as a convenient designation. Domestics had their own hierarchy, which assigned rank based both on the domestic's occupation and on race or ethnic background. White housekeepers in slave households stood above all the slaves by both criteria. When southern housekeepers emphasized their superiority to slaves, as Ann Perry did by demanding the use of an honorific, insisting on retiring to her own quarters, and finally asserting her status as a free white by leaving her employers, they threatened the symbolic boundaries that separated privileged white families from their servants of both races.[12]

For the Wirts, a family with a strict class- and race-specific definition of family, upholding the demarcation between the master and mistress and their servants and slaves was crucial. Elizabeth and William Wirt were committed to a private family that excluded slaves and white servants. As Elizabeth's reaction to Ann Perry's wish to "withdraw to her closet" indicated, one of the most effective ways to demonstrate the boundaries between family members and servants was through household architecture. Workspace and family space were clearly marked out in the Wirts' "elegant and well-furnished establishment" in Richmond. Insurance records show that the rooms for storage and laundry were located in two wings attached to the center building by covered walkways, while the dairy and stable were detached from the house and located in the yard. Even the yard was divided. An area

11. EW to WW, December 6, 1812, MHS. For an example of warnings to avoid using servants in childcare, see Anne M. Boylan, "Growing Up Female in Young America, 1800–1860," in *American Childhood,* ed. N. Ray Hiner and Joseph M. Hawes (Westport, Conn.: Greenwood Press, 1985), 154–55. The Wirts were not alone in hiring white servants for certain tasks; the Washingtons hired a white housekeeper in the late 1790s. Miriam Anne Bourne, *First Family: George Washington and His Intimate Relations* (New York: Norton, 1982), 195–96.
12. Sutherland, *Americans and Their Servants,* 82–89, 92–94, 126–32.

planted with trees to form a "romantic grove" for the children's play and for entertaining guests was separated by a picket fence from the vegetable garden and compost heap located in the working yard. Such distinctions served to insulate family members from the servants and slaves who provided the labor for continuing household production. Restricted to the back of the house, to cellars or attics, or to out-buildings, servants and slaves were virtually invisible. This was clearly what Elizabeth had in mind when she designed "a snug little family room, or morning parlour." She made sure "to cut off all back views of staircases, entries Mammoth presses, & old trunks." In 1809 William wrote from Richmond to Elizabeth and the children, who were away for the summer, complaining that he was "surrounded only by silent walls or beings equally uninteresting," despite the presence of five adult slaves, several slave children, and a housekeeper. William's comment demonstrates how architecture and a narrow definition of the family could obscure the presence of "uninteresting" servants and slaves.[13]

Mistresses in the upper South attempted to reconcile the need to recognize housekeepers' superior standing relative to slaves and their own desire to maintain class lines. Martha Washington, for example, decided in the 1790s that her housekeeper would have "a warm decent and comfortable room to herself, [and] Victuals from our Table" but would not "set at it, at any time *with us.*" Similarly, Elizabeth Wirt permitted Ann Perry to have a room of her own but expected her not to use it to withdraw from the presence of slaves. Although Elizabeth insisted on hiring white women for specific tasks and admitted her housekeepers' superiority to the slaves and lower servants, she was reluctant to concede all the privileges her housekeepers desired, fearing that by doing so she would weaken her own position as mistress.[14]

Being mistress was Elizabeth Wirt's chief opportunity to exercise her privileges as a well-to-do white woman in the South. Like other married women of her time and place, she was legally dependent on, and inferior to, her husband. William Wirt's directive to one

13. WW to Benjamin Edwards, June 23, 1809, EW to WW, July 18, 1810, WW to EW, September 8, 1809, MHS; Mutual Assurance Society Fire Insurance Policy #1721, October 13, 1815, VSLA; WW to EW, April 9, September 11, October 4, 1809, MHS.

14. Bourne, *First Family,* 195–96. For similar uses of space in the north, see Dudden, *Serving Women,* 196; Sutherland, *Americans and Their Servants,* 114–17.

housekeeper to command the slaves in his name suggested that even Elizabeth Wirt's authority as mistress was derived from that of her husband. In the mistress-servant relationship, however, Elizabeth was dominant. By demanding recognition as mistress, she confirmed her superiority over servants and slaves, thereby strengthening her sense of herself as a member of the powerful class of slaveholders and employers and justifying the class and racial privileges that gave her authority.[15]

Although ultimately Elizabeth's authority as mistress was compromised by her husband's authority as master—in 1802 William referred to his wife as "mistress of her Williams household"—in practice William ceded authority over household operations to Elizabeth. William may have been willing to share authority over the household because of the lengthy absences from home that traveling from court to court required of antebellum lawyers. Already by 1804 William had bowed to his wife's judgment on matters pertaining to their household economy. In a letter to Elizabeth, he referred to the Wirt household as "your home." Elizabeth never indicated in her letters that she feared her husband would deprive her of a mistress's authority. Her letters to William were written not as an appeal for assistance or approval but simply to vent the frustration she felt in the contests for power within the household that took place during her husband's absences. Elizabeth did not acknowledge that her problems in household management were shaped by the circumstances that gave her the privileges of race and class but the disadvantages of her sex. As a woman, Elizabeth had only tacit authority over the household she managed. Her difficulties in William's absence suggest that Elizabeth relied on her husband to maintain order when he was at home. When he was away, Elizabeth may have found that her authority was compromised by her standing as mistress, rather than master. Possibly Elizabeth felt some uncertainty about her ability to wield authority on her own. If so, she directed her frustration toward her housekeepers, over whom she could exercise the dominance of class. Elizabeth Wirt jealously guarded her own position as mistress, an attitude that made it all the

15. See especially Elizabeth Fox-Genovese, *Within the Plantation Household: Black and White Women of the Old South* (Chapel Hill: University of North Carolina Press, 1988), chap. 1.

more crucial to define the housekeepers' unique position in the Wirt household, between mistress and slave.[16]

Because white housekeepers were not distinguished by legal status or race from their employers, symbolic expressions of status were of vital importance for both mistresses and their white servants. Whenever one of Elizabeth's housekeepers emphasized her rights as a free worker and capitalized on her status as "second mistress," Elizabeth defended herself against what she perceived as her housekeeper's attempts to be "*sole mistress*—which would never suit me." Elizabeth Wirt's assertions of dominance took two forms. First, she sought to limit her housekeepers' contractual rights, thereby minimizing their rights as free women. Second, by insisting on her exclusive enjoyment of the privileges of a mistress, Elizabeth symbolically reminded her "second mistresses" that, although they were white, their lower class set them apart from the one true mistress. Elizabeth's words and actions grouped her free, white housekeepers with the Wirts' other "servants," slaves. Her housekeepers resisted their mistress by insisting on recognition of their differences from slaves. Situated as they were between their mistress and the slaves, when the housekeepers attempted to better their position, they often overstepped the upper boundaries of their role. The letters Elizabeth Wirt wrote to her husband and other family members from her homes in Richmond and Washington between 1808 and 1825 reveal the conflicts created when her housekeepers tested the limitations of their ambiguous position in the Wirt household.[17]

Between 1808 and 1825, the Wirts employed at least seven housekeepers, a special group set apart from both the white women who laundered and sewed for the Wirts on a contract basis and the enslaved black servants. Like Ann Perry, the Wirts' subsequent housekeepers were native-born white women. When the Wirts searched for housekeepers, they first approached "poor widows" or "elderly single wom[e]n." The Wirts correctly assumed that the gendered experiences of widowhood, abandonment, or singlehood forced white women into poverty and led them to seek domestic employment. For example, one woman the Wirts inquired of as a likely applicant was a woman whose husband had abandoned her; one came to the Wirts after

16. WW to EW, August 31, 1802, October 21, 1804, MHS.
17. EW to WW, January 22, 1825, MHS.

leaving her abusive husband; and still another potential housekeeper, who was unmarried, was perennially without a home because she quarreled with her relatives.[18]

Although forced by circumstances to seek labor as domestic servants, the Wirts' housekeepers, like northern domestics, were keenly aware of their rights as free white workers. As William commented with disappointment of a family acquaintance who proved unsuitable as a housekeeper, "I always knew her pride but hoped that adversity had schooled her into more sense." Women who expressed interest in working as Elizabeth Wirt's housekeeper refused to be schooled by adversity, exhibiting instead a keen sense of their ability to use the demand for their labor to their own advantage. When in 1820 Elizabeth attempted to talk one domestic known only as Margaret into accepting lower wages, she found that Margaret was not as biddable as she had hoped: "dull as she appears to be upon other subjects she is *cute* enough upon that," she noted.[19]

The perennial "servant shortage" caused by the ability of free servants to leave their employers gave domestics an important bargaining tool in setting wages and work and living conditions. Like northern mistresses, Elizabeth was reluctant to acknowledge the bargaining power of free domestics, and she, like her northern counterparts, relied on the recommendations of other mistresses when hiring housekeepers. Northerners' incomplete acceptance of the market ethic in their dealings with servants reflected the persistence of a personalistic bond between servant and mistress reminiscent of indentured servitude. In the South, where slavery continued to flourish, uncertainty about servants' rights as free laborers may have been even more acute. Undoubtedly the connection between involuntary service and domestic service was more evident. In the Wirts' case, obtaining "character" references for housekeepers was a technique they adapted from their

18. EW to WW, January 4, 1816, December 15, 1825, MHS. Antebellum servants were overwhelmingly native-born, and 90 percent were women. Native-born white servants were usually unmarried, divorced, or widowed. Sutherland, *Americans and Their Servants,* 45, 55.

19. WW to EW, December 3, 1818, EW to WW, September 4, 1820, MHS. For comparison to the North, see Carol Lasser, "The Domestic Balance of Power: Relations between Mistress and Maid in Nineteenth-Century New England," *Labor History* 28 (winter 1987): 5–22.

experiences in purchasing slaves. In order to exercise some control over white domestics' bargaining ability, Elizabeth used a network of other well-to-do mistresses to locate and recommend potential housekeepers. Although away from her Richmond home during the winter of 1812 and 1813, for example, Elizabeth was able to locate five prospective housekeepers, one as far away as Staunton, through her mother, Catharine Gamble, and other friends and neighbors in Richmond. Elizabeth's mother screened some of the Richmond applicants herself and obtained recommendations for others through consultation with two of her neighbors. "She prefers Mrs. Harrie's recommendation," William updated Elizabeth on developments, "and tomorrow . . . the two ladies go to see Miss Johnson, the proposed housekeeper—Mrs. H. knows her [and] speaks of her in the highest terms." For unspecified reasons, Miss Johnson did not accept the post, but a housekeeper named Miss Porter was soon hired for a month's trial through the offices of yet another female acquaintance.[20]

Neighbor women continued to assist Elizabeth in finding domestic servants after the Wirts moved to Washington in 1817. In the mid-1820s, Elizabeth rejected one candidate when she learned from her friend and neighbor Mrs. Elzey that a potential servant was "*a fire brand,*" and hired another housekeeper, "tho' I have not yet seen her," on the recommendation of a Mrs. Watson. A reliance on such personal recommendations led Elizabeth to limit the pool of potential candidates. In 1825, William suggested that Elizabeth, once again in search of a housekeeper, "had better get one in Washington, where you can see the candidate, beforehand, yourself and make your own bargain." "I beleive [*sic*] it is best," Elizabeth agreed, "to take my chance for a housekeeper in our own neighbourhood, to having one from a distance, with the uncertainty of her pleasing."[21]

Once a mistress located a "pleasing" housekeeper, she often behaved as if housekeepers had no right to bargain with other potential employers. An 1816 letter suggests that Elizabeth believed she had

20. EW to WW, December [13?], 1812, WW to EW, December 17, 1812, January 6, 13, 1813, EW to WW, November 25, 26, 1817, EW to Catharine Gamble, May 3, 1825, MHS. On the "servant shortage," see Dudden, *Serving Women,* 51–55, 232–34; Sutherland, *Americans and Their Servants,* 130–32.

21. EW to WW, January 22, 1825, May 11, 1824, WW to EW, November 8, 1825, EW to WW, November 9, 1825, MHS.

a prior claim on all of the women who had once worked for her. Betsey Jordan and her mother had jointly served Elizabeth Wirt as housekeepers in 1814. In 1816, when the younger Jordan refused to come in response to her former employer's call, Elizabeth was outraged. "I sent twice for Betsey Jordan to stay with me," she informed William, "But her Mother could not spare her at those times—and I shall never send for her again."[22]

Elizabeth's attitude was shared by other urban mistresses in the border South. In 1817 Elizabeth sought to regain the services of Ann Perry, but the attempt was complicated by the general reluctance of employers to allow housekeepers to sell their labor to the highest bidder. Having searched in vain in Washington for a woman to serve as housekeeper in the Wirt's new home, William looked again to the possibilities in Richmond, suggesting to Elizabeth that "Miss Ann" might be willing to engage herself to them a second time. In the six years since she had left the Wirts, Perry had used the demand for her skills to shift employers at least twice, working first for a Mrs. McClurg and then for a Mrs. Wickham. The Wirts hoped that high wages would induce the housekeeper to change yet again. "I wish it were possible without any breach of propriety towards Mrs. Wickham, to tempt Ann Perry to follow your fortunes," William wrote to Elizabeth. William meant that Elizabeth must not appear to lure Perry away or steal her from her mistress—a definition of "propriety" that suggested that Perry was Mrs. Wickham's property. This was not the first time the Wirts had hoped to rehire Perry. When they had tried four years earlier, it was her mistress, Mrs. McClurg, who had responded firmly that she "*never intended* to part with Miss Ann." The Wirts hoped to avoid a repeat of this embarrassing incident by concealing their effort to induce Perry to accept their offer. "*You* must not be seen in it," William warned Elizabeth, although "your mother & Mrs. Vanet [a neighbor] may do what they please." It would be best of all, William slyly suggested, "if Ann shd. take it in head to quarrel with Mrs. Wickham, or the servants," so that the Wirts could not be blamed.[23]

Elizabeth promptly visited Mrs. Vanet, telling her friend that "if [Ann Perry] had any notion of a change I wished she would go to

22. EW to WW, January 4, 1816, MHS.
23. WW to EW, November 23, 1817, WW to EW, January 6, 1813, MHS.

Washington with me." Elizabeth secured her friend's assistance by mentioning "that she would oblige me if she would see [Perry] and tell her so in a suitable manner—that money was not a consideration with me, if she found her disposed to go, or wished to change, I would satisfy her in that respect." William approved but worried that Elizabeth's offer of higher wages—even when communicated in such a roundabout manner—might subject her to criticism. "I pray you not to be seen if possible in the affair of Ann Perry," he wrote. "Let it be so managed as to make the affair one of Ann's own, if she comes, at all. I should be extremely unhappy to have it said that you had seduced her to leave the services of another lady: and it will be said, unless it is managed with extraordinary delicacy." Even if Perry offered to come herself, William wrote, he felt that Elizabeth should confer with Mrs. Wickham before employing her, "and state the fact, with an inquiry whether *she* has any objection to your accepting her offer or something to that effect—perhaps it will be sufficient for you to express your reluctance at promoting your own convenience at the expense of her's—or any thing else that occurs to you as better to satisfy her of the propriety and dignity of your conduct."[24]

As the Wirts' hopeful efforts to rehire Perry away from first Mrs. Mc-Clurg and then Mrs. Wickham suggest, Elizabeth and her fellow mistresses did not always succeed in curbing their free white domestics' bargaining power. Despite Mrs. McClurg's presumption that she could dictate Ann Perry's movements, the housekeeper soon moved on to work for Mrs. Wickham. The Wirts recognized that a housekeeper could offer herself to them on her own, even though they worried that accepting such an offer might subject them to charges of having "seduced" a servant. Some housekeepers may have learned to manipulate their employers by intentionally provoking quarrels as an alternative to quitting outright, as William suggested "Miss Ann" might do if she chose to leave Mrs. Wickham to work for the Wirts a second time. Housekeepers in the border South may have been encouraged to take such oblique actions to protect their new employers from criticism and ensure themselves new posts. Perry did not follow the Wirts to Washington (after her successes in finding other employers, she probably did not relish the thought of another stint with Elizabeth

24. EW to WW, November 26, 1817, WW to EW, November 28, 1817, MHS.

Wirt), but the battle for her services indicates that employers like the Wirts, who often relied on recommendations to eliminate troublesome housekeepers from their list of candidates, were sometimes willing to hire a housekeeper who lost a position by quarreling with her mistress.

While some housekeepers may have cloaked their determination to exercise their right to bargain, many housekeepers were forthright in stating their expectations before they took a post. Elizabeth Wirt indicated in her letters that many housekeepers preferred to keep searching for a less demanding employer rather than submit to her terms. One woman informed Elizabeth "that it did not agree with her to loose her rest, [and] that she must be in bed by 10 o'clock. or she would have a nervous head ach. None of this suited me," Elizabeth complained. Another woman, Mrs. Hyland, "would not suit us" because she required "a room in the house *to her self.*" Elizabeth concluded with a succinct statement of her displeasure with this housekeeper's attempts to set her own terms: "Unless she has more correct notions—or at least notions that would suit me better—we do not touch."[25]

Elizabeth's phrasing suggests that she, the employer, decided against hiring the applicants, but the women who interviewed with Elizabeth Wirt were also screening her. A series of meetings between Elizabeth and a woman named Mrs. Gardiner in 1825 demonstrates that negotiating terms was a two-way process. Mrs. Gardiner proposed to work for the Wirts for a wage, Elizabeth noted, that was "more than she gets from any one else" in Washington. In addition, Mrs. Gardiner refused to work for the Wirts unless they fired their cook, "as that woman is her greatest antipathy." Desperate for household help, Elizabeth conceded these points on the condition that the housekeeper would add cooking to her duties, "but that she would not—so we did not agree."[26]

Negotiations did not end with an initial agreement. At least one housekeeper who agreed to start working for Elizabeth on a specific date continued to search for a better position and backed out of her job with the Wirts when her search proved successful. "I sent to day to my housekeeper to say that I should look for her on Monday," Elizabeth

25. EW to Catharine Gamble, May 3, 1825, EW to WW, December 13, 1812, MHS.
26. EW to Catharine Gamble, May 3, 1825, MHS.

recorded with dismay in 1825, "& had for her answer, that she had made a different arrangement with [another] lady."[27]

Elizabeth had no legal recourse, for she herself refused to give her housekeepers a written contract. In 1817, the Wirts had hired a governess named Miss Gray. Her contract was for the year, although she was paid by the quarter. When their move to the capital prompted the Wirts to discharge Miss Gray early, she insisted on her contract rights, informing her employers that "an *engagement was easier formed than broken.*" Eventually the Wirts agreed to pay her for the year, but the experience made them unwilling to agree to contracts with other household employees. Instead, Elizabeth made verbal agreements with housekeepers to pay them by the month, with both parties reserving the right to terminate the relationship at the end of each month. Informal monthly arrangements like these potentially permitted Elizabeth and her housekeepers to renegotiate salaries and other terms on a regular basis. Elizabeth attempted to reserve the right to change the conditions of employment. When one housekeeper requested a raise, Elizabeth refused: "I have given *my dame* notice that I can not agree to *her* terms," she told her husband, "that I shall reduce her pay . . . & that I must have a reform &c &c." The housekeeper was not so easily put off, however, responding that "she only took the place for a time— until some of her family affairs were settled." When her housekeeper threatened to quit unless her "terms" were met, Elizabeth refused to back down. "I hope she will be off," Elizabeth wrote, "upon what I have already said."[28]

Typically Elizabeth did not indicate in her letters who chose to end the informal agreement between housekeeper and mistress. She rarely commented at all on her housekeepers' departure; following an argument with their mistress, housekeepers simply dropped out of the Wirts' correspondence. Contemporary studies of domestics suggest that the Wirts' housekeepers reasserted their rights as free workers by leaving the Wirts after such disagreements. One history of southern domestic workers concludes that household servants often have requirements for staying on a job that they do not state explicitly to their

27. EW to WW, December 30, 1825, MHS.
28. EW to WW, November 19, 1817, WW to EW, November 22, 1817, EW to WW, July 1, 1825, EW to WW, November 14, 16, 1824, MHS.

employers. When those requirements are not met, they leave without notice or a confrontation with the employer. For Elizabeth Wirt's housekeepers, as for these later domestics, there was a fine and often indistinct line between being fired for dissatisfactory performance and quitting because of dissatisfaction with the mistress's requirements.[29]

A housekeeper's reasons for not liking the job and Elizabeth's reasons for not liking a servant often coincided. Elizabeth Wirt made demands on her housekeepers that, like the limits she placed on their right to make contracts, reinforced the notion that mistresses owned their housekeepers, at least for the duration of their stay. Rather than requiring her housekeepers to fulfill specific duties, Elizabeth expected them to perform any task she requested of them. She once described a well-recommended housekeeper as "a first rate housekeeper—semstress—& every thing—and not too much pride & folly, to put her hand to any thing." In their turn, housekeepers in the Wirt household focused their demands on establishing a firm job description and set work hours, conditions of employment that were denied slaves. Employers and domestics throughout the nation clashed on this point. In her *Letters to Persons Who Are Engaged in Domestic Service*, for example, Catharine Beecher noted, "There is one frequent cause of difficulty between employers and domestics, that ought to be taken care of, when first making an agreement. Employers always wish to *hire the time* of domestics, instead of hiring them to do some particular parts of family work. But some domestics feel that they are hired to do some particular part of the work, and when this is done, that their time is their own."[30]

Although the conflict over work hours and duties was a common one in nineteenth-century households, it took on additional significance in the South. One historian of urban slavery notes that "constant service was part of the expectation, if not always the fulfillment, of slavery." Well after the end of slavery, southern domestic workers identified

29. Even when EW explicitly noted a parting of the ways, no agency was assigned. "Mrs Lane goes home to day," EW wrote in 1819, "we part friends I believe." See EW to Catharine Gamble, [February 1, 1819], MHS. See also Tucker, *Telling Memories*, 211; Rollins, *Between Women*, 142.

30. EW to WW, November 29, 1825, MHS; Catharine E. Beecher, *Letters to Persons Who Are Engaged in Domestic Service* (New York, 1842), 170–71.

live-in service with involuntary servitude.[31] Nineteenth-century domestic servants attempted to differentiate themselves from slaves by exerting some control over the definition of their responsibilities. One way to obtain some relief from Elizabeth Wirt's unceasing demands was to define set job duties rather than standing ready to serve in any capacity the mistress required. Jane Redin made her position clear in 1822. When Elizabeth reminded her to organize the children's combs to be sure that each child used only his or her own comb, Redin "got into a towering passion—said that she *was not a chamber maid*—to keep the combs either in order, or in their places . . . . That she would never comb their heads again—and a great deal more with a great deal of passion." Redin was determined to define her duties strictly and not to deviate from them, particularly if by doing so she lowered her status to that of a chambermaid. "Miss Jane" may have quit following her unsuccessful bid for a more clearly defined—and superior—job description. Elizabeth next mentioned her the following year, commenting with regret that she had been unable to find a replacement who matched Redin's prowess at organizing dinner parties. She attempted to rehire Redin, who was then working for a Mrs. Mason, but the housekeeper refused to return to the Wirts. Perhaps she had found an employer more receptive to her pressure for a job with set tasks.[32]

Housekeepers also objected to Elizabeth's expectation that they ought to be constantly on call. This was a common complaint among domestics in general. Catharine Beecher's tract, *Letters to Persons Who Are Engaged in Domestic Service* was intended to offer household workers tips on how to please their employers and to reconcile them to their position. To counteract domestics' tendency to lay claim to their own time after their tasks were completed, Beecher admonished:

> You perhaps may feel that it is your own concern what company you visit, and who visit you, and that, after your work is done, you have a right to go where you please without asking leave of your employers. But here I wish you would try yourselves

31. Richard Wade, *Slavery in the Cities: The South, 1820–1860* (New York: Oxford University Press, 1964), 29–32; Clark-Lewis, *"This Work Had a' End,"* 29; Rollins, *Between Women,* 63–69.

32. EW to WW, November 17, 1822, November 14, 1824, MHS. Sutherland, *Americans and Their Servants,* chap. 5.

by "the golden rule." Suppose you to look forward to a time when
you are the mistress of a family, and hire persons to help you do
the work, would you not in such a case feel thus: I have hired
these persons and pay them for their time, and they have agreed
to do my family work at the time and in the way I wish. Now they
cannot know, without asking, when I can spare them and when I
shall need their help. There are always times when, if the regular
work of the day is done up, some extra work, or some sickness,
or other causes, may make it needful for them to stay at home.
Therefore, I think it right to expect that those I hire will not either
go out, or invite company to come and see them, without first
inquiring of me whether it will be convenient.[33]

Elizabeth Wirt's housekeepers resented this "golden rule" and resisted it in a variety of ways. One housekeeper preferred to continue
looking for a position when Elizabeth refused to concede a ten P.M.
end to the workday and called such a requirement more suited to "a
pet child" than a domestic. Other housekeepers worked slowly or not
at all when unsupervised. "As to my present Housekeeper," Elizabeth
wrote in 1824, "I do not like her—she most unconscientiously requires
to be watched to keep her at her work—sets with a book in her lap, or
before her on the table—and is very slow at her needle."[34]
A particularly telling conflict took place between Elizabeth and
a housekeeper named Nancy Porter in 1816. "Nancy Porter . . . has
been sick," complained Elizabeth to her husband, "and when well is
the half of her time entertaining a sweetheart of hers, who spends
a great part of his time here. He comes to *dinner*, or to *Tea* at pleasure." As a housekeeper in a slaveholding household, Nancy Porter
had few opportunities for the kind of servants' hall socializing that
was available to domestics in establishments with a larger force of
white household workers. Entertaining a sweetheart at the Wirts' was
probably her only opportunity to find a husband and escape domestic
service to be mistress of her own household.[35]
Elizabeth's reaction, which was to begin searching for a replacement, suggested that she thought housekeepers, like her family's slaves,

33. Beecher, *Letters to Persons Who Are Engaged in Domestic Service,* 110–11.
34. EW to WW, May 9, 1825, November 14, 1824, MHS.
35. EW to WW, January 4, 1816, MHS. Sutherland, *Americans and Their Servants,*
78.

should not be permitted personal ties. Nancy Porter probably did not miss the connection between domestic service and servitude that was expressed in her mistress's refusal to allow the housekeeper to entertain visitors. Elizabeth's ire with Porter also may have been provoked by a feeling that in offering her male visitor *"dinner"* and *"Tea"*—words heavily underscored in Elizabeth's letter to her husband—the housekeeper was engaging in activities properly reserved for the mistress of the house. Dinner and tea were commonly offered in the parlor, a room that was strictly reserved for mistresses and their daughters to "wear fine clothes, and sit in beautiful rooms, and have nothing to do but sew on fine things," as a fictitious kitchen domestic complained to a similarly fictitious clergyman in Beecher's tract. In serving her male visitor tea, Porter appropriated an activity that well-to-do white women claimed for themselves and, perhaps intentionally, reminded her mistress that there was little to distinguish Elizabeth Wirt from her white female housekeeper.[36]

In his reply to Elizabeth's complaints about Nancy Porter, William suggested that free white help, in contrast to slaves, had to be cajoled rather than punished or summarily sold. "As to Nancy Porter, it is *natural* enough for her to encourage a sweet heart," he soothed, "but not altogether so just to do it at the expense of your convenience—can you not contrive to get more of her service by a gentle and jocular remonstrance." The "gentle and jocular remonstrance" William advised for the better management of white domestics was a method ill-suited to Elizabeth Wirt, who, as a slaveholder, was used to exercising the power of ownership to control her servants. At the same time that she was complaining about Porter, Elizabeth was making arrangements to sell two female slaves because "of Both of them I am heartily, thoroughly sick." A male slave was also to go, and all three were to be replaced by slaves currently being offered for sale in Richmond. Within a week Elizabeth's objectives had been reached. Nancy Porter also left the Wirts. Whether she quit or was fired is not recorded, but the incident did not end Wirt's difficulties in managing her housekeepers.[37]

36. EW to WW, January 4, 1816, MHS; Beecher, *Letters to Persons Who Are Engaged in Domestic Service*, 30.
37. WW to EW, January 6, 1816, EW to WW, January 4, 7, 11, 12, 13, 1816, MHS.

An even more contentious struggle between a housekeeper known as Mrs. Lane and Elizabeth Wirt in late 1818 illustrates the tense situation created when housekeepers attempted to maximize their position as free white supervisors, thus threatening Elizabeth's authority as mistress. Elizabeth was already dissatisfied with her housekeeper, who was reluctant to take effective control of the operation of the Wirts' Washington household. Instead, Mrs. Lane delegated responsibilities—even to the holding of the keys to the house's storerooms and closets—to the slaves. "She can complain and find fault, as well as heart can desire," Elizabeth wryly remarked, "But effects no change for the better in any one department of house keeping."

A more important source of tension was Mrs. Lane's refusal to show deference to her mistress. Mrs. Lane repeatedly challenged her mistress's authority, in part by claiming superiority over the Wirts' slaves and other servants. As Elizabeth described it, "Last Sund[a]y, the carriage had been ordered in the *morning* to carry my nurse [Mrs. Barclay] to see her family, but receiving a message from Mrs Lane to enquire if she could have the carriage in the *evening* to attend church at the *Navy Yards*—I told Mrs Barclay to put off her visit and she could go at the same time," an arrangement which would use the horses and carriages only once that day, as well as giving Stephen, the white coach driver, a half day to attend church as he had requested. "I thought this, a very proper & comfortable arrangement for all parties," Elizabeth recalled, "But behold when evening came, and the carriage brought to the door, Mrs Barclay enquired of [Mrs. Lane] if she were not going to the *meeting* aforesaid—she answered with great solemnity & emphasis—No-I-am-not-. Remarking immediately afterwards to the servants—that when she went out, she *chose* to have the carriage to herself."

In assigning carriage use and free time, Elizabeth acknowledged the internal hierarchy of her servants by race, legal status, and job description. Of the servants, the white housekeeper, as head servant, had first claim to the carriage and was allowed to set her own working hours, with her desires dictating when the carriage would be used. The white children's nurse, her elevated station suggested by the title Mrs. Barclay, had second claim to the carriage, although she had to rearrange her scheduled free half-day to suit Mrs. Lane, the housekeeper. The coachman, whose name was not preceded by an honorific, was allowed free time, though not carriage use, when the carriage was not needed. The slaves, of course, were conceded neither free time nor carriage use. Although she extended limited recognition to the servant hierarchy, Elizabeth was determined to remind her servants that no matter what their position on that hierarchy, they were all subject to her preferences as the mistress. Having "the carriage to herself," as Mrs. Lane no doubt knew, was the mistress's prerogative, and the housekeeper went too far for her mistress's comfort when she refused to share the carriage with her fellow servants. Although not yet ready to challenge Elizabeth directly, Mrs. Lane felt free to communicate her wishes to "the servants," the slaves and lower white domestics she supervised. Mrs. Lane's attitude of superiority did not go unremarked by the other domestic workers, who resented the housekeeper's determination to maximize her status as "second mistress." Other white servants in the household may have been particularly annoyed at the housekeeper's attempts to capitalize on her race and position. The hired coachman, Stephen, was "head hand among them all" in stirring up "the contention & grumbling spirit, which they all evince towards Mrs Lane," Elizabeth remarked.

The next week Mrs. Lane again used her position as supervisor to convey a challenge to her mistress. One afternoon Mrs. Lane handed the keys to the house to a slave and directed the slave to deliver the keys to Elizabeth with the message that the housekeeper "was going out[.]" Elizabeth intercepted the housekeeper on her way out the door. She described the encounter: "I met her on her way to the door, and asked if she had dined?—'No.'—when shall we see you again?—'I suppose to night'—which way do you go?—'To George Town'—and off she *walked*—She did not return," Elizabeth added, "Fine airs these[.]" "I wish for my part she never would come back," announced Elizabeth after this affair, "for I have no idea of submitting to her airs."

Mrs. Lane did come back, however, and the following day she again claimed the carriage for her own use. This time she challenged her mistress's authority even more directly. "This morning while at Breakfast," Elizabeth described the scene to her husband, "I gave orders not to get the carriage—as I prefered for the children to walk—she spoke up, and said she was going to the Capitol Hill—where she might probably remain all day," and would need the carriage herself. "I had the *hardihood*," Elizabeth wrote, "to say that I had promised

Mrs. Barclay to send her home this morning—and wish to know if the carriage could be used by *both* at the same time—Beleiving it to be impossible she could have the effrontery to shew any offence at such a natural proposition[.]" Although Mrs. Lane, to Elizabeth's satisfaction, "was obliged to gulp it down," she was not ready to surrender. "When she got out of the carriage," Elizabeth continued, "she said [according to the coachman and Mrs. Barclay] 'she had a good many visits to pay But that if Mrs W. chose to send for her in the evening she would come home—if not, she would get home as she could'—not saying where she was to be found. I shall *not* send for her," concluded Elizabeth angrily. "Tis time for her to find out that this very independant conduct does not become one in her station. I shall have no difference with her in words. But she may discover from my conduct if she chooses, . . . that I have the proper dignity of the Mistress of a House."[38]

Elizabeth Wirt's housekeepers resisted all her efforts to reduce them to the status of the other servants in the Wirt household. Housekeepers minimized their contact with and announced their superiority to slaves by retreating to their own quarters as well as by claiming the parlor. Ann Perry gave the slaves orders and then escaped to her own room. Probably Mrs. Lane acted similarly in the Wirts' Washington home when Elizabeth complained that she was "too fond of her own ease, to attend . . . to the management of the servants." As Elizabeth's wrath with Nancy Porter, who served her suitor tea, suggests, housekeepers' efforts to differentiate themselves from slaves often shaded over into what Elizabeth considered a usurpation of her role as mistress. When "Miss Jane" refused to take care of the children's combs, Elizabeth angrily reported that it seemed, as one of the Wirts' seamstresses had remarked, "that Miss J. did not seem to consider herself as a housekeeper—but as on a perfect equality with me,—the mistress." Jane Redin may well have considered herself the true mistress of the Wirt household, which she apparently managed very capably. While working for the Wirts, "Miss Jane" took such thorough control that Elizabeth feared her own authority was depleted. When she considered rehiring Redin at reduced wages in 1823, Elizabeth told William that

38. EW to WW, September 17, November 29, December 2, and December 9, 1818, MHS.

"I will never again give up the reins entirely, & be afraid to inspect, (& that closely,) my own affairs."[39]

The altercations between Elizabeth Wirt and her housekeepers suggest the extraordinary complications that ensued over issues of dominance and control in the urban upper South, where slavery and the free market intersected in the household. Elizabeth was distressed at the freedom and assertiveness displayed by her troublesome housekeepers, claiming that between their insolence, laziness, and brief tenures they were "of very little use." Yet despite her complaints, Elizabeth repeatedly found that she could not manage without a housekeeper to help her.[40]

Elizabeth Wirt hoped that having a white housekeeper would provide another level of supervision between herself and her troublesome enslaved, hired, and free help, and would ease her own burden as mistress of a large and productive household. Like many of her contemporaries, she was convinced that an intermediary was necessary to separate the mistress and her family from their slaves and servants and provide her with the leisure to attend to the needs of a privatized, affectionate family. "I am on the look out for a respectable woman, as housekeeper to enable me . . . to take a run up [to Richmond] to see you this summer," she wrote to her mother. "But," she concluded from her experiences thus far, "such an article is not easy to find."[41]

By using the demand for their labor to their best advantage, free white women who had been forced by economic distress to seek positions as domestics increasingly demanded rights and privileges that set them apart from slaves. Although troubled by her housekeepers' "airs," Elizabeth Wirt could not force the women to adapt completely to her preferences because the demand for white domestics was rising in the border cities out of proportion to the supply. As the century progressed, increased foreign immigration made it difficult for the Wirts to find the type of white, female, native-born servant they required for a housekeeper. Housekeepers knew how to manipulate the labor

39. EW to WW, September 17, 1818, November 17, 1822, June 17, 22, 1823, MHS.
40. EW to WW, September 20, 1813, MHS.
41. EW to Catharine Gamble, May 3, 1825, MHS.

market to their own advantage. Elizabeth Wirt's housekeepers, like other domestics, used the high demand for their labor to elevate their own status, distinguish themselves from lower servants and slaves, and even, Elizabeth believed, assume the liberties that properly belonged only to "the Mistress of a House."[42]

42. EW to WW, November 29, December 2, 1818, MHS.

Enthusiasm, Possession, and Madness

Gender and the Opposition to Methodism in the South, 1770–1810

CYNTHIA LYNN LYERLY

 In the late eighteenth century, Doctor Thomas Hinde of Hanover County, Virginia, began losing control of the women in his family. It started when his daughter Susanna joined the Methodist church against his wishes. Enraged when he learned of this, he rushed her off to live with an aunt forty miles distant and told her that unless she gave up Methodism, she was "never to see his face again." The aunt was a poor choice of guardian, for unbeknownst to Hinde, she, too, had converted to Methodism and hosted services regularly in her home. Meanwhile, Mary Hinde, the doctor's wife, was also under a "deep impression" of religion, and she, too, began attending Methodist services against her husband's will. Thomas became convinced that the Methodists made their followers "crazy" and "that his wife and daughter were really deranged." He "applied a blister to [his wife's] neck to bring her to her senses." The treatment failed; Mary Hinde went to church with the plaster still on. Ultimately the Hinde women won this religious battle, and Thomas himself converted to Methodism.[1]

In homes and churches across the Revolutionary and early national South, numerous such contests took place. The Hindes' story is a

This essay was completed with the assistance of a National Endowment for the Humanities Doctoral Dissertation Fellowship.

1. Rev. A. H. Redford, *The History of Methodism in Kentucky* (Nashville, Ky., 1868), 374–75. Although the years under consideration here are precise—1770 to 1810—the shifting values and ideas described herein admit of no easy dating. Accusations that Methodist women were mad or possessed decreased during the early nineteenth century for reasons discussed below but did not disappear in 1810.

common one. A white man directed women in his family to avoid the Methodists. The women disobeyed and exhibited what was considered strange behavior. The man accused the Methodists of having a pernicious effect on women and attempted more forcefully to put a stop to it. And the drama reached its successful, although not universal, resolution with the winning over of the man to the church he had previously despised.[2]

To the non-Methodist world, white women in the church often seemed deviant, for they violated southern gender conventions in the service of their religion. Bolstered by their beliefs in individual communion and revelation from God, some women defied male relatives. By speaking in public assemblies, aggressively proselytizing, and critiquing others' behavior, women assumed moral leadership previously reserved for men. Women's religious enthusiasm, sensually experienced and often physically evident, allowed them a means of self-expression generally denied outside of marriage.

Critics blamed Methodism for women's unconventional behavior. Many white men tried to keep women in their families from the church, and when they failed, they sought to define Methodism as deviance. Whether they earnestly confused religious and sexual passion or deliberately attempted to discredit women's religious expression, critics accused Methodists of sexual license. Some exasperated observers concluded that Methodism incited women to madness or brought them under diabolical influence. By redefining Methodist women's actions as pathology, critics muted the threat that these women posed to the social order.[3]

2. See J. B. Wakeley, *The Patriarch of One Hundred Years* (New York, 1875), 189; John Littlejohn journal, January 7, 1777, Louisville Conference Historical Society, Louisville, Ky.; Thomas Ware, "Sketches of the Life and Travels of Rev. Thomas Ware," in *Thomas Ware, a Spectator at the Christmas Conference*, ed. William R. Phinney, Kenneth E. Rowe, and Robert B. Steelman (Rutland, Vt.: Academy Books, 1984), 168–69.

3. This essay will deal only with white women and white gender ideology. The conjunction of racism and sexism made the experience of black Methodist women distinct from that of white Methodist women. For an exploration of religion and gender ideology as they relate to African American women, see Cynthia Lynn Lyerly, "Religion, Gender, and Identity: Black Methodist Women in a Slave Society, 1770–1810," in *Discovering the Women in Slavery*, ed. Patricia Morton (Athens: University of Georgia Press, 1995).

The Revolutionary and early national South witnessed several crucial transformations that formed the backdrop for conflicts like that in
the Hinde family. First was denominational rivalry, which intensified
after the disestablishment of the Church of England. The second shift,
the expanding influence of the secular Enlightenment, was under way
long before the Revolutionary War, but it played a pivotal role in changing conceptions of insanity. Methodism entered the competitive marketplace of southern religion in the 1760s, when numerous men and
women were turning to new evangelical sects like the Presbyterians
and Baptists and away from the Church of England. Anglican gentry
and evangelical plain folk battled for the hearts and minds of southerners; religious and class conflict was often indistinguishable. Evangelicals, with their rejection of worldly ways and criticism of elite lifestyles,
challenged the ideological dominance of the southern gentry. By the
end of the eighteenth century, two distinct worldviews had emerged.[4]

Gender was just as pivotal a factor as class in the contests for
religious authority in this era. Clergy of all stripes recognized the
importance of women to their success. Women usually outnumbered
men in church attendance and membership, and thus clergy were, to a
large extent, competing for female converts. Women's opinions could
make or break a minister; their money, time, and labor kept many
a poor preacher fed, clothed, and sheltered. With disestablishment,
church membership became a matter of choice, and white women
found that they had the same religious options as the men in their
families. And women sometimes made choices of which their male
relations disapproved.[5]

Prevailing views about mental illness, derived from Enlightenment
thought, help explain why male disapproval of Methodism could take

4. Rhys Isaac, *The Transformation of Virginia, 1740–1790* (New York: W. W.
Norton, 1988); John B. Boles, *The Great Revival, 1787–1805: The Origins of the
Southern Evangelical Mind* (Lexington: University Press of Kentucky, 1972); Don-
ald G. Mathews, *Religion in the Old South* (Chicago: University of Chicago Press,
1977); Sylvia R. Frey, *Water from the Rock: Black Resistance in a Revolutionary Age*
(Princeton, N.J.: Princeton University Press, 1991).

5. Mathews, *Religion in the Old South*; Joan R. Gundersen, "The Non-Institu-
tional Church: The Religious Role of Women in Eighteenth-Century Virginia,"
Historical Magazine of the Protestant Episcopal Church 51 (December 1982): 347–57;
Nancy Cott, "Young Women in the Second Great Awakening in New England,"
Feminist Studies 3 (fall 1975): 15–29.

the extreme form of accusations of madness or satanic possession. In the late eighteenth and early nineteenth centuries, a profound shift in Anglo-American ideas about the causes and treatment of insanity was taking place. Mental disorders had long been viewed in a religious framework. Satan, witches, and evil spirits drove men and women out of their senses. Madness required a religious cure, and ministers, as physicians of the soul, prayed and prescribed for the insane. The most incurably mad were put in chains and locked safely away. But as secular Enlightenment views gradually gained ascendance, explanations of the causes of deviance began to shift away from the supernatural toward the "scientific." Experts looked to factors such as diet, physiology, and environment as leading causes of insanity. Physicians began to take over the diagnosis and treatment of the mad; the age of "humane treatment" and the asylum had begun.[6]

As secular explanations for madness replaced religious ones, British physicians spearheading the paradigm shift increasingly drew distinctions between what they saw as the rational, enlightened faith of moderate Anglicanism and the emotional, deluded religion of evangelicals. Satan and witches gradually disappeared as causal agents; demonstrative religion, especially the exuberant religion of dissenters, was now seen to be more likely to cause insanity. Certain kinds of religious expression were thus effectively stigmatized. Church of England clergy joined forces with doctors to charge that emotional, enthusiastic religion, especially that of John Wesley's Methodists, was driving people mad.[7] Methodists were neither the first nor the last sect to stand accused of producing dementia, but the fact that their rising popularity in Britain occurred simultaneously with this shift in psychiatric epistemology was not, as British historians have shown, coincidental. Anglican clergy had a vested interest in discrediting their Methodist competitors. Doctors had a vested interest in wresting

6. Michael MacDonald, *Mystical Bedlam: Madness, Anxiety, and Healing in Seventeenth-Century England* (Cambridge: Cambridge University Press, 1981), esp. 198–231; Michael MacDonald, "Insanity and the Realities of History in Early Modern England," *Psychological Medicine* 11 (1981): 11–25; Michel Foucault, *Madness and Civilization: A History of Insanity in the Age of Reason* (New York: New American Library, 1965); Roy Porter, *Mind Forg'd Manacles: A History of Madness in England from the Restoration to the Regency* (London: Athlone Press, 1987).

7. MacDonald, "Insanity and the Realities of History in Early Modern England," 11.

treatment of the insane from ministers, and British elites had a vested interest in distancing themselves from and controlling popular beliefs. The result was what one historian has labeled "the stigmatization of religious rapture as disease."[8]

Gender ideology played a role in the association of religious enthusiasm with madness. Historians of Britain have noted that the dreaded term *enthusiasm* was largely used against dissenting English women.[9] As the experience of white Methodist women in the American South will suggest, the gendered characteristics of evangelical religion may also have influenced the change in Anglo-American views about insanity and about what constituted "proper" religion. By stigmatizing enthusiasm, critics effectively closed off one of the only avenues white southern women had to proclaim public moral authority and practice uncensored self-expression.

Methodism became identified with madness in England, and British physicians first catalogued symptoms, diagnoses, and treatments for religious mania. The author of one treatise on insanity, William Pargeter, even claimed that most of his patients at a London psychiatric hospital had been driven mad by religious, primarily Methodist, enthusiasm. To men of reason like Pargeter, who was both an Anglican clergyman and a doctor, it seemed the ranting, mystical, and enthusiastic religion of the Methodists pushed some over the edge of reason. Pargeter was expansionistic in his view of what constituted insanity. He diagnosed one woman as mad because she claimed "to have seen" and have "been talking with, her dear Christ." Thus, even religious behavior that was normal for Methodists was considered symptomatic by some physicians.[10]

The Methodists' reputation as enemies of reason preceded them into the New World both through the transatlantic community of scientists and through popular accounts of Methodist revivals in Britain that appeared in the American press. In the 1760s and 1770s, the

8. Porter, *Mind Forg'd Manacles*, 79.

9. Cynthia J. Cupples, "Pious Ladies and Methodist Madams: Sex and Gender in Anti-Methodist Writings of Eighteenth-Century England," *Critical Matrix* 5 (spring/summer 1990): 30–60.

10. William Pargeter, *Observations on Maniacal Disorders* (New York: Routledge, 1988), 33–34; William Perfect, *Annals of Insanity* (n.p., n.d.; reprint, New York: Arno Press, 1976), 17–20, 87–92, 166–70, 237–43, 295–309, 363–66.

Virginia Gazette published accounts of British Methodists allegedly gone mad as well as letters to the editor and satirical poems that claimed Methodism drove people insane. Southern whites had thus been exposed to the notion that Methodism could cause insanity before most had ever seen a Methodist.[11]

Despite the changing views on insanity, supernatural explanations for deviant behavior did not disappear. Many men and women continued to believe that Satan, witches, and evil spirits could possess humans and cause insanity. Others were comfortable with a mixture of secular and religious explanations for madness, and Methodists were among this group. John Wesley cured the insane with a combination of modern physic, mystical faith, and fervent prayer. Because of the temporal overlap of these two paradigms, it is not surprising that white Methodist women in the South were accused both of being possessed and of being mad. In terms of gendered archetypes, Methodist madwomen may be seen as marking the transition from the witches of the seventeenth century to the hysterical women of the nineteenth.[12]

In the American South, accusations that white Methodist women were mad or possessed were surprisingly common. A German reformed minister of Baltimore accused Deborah Owings of being "beside herself." Mary E.'s family in Dorchester County, Maryland, likewise feared she was "beside herself" after becoming a Methodist, and a male relation tried to stop her from visiting his wife, for he feared she would "drive his wife out of her senses." A Methodist woman of Virginia was said to be "deranged." A New Jerusalem minister published his accusation that Methodist clergy exploited the "faint hearted and weak nerved" members of their audience, language normally used in this era to describe women.[13]

11. Robert Alexander Armour, "The Opposition to the Methodist Church in Eighteenth-Century Virginia" (Ph.D. diss., University of Georgia, 1968), 21–23, 27–29.

12. Carol Karlsen, *The Devil in the Shape of a Woman: Witchcraft in Colonial New England* (New York: W. W. Norton, 1987); Carroll Smith-Rosenberg, "The Hysterical Woman: Sex Roles and Role Conflict in Nineteenth-Century America," *Social Research* 39, no. 1 (winter 1972): 652–78.

13. John Lednum, *A History of the Rise of Methodism* (Philadelphia, 1859), 89–90; Robert Drew Simpson, ed., *American Methodist Pioneer: The Life and Journals of the Rev. Freeborn Garrettson, 1752–1827* (Rutland, Vt.: Academy Books, 1984), 94; John Littlejohn journal, October 10, 1776; "A Layman of the New Jerusalem

Methodist clergy were so often accused of driving people mad or of working for Satan that it is worth asking to what extent white women were singled out for ignominy.[14] A substantial number of Methodists were black, and they exhibited the same "symptoms" as those identified in white women. Although black Methodists were called fanatics and enthusiasts, they do not seem to have been considered mad. Perhaps this was because most black Methodists were enslaved and thus subject to a greater range of overtly coercive controls on their behavior. Masters who were averse to violence could sell a religious slave. The fortunate but rare experience of a Methodist bondswoman indicates that, in her case, religious differences between master and slave worked to her advantage: her master freed her *because she had too much religion for him.*[15]

While black Methodists were not labeled mad or possessed, some white male church members were, although they were less likely to be accused than white women. Most fell into two groups—clergy and young men still living in their parents' households. Clergy, as producers of insanity in others and as celibate itinerants without honor, property, and status, had chosen to separate themselves from traditional white male culture. Young men who converted to Methodism against their fathers' wishes were in a somewhat analogous position to white women in southern society—they were dependents, though for sons dependence was temporary. Thus, those white men accused of madness were often, like Methodist "madwomen," violating gender conventions and patriarchal standards.[16]

Church," *A Short Reply, to Burk and Guy, with Some Ripe Fruit for a Friend to Truth* (Baltimore, 1804), 11. Allegations that Methodist women were mad were not confined to the South, nor was Methodism the only sect that was seen to drive people mad.

14. See, for example, Lednum, *Rise of Methodism*, 94, 400–402; William Colbert journals, September 21, 1794, Garrett-Evangelical Theological Seminary, Evanston, Ill.; Simpson, *American Methodist Pioneer*, 183–84; Jacob Young, *Autobiography of a Pioneer: Or, The Nativity, Experience, Travels, and Ministerial Labors of Rev. Jacob Young, with Incidents, Observations, and Reflections* (Cincinnati, 1857), 136.

15. Elmer T. Clark et al., eds., *The Journal and Letters of Francis Asbury* (London: Epworth Press, 1958), 1:656 (italics in original). For membership statistics, see *Minutes of the Annual Conferences of the Methodist Episcopal Church, for the Years 1773–1828*, vol. 1 (New York, 1840).

16. A. Gregory Schneider, *The Way of the Cross Leads Home: The Domestication of American Methodism* (Bloomington: Indiana University Press, 1993); Lednum,

White Methodist women, because of their values, beliefs, and actions, were more frequently charged with insanity or possession than were white men, and these accusations of madness must be understood in the context of southern gender ideology. Women's access to and influence in the public sphere was much more circumscribed than men's. White men prized honor and independence, ideals that placed a premium on women's obedience and submission. Additionally, the white South's commitment to patriarchy, doubly strong because of its dual emphasis on gender and racial hierarchy, limited secular tolerance for women behaving unconventionally.[17]

Within this ideological setting, there were a number of reasons that Methodist women might have been accused of insanity. One primary reason was the way white women behaved in Methodist services. Evangelicals' physical and verbal displays have been documented by numerous historians. Shouting, weeping, falling, and, to a lesser extent, paralysis, unconsciousness, and seizures were visible among both male and female worshippers at many Methodist meetings. What has been less explored is the extent to which white women were more often described as exhibiting enthusiasm than men, and the degree to which their enthusiasm was also often described as more pronounced than men's. French traveler Charles Janson, for example, noted marked gender differences in camp meeting behavior: "I have seen women jumping, striking, and kicking, like raving maniacs; while surrounding believers could not keep them in postures of decency . . . . The men under the agony of conversion find it sufficient to express their contrition by loud groans, with hands clasped and eyes closed."[18] Such gendered enthusiasm was a regular component of Methodist services. A South Carolina woman was "deeply affected" during a communion service, lost "the use of the members of her body, and lay for some

---

Rise of Methodism, 94, 146, 357; M. H. Moore, *Sketches of the Pioneers of Methodism in North Carolina and Virginia* (Nashville, 1884).

17. Bertram Wyatt-Brown, *Southern Honor: Ethics and Behavior in the Old South* (New York: Oxford University Press, 1982); Kenneth Greenberg, *Masters and Statesmen: The Political Culture of American Slavery* (Baltimore: Johns Hopkins University Press, 1985).

18. Charles William Janson, *The Stranger in America, 1793–1806* (1807; reprint, New York: Press of the Pioneers, 1935), 107–8; Mathews, *Religion in the Old South*; Isaac, *Transformation of Virginia*.

time without apparent power to rise." In Maryland, a woman cried out so loud in a 1789 service that people nearby thought there was a fire. A rural North Carolina woman got "uncommonly happy" at a service in 1805; her minister reckoned "she knew nothing of this world for one hour or more."[19] To non-Methodists, ecstatic behavior was frightening, and some people could best understand it as maniacal.

A second reason some Methodist women might have been labeled mad should be traced to the meaning behind these displays. In Methodism, as in other evangelical sects, women's entry into the church began with unique and unmediated communion with God. After publicly testifying about their conversions, Methodist women continued to seek intimacy with God, which, when achieved, often caused them to shout, fall, or weep. In Methodist views, God could directly communicate to the body and soul of a believer, and this subjective element in Methodism conferred religious power on women in the church. Although other evangelicals shared Methodists' belief that people could establish a close personal relationship with God, they did not fully share Methodists' views about human agency. As Arminians, Methodists placed the responsibility for salvation on the individual. God through His grace had sacrificed His Son for the sins of all, and humans had the free will to accept or reject this gift. Because of these rituals and beliefs, Methodism granted individuals much authority over their spiritual life and destiny, authority previously vested in educated male divines. Each time Methodist women shouted or fell, they publicly dramatized their individual moral agency and their direct access to God.[20]

Some Methodist women were labeled deviant because they assumed active, vocal roles in their congregations. Evangelical churches were one of the few public forums open to southern women. Lay participation was integral to Methodist services, and women often

19. Jeremiah Norman diary, November 24, 1799, Stephen B. Weeks Papers, Southern Historical Collection, University of North Carolina at Chapel Hill, Chapel Hill; Ezekiel Cooper journals, August 9, 1789, Garrett-Evangelical Theological Seminary; Thomas Mann Papers, November 18, 1805, Special Collections, Duke University, Durham, N.C.

20. Nancy Hardesty, *Your Daughters Shall Prophesy: Revivalism and Feminism in the Age of Finney* (Brooklyn, N.Y.: Carlson Publishing, 1991); Linda Kerber, "Women and Individualism in American History," *Massachusetts Review* (winter 1989): 589–609; Mathews, *Religion in the Old South*, 104–5.

led the way. Women gave oral testimony, led congregations in prayer, displayed verbally and physically their communion with God, and also sometimes exhorted or preached.[21]

Women's duties as Methodists extended beyond the church proper, and women who counseled and rebuked others violated southern gender norms by assuming authority normally reserved for men. Methodists were expected to set pious examples and to bring others into the church fold, and women actively recruited and converted their neighbors and family members. Major John Martin, a Kentuckian "of standing in society" was converted from Deism to Methodism by Mary Hinde. Martin recalled that when he denied "the resurrection of the dead," Hinde "set out zealously upon me respecting the reality of these things and the great necessity there was for a preparation for them." Although Martin "conceived it a disgrace to take an insult, or to bear even a rebuke from any man," the "indefatigable" Hinde "put to flight" his courage; he resolved to seek God that day. John Owen was separated by many miles from his zealous sister, Elizabeth Anderson, but he was not spared her sermons. By mail, she reminded him that "life is uncertain and death is shure." "I charge you," she wrote, "to meet me in heaven." Women like these could be found throughout the South, and their evangelism made them visible outside their local Methodist congregations.[22]

21. Lednum, *Rise of Methodism,* 115; Charles F. Deems, ed., *Annals of Southern Methodism for 1856* (Nashville, Tenn., 1857), 243; James B. Finley, *Sketches of Western Methodism* (Cincinnati, 1855), 532–35; Sarah Jones, *Devout Letters: or, Letters Spiritual and Friendly. Written by Mrs. Sarah Jones.,* ed. Jeremiah Minter (Alexandria, Va., 1804), 124–25, 130–31; Jeremiah Norman diary, June 14, 1796 and April 23, 1797; Clark, *Journal and Letters of Francis Asbury,* 2:360; "Diary of John Early, Bishop of the Methodist Episcopal Church, South," *Virginia Magazine of History and Biography* 34 (April 1926): 2, 133; Joseph Travis, *Autobiography of the Rev. Joseph Travis, A.M., a Member of the Memphis Annual Conference, Embracing a Succinct History of the Methodist Episcopal Church, South* (Nashville, Tenn., 1856), 62; William E. Smith, ed., *Memoirs of a Methodist Circuit Rider—Francis Wilson* (Austin, Tex.: for William E. Smith, 1983), 11; William Colbert journals, March 4, 1794; "A Journal and Travel of James Meacham, Part II" [Trinity College] *Historical Papers* 10 (1914): 92–93.

22. For the story of Hinde and Martin, see Rev. John Kobler journal, July 28–29, 1798, Baltimore-Washington Conference United Methodist Historical Society (hereinafter B-W CUMHS); Redford, *History of Methodism,* 368–69; *Methodist*

Methodists were also encouraged to reprove ungodly behavior both inside and outside the church. Many southern women became neighborhood Jeremiahs, warning friends and family to forsake sin or be damned. Sister Sarah Jones, one such woman, "reproved with pointed severity" all those around her in sin. Elizabeth Russell of Virginia was also famous for her boldness. At a party given by her irreligious son-in-law, Francis Preston, "she ordered the Bible to be laid on the stand, and then, with great solemnity rose to her feet." "Colonel Preston," she commanded, "go to prayer!" On another occasion Russell was said to have pushed James Madison, just elected president, to his knees for prayer.[23] Madison and Preston were reportedly chastened or inspired by their encounters, but many southern men resented the effrontery of zealous Methodist women. On a trip from Delaware to Maryland in 1802, James Hemphill encountered a bold Methodist. "Mrs. K," he confided in his journal, "attacked in the most severe Methodist strain I ever heard, told me I was in the broad road to hell. . . . I was lost in surprise at such a salutation from a person I had never seen before." As these examples show, Methodist women exercised what they viewed as religious and moral leadership and at times either implicitly or explicitly threatened male authority.[24]

Another reason Methodist women might have seemed mad or possessed to some southerners was that their religious behavior often put them beyond the reach of traditional controls. In Sheperdstown, Virginia, in 1791, Methodist women were "in such dir[e] agoney" in a service that "it took three or [four] men to hold them." The Connor family locked up their daughter's "best apparel" to keep her from going to hear the Methodists, but she went anyway. Sarah Jones's husband threatened to shoot her for attending a service; she informed him that it was the will of God—her "Heavenly spouse"—for her to defy his

---

Magazine 10 (July 1827): 312; *Methodist Magazine* 10 (August 1827): 369–70. For Anderson, see Elizabeth Anderson to John Owen, October 21, 1810, Campbell Family Papers, Special Collections, Duke University.

23. Clark, *Journal and Letters of Francis Asbury*, 2:34; Young, *Autobiography of a Pioneer*, 129; Elva Runyon, "Madame Russell, Methodist Saint" (M.A. thesis, University of Virginia, 1941), 57–58.

24. John A. Munroe, ed., "James Hemphill's Account of a Visit to Maryland in 1802," *Delaware History* 3 (September 1948): 67.

orders. The "furious" husband of a woman who attended a Methodist service against his wishes came "in a rage" to the preacher's lodging later that evening "in pursuit of his poor wife, that came to prayers." The woman had fortunately already departed.[25]

Methodist women like these, by defying male wishes or by being unreachable while in religious ecstasy, were, in a way, uncontrollable. White men found it difficult to compete with God for women's allegiance, and those women who believed they had divine sanction for disobedience were especially resolute. Wives and daughters of unconverted husbands and fathers, moreover, could claim moral superiority because of their exclusive connection to God. By labeling such women mad or satanically possessed, critics could discount their words and actions and, at least ideologically, contain the threat to patriarchal authority that these women posed.

Some men accused Methodist women of violating biblical decrees requiring women's submission but did not link their behavior to insanity. One Presbyterian minister condemned camp meetings in part because women at those meetings routinely disobeyed Paul's command for women's silence in churches. An 1804 anti-revivalist tract denounced women's testimony and teaching in services as "inconsistent with the due subordination and modesty of their sex." Other detractors, such as the Presbyterian clergyman Adam Rankin, explicitly denounced women who were "in open defiance of the divine interdiction" for silence as insane. Rankin was most troubled by the fact that women in revivals were looked upon as authorities, with crowds paying "ardent attention" and "eating every word, as if their eternal all depended upon their information." Instead, he suggested, such women should be subjected to "close confinement" in insane asylums. Authoritative, outspoken Methodist women clearly threatened some critics' sense of order and hierarchy.[26]

25. Rev. George Wells journal, August 11, 1791, B-W CUMHS; Lednum, *Rise of Methodism*, 164; Ware, "Sketches of Life and Travels," 168–69; James Meacham Papers, March 30, 1792, Special Collections, Duke University.

26. Matthew Lyle to William Spencer, December 21, 1808, copy, William Spencer copybook and memoir, B-W CUMHS; John Cree et al., *Evils of the Work Now Prevailing in the United States of America, under the Name of a Revival of Religion* (n.p., 1804), 40; Adam Rankin, *A Review of the Noted Revival in Kentucky, Commenced in the Year of Our Lord, 1801* (Lexington, Ky., 1802), 84–85.

Rankin also made more subtle allegations about women's camp meeting behavior, linking enthusiasm with sexual license and "delusion" with the "passions." Other southern men seem to have agreed that Methodist women were violating norms of female modesty. In Iredell County, North Carolina, Hannah Arrington "fell from her seat and begged for mercy" during a Methodist service. Her brother Joel "rushed to her caught her arm, snatched her from the house and literally dragged her home!" When he described his sister's episode to his parents, they forbid her to return. In Virginia, two sisters "were down on the floor, crying to GOD to deliver them." Their brother forcibly removed one of them "swearing that she should not expose herself there."[27]

His wording—"expose herself"—is typical of the most extreme charges of Methodist opponents. One detractor claimed that at "indecent and unseemly" Methodist services, "prostitutes of both sexes meet under the mask of a sanctified face and plain bonnet." Methodist clergy, whom he called "ignorant," were much to blame in his view, "for the freedom they take on such occasions with the young female converts . . . is the most objectionable and unseemly spectacle to behold." Critics' frequent allegations of sexual impropriety tell more about their own values than about Methodists' actions. Nonetheless, it is clear that the sensual and emotional behavior of Methodist women defied southern secular norms of female modesty and self-control.[28]

Methodist women physically experienced their religion and described these experiences in sensual terms. Women's correspondence reveals the passionate nature of their faith. Mary Browder wrote that during prayer, she felt God's power "in so wonderful a manner, that it occasioned my trembling body to fall down befor[e] Him." Another woman described her communion with Christ in similar terms: "How I tremble! Some days I can hardly work, for shaking of nerves, strugling amid the flames of Jehovah's Beams." When publicly displayed, many observers found women's passion threatening—so threatening that their first instinct was to flee. At a service in Middlesex, the audience

27. Rankin, *Review of the Noted Revival*, 85–86, 102; Nancy Campbell King, "Sketch of Methodism in Statesville, North Carolina," [c.1872], Historical Sketches, Methodist Church Papers, Special Collections, Duke University; Philip Cox to Bishop Coke, July 1787, *Arminian Magazine* (February 1790): 93.

28. *A Short Reply, to Burk and Guy*, 8, 14.

became "discompos'd" when a girl and a woman fainted. In a 1776 Methodist meeting, a woman affected by the sermon "cried so loud for mercy as to make the church ring." The audience, "being unacquainted with such things, strove to get out" of the church but was prevented by the standing-room-only crowd. Women's public passion provoked anger in hostile onlookers. In a 1791 service, one woman stood up and "with a loud voice gave praise," another "fell to the floor," followed by a third who "broke out in the language of the Virgin Mary." At this point, the crowd of curious onlookers and scoffers that had gathered outside "broke the door open and all came in." During a prayer meeting in a Maryland home, while some critics stood outside the house or peeped in the windows, Sister Shore and Sister Clark became "filled with the power and love of God." A man listening to these women was "filled with anger" and shocked that a preacher "should suffer such noise and crying among the people."[29]

The spontaneity and exuberance of women who exposed their passions in public, as well as the angry or frightened reactions of their critics, are best understood when placed in a wider context. Historically, women under divine or supernatural influence have provoked criticism. Women's unmediated contact with the spiritual world— whether by Anne Hutchinson, the French Prophetesses, Mother Ann Lee of the Shakers, or the so-called witches of Salem—threatened not only clerical authority but also the social order. Many of these women were charged with sexual license and "fanaticism," much like their Methodist successors.[30]

Some southern Methodist women defied racial and gender conventions. Two white North Carolina women, for example, joined a society headed by a black man and composed of fifty black Methodists, because they "would not join the [Baptists]." In Georgetown, Maryland, a Methodist class was composed of twenty white women and one black man. At a 1790 service for blacks, some "dear humble white

29. Mary Avery Browder to Edward Dromgoole, November 1777, and Sarah Jones to Edward Dromgoole, September 1, 1788, Edward Dromgoole Papers, Southern Historical Collection; Nelson Reed diary, March 28, 1779, B-W CUMHS; Simpson, *American Methodist Pioneer*, 58–59; Rev. John Kobler journal, July 2, 1791; Ezekiel Cooper journals, September 6, 1791.

30. Karlsen, *Devil in the Shape of a Woman*; Hardesty, *Your Daughters Shall Prophesy*.

sisters" attended and "God poured out his divine Spirit and love upon them." A schoolmistress was the first white to join the persecuted black Methodist congregation in Fayetteville, North Carolina, a group also under the direction of a black preacher. In some 1795 services in Charleston, South Carolina, the only whites who worshipped with the overwhelmingly black congregations were women.[31]

The emotionalism and physical demonstrativeness of Methodist gatherings led some observers to suspect white women were breaking taboos against interracial sex. A poem authored by the pseudonymous "Druid of the Lakes" made such an allegation in verse. Entitled "The Camp Meeting," the poem described a white "trollop" at a meeting "[w]ith her bosom all bare." "Druid," who was careful to describe her seducer as a Methodist, continued, "Then a negro so strong, / Full of faith and of song, / View'd her charms thus expos'd to the weather; / He pity'd her case / In the tone of free grace, / 'Till they lovingly walk'd off together." The poet stopped short of describing a sexual encounter, but his implication was clear. In the racist climate of the early national South, it is not surprising that some critics would connect women's passionate "exposure" at biracial meetings to their nightmares of sexual contact between white women and black men.[32]

Men (and some women as well) who objected to female Methodists did not silently acquiesce to their challenges to the social order. They attempted in a variety of ways to stamp out women's participation in Methodism. Throughout the late eighteenth century, opponents tried to discredit Methodists by claiming their rituals and practices were not godly. In a pamphlet condemning Methodist camp meetings, five Presbyterian ministers accused Methodists of a host of unbiblical ways. A theme running through the discussion was their insistence that what Methodists called divine may instead have been, in their words, "delusions of Satan." What these ministers subtly suggested,

31. Thomas Mann Papers, July 21, 1805; John Ffirth, *The Experience and Gospel Labours of the Rev. Benjamin Abbott* (New York, 1892), 98; James Meacham Papers, April 20, 1790; Clark, *Journal and Letters of Francis Asbury,* 2:41.

32. *The Camp Meeting* (1810), 7; Catherine Clinton, " 'Southern Dishonor': Flesh, Blood, Race, and Bondage," in *In Joy and in Sorrow: Women, Family, and Marriage in the Victorian South, 1830–1900,* ed. Carol Bleser (New York: Oxford University Press, 1991); Victoria E. Bynum, *Unruly Women: The Politics of Social and Sexual Control in the Old South* (Chapel Hill: University of North Carolina Press, 1992).

others made explicit. Methodist clergyman Benjamin Abbott, who was powerfully appealing to women, was so often accused of being the devil's servant that he recited a standard caveat whenever a Methodist woman fell: "if it is [the work of the devil] . . . when she comes to, she will curse and swear, but if it is of God, she will praise him." Preachers who led enthusiastic services were sometimes linked with magic and witchcraft. One Methodist minister was accused of working "the magic art." After an enthusiastic meeting in western Virginia, a preacher reported, "Some said we had bewitched the people."[33]

Another common tactic was to allege that Methodist women were mad and that clergy were making them so. Charges of madness were leveled against Methodists from Edisto Circuit, South Carolina, to Maryland.[34] Some men, like Thomas Hinde, who applied the blister to his wife, tried medical remedies. A woman who burned her hands deliberately in a fire was "diagnosed" by her friends as deranged and then taken to a physician. The doctor's "prescription" was "1st To keep the praying people from her, 2. to watch her closely, then to cut of[f] her hair." A Methodist preacher, violating the doctor's orders, recommended "a Physician called Jesus" to her, and she "got her right mind" again. Mr. Johnson of Maryland wanted to send for a doctor when his wife "fell on the floor" during her conversion, but she responded only to a Methodist clergyman. A North Carolina doctor brought "salts of hartshorn," the forerunner of smelling salts, to a meeting to "apply to those who fell."[35]

Another way opponents of Methodism, who were overwhelmingly men, responded was to reassert their authority, especially when women were "struck" by divine power. Non-Methodist men commonly entered services to remove female relatives by force. In July 1794

33. Cree et al., *Evils of the Work Now Prevailing*, 6; Ffirth, *The Experience and Gospel Labours of the Rev. Benjamin Abbott*, 59; James Meacham Papers, June 1, 1793; Rev. John Kobler journal, October 9, 1792.

34. Lednum, *Rise of Methodism*, 402; Rev. George Wells journal, December 2, 1791; Ware, "Sketches of Life and Travels," 67–68, 122; Simpson, *American Methodist Pioneer*, 184.

35. John Littlejohn journal, October 10, 1776; Ezekiel Cooper journals, August 10, 1790; Daniel Asbury to [Francis Asbury?], August 20, 1802, *Extracts of Letters, Containing Some Account of the Work of God since the Year 1800* (New York, 1805), 59.

a man hauled his two daughters from a Methodist meeting. A woman was affected in a service at which a minister named George Wells preached, and her husband tried to drag her off. At an enthusiastic meeting in North Carolina, a man came and removed his sister. At an Alexandria, Virginia, service, the audience got so animated that "the men came to take away their wives. Some went, others would not."[36] Men who succeeded in removing their female relations from church had publicly asserted their authority, reordering their world as they wanted it to be, and by doing so in front of a crowd, restored their honor. Perhaps bullying their wives, daughters, or sisters in public settings accomplished their purpose. Yet they unwittingly played a part in a drama that was centuries old, a part they probably had no desire to play.

Methodists fit these recurring dramas into a framework of good and evil: God's people (the part they saw themselves playing) struggling against Satan's people (those who opposed them). When a Delaware woman fell unconscious in a service, her mother grew angry and "seized her by the arm" to arouse her. When her daughter did not respond, the mother "began to pinch her, as if she would pinch pieces out of her flesh." The Methodist preacher interpreted the scene according to the biblical script; he "prayed to God to have mercy on this old hardened sinner."[37] In a Virginia service, a young woman fell under preaching, and some people tried to "drag out the Slain [woman] . . . by force." Preacher James Meacham described the events in classic terms, pitting "Hell" and "Satan" (those trying to remove the woman) against "Israel's camp" (the Methodists.) From his account, it appears that the woman was dragged back and forth between the two groups "until Satan made a small retreat then we boldly marched forward and took the slain . . . again." In this case, the Methodists won the battle over the female convert.[38]

36. Rev. George Wells journal, November 11, 1792; Thomas Mann Papers, November 18, 1805; Jeremiah Norman diary, April 29–30, 1800.

37. Ffirth, *The Experience and Gospel Labours of the Rev. Benjamin Abbott*, 286. Opposition by non-Methodist women was much rarer than opposition by non-Methodist men, but it did occur. These rarer incidents between women usually involved a persecuting mother and a Methodist daughter.

38. "Journal and Travel of James Meacham," May 25, 1789, [Trinity College] *Historical Papers*, series 9 (1912): 67.

People who came to services to physically force female relations home were, in effect, confirming the Methodist worldview. Methodists believed persecution was one sign that Christians were doing their duty, and thus pious women whose men attempted to remove them saw their stature raised among church members. Many Methodists wore persecution like a badge of honor. Consider the following passage from Methodist Sally Eastland's letter to her clergyman: "[T]he Devil often asaults me[,] tho in the kings high way I have waged war against Hell, but alwais when I can venture on Jesus[,] Hell retracts, it is now twilight I am just going, into an ingagement, with the powers [of] darkness, I feel as if Id die rather than yeald."[39] As a militant soldier in the Christian army, Eastland knew there would be assaults from the devil and his forces. And she knew how to place opposition in a context where she would be on the side of God. Methodist women like Eastland could wage war against hell—and earthly opposition—because they drew strength from their religion. They claimed sanction for their actions from God, and He answered to no man. It mattered not that the ungodly believed them to be mad or possessed by Satan, for pious women would reap the ultimate victory in Heaven.

In the South, a number of white Methodist women defied the gender conventions of their society in the service of their God. They disobeyed fathers and husbands who tried to keep them from Methodist influence. They asserted moral authority in their homes, churches, and communities, confidently proclaiming their values and beliefs and reproving those whom they saw as ungodly. Through their enthusiastic behavior in services, they demonstrated their closeness to God and flouted secular restrictions on the public display of their emotions and passions. Their religion equipped them with a worldview through which they interpreted persecution as a sign of their moral rectitude, a view that bolstered them despite derision, criticism, and sometimes, violence. It is not surprising that some white men attempted to discredit these bold, assertive women by labeling them mad or possessed, for this was the only way these men could comprehend such behavior. To a large extent, these women were deviant, and their

39. Sally Eastland to Edward Dromgoole, February 21, 1790, Edward Dromgoole Papers.

male relations used the available intellectual frameworks to explain the women's actions. For men of a more traditional bent, the vocabulary of possession and witchcraft seemed appropriate. Men embracing the secular views of the Enlightenment chose the vocabulary of insanity.

During the nineteenth century, madness became dissociated from the soul and located in the body—typically a female body.[40] Charges that women were bewitched or possessed by Satan grew less common as secular physicians looked to environmental or physiological explanations for deviance. Religious enthusiasm seemed anachronistic in the age of reason and was eventually stigmatized. When the era of the great camp meetings passed, even many Methodists abandoned their earlier demonstrativeness for more formal worship.

The religiously motivated radicalism of southern Methodist women affected the family and society, subtly shaping but not subverting secular gender ideology. To fulfill their religious responsibilities, some Methodist women challenged husbands, fathers, and societal norms of femininity, but they defied gender conventions in the service of their church and their God, and not for the sake of overturning gender roles. Perhaps because they viewed their defiance in terms of religion, not gender, their ability to translate religious victories into a revision of secular gender ideology was severely limited.

In the nineteenth century, the opportunities for women's leadership in mixed-gender adult audiences and their public roles in the church diminished. As Methodism gained respectability, opposition to the church decreased, as did criticism of Methodist women. The image of the impertinent Methodist woman aggressively reproving all those who sinned around her gradually waned. In several ways, women's religious radicalism was muted over time. First, the success of many women in converting their male relatives had, ironically, a negative effect on women's moral primacy. The dynamics of relationships changed when, for example, a husband joined the church, for no longer could his wife claim exclusive moral authority. By converting, men gained the ability to communicate directly with God and could then challenge their female relations in religious matters. The effects of women's success became more evident in the course of the nineteenth century when male enthusiasm became more commonplace. As early

40. Smith-Rosenberg, "The Hysterical Woman."

as 1802, one minister noted that as many men as women had exhibited physical and emotional enthusiasm at a camp meeting.[41]

A closely related development was that after converting, men could subtly appropriate women's narratives. The tale of Thomas Hinde is a perfect example. When the doctor was won over by his wife to the Methodists, the blister plaster story became his. He told it over and over, in class meetings and love feasts, exclaiming that he had been converted by the treatment he applied to his wife. What could have been her tale of persecution became his tale of an errant man who finally saw the light. The persecutor became the hero.[42]

Third, as the church evolved from a sect into a denomination in the nineteenth century, several developments worked to limit women's authority. Love feasts and class meetings—enthusiastic and emotionally charged rituals in which women had played such a large part—were neglected. Instead, as a recent author has shown, the church turned to Sunday schools to impart its ways and values, socializing children and not adults. The church's phenomenal success also meant that women had less evangelizing to do. As Methodism slowly turned to an educated ministry, the role of lay testimony and leadership became less important. Women's piety was increasingly confined to the domestic sphere, thereby limiting women's public role in mixed audiences.[43]

Last but not least, the muting of women's radicalism can be connected to changes in the discourse of deviance. Male clergy and physicians who secularized madness in the late eighteenth and early nineteenth centuries succeeded both in stigmatizing popular beliefs and in limiting women's unmediated access to God.[44] Women's enthusiasm had posed a threat to patriarchal authority, and by equating religious enthusiasm with insanity, the threat was recast as illness. As medical explanations for madness replaced supernatural ones, the treatment of the insane became the purview of educated male physicians, and these men believed women who had contact with the divine and spirit

41. James Ward to [Francis Asbury?], October 23, 1802, *Extracts of Letters,* 61.
42. Redford, *History of Methodism,* 377.
43. Schneider, *The Way of the Cross Leads Home;* Mathews, *Religion in the Old South;* Cynthia A. Kierner, "Women's Piety within Patriarchy: The Religious Life of Martha Hancock Wheat of Bedford County," *Virginia Magazine of History and Biography* 100 (January 1992): 79–98.
44. Porter, *Mind Forg'd Manacles,* 79.

worlds were deluded. Gradually, Methodists modified their ways to conform with notions of acceptable religious behavior.

The experience of Methodist "madwomen" of the late eighteenth and early nineteenth centuries suggests that gender was a significant factor in the intellectual shifts of this era. Critics and adherents alike described evangelical religion like that of the early Methodists as a religion of the passions, emotions, and heart. Critics, however, exploited the new ideas about insanity and used the language of the secular Enlightenment to discredit religious enthusiasm by linking it with the alleged weaknesses of women. Methodists' opponents persistently derided religion based on the "lower faculties" of the "imagination," "affections," and the "body," while exalting religion based on the "higher faculties" of the "understanding and the will."[45]

As ideas about insanity became secularized, irrationality became a female trait. Although the ideology of separate spheres deeded to women control of piety and religion, the new secular views about madness set limits on the ways women could express their religious beliefs. At least when supernatural phenomena were believed to account for deviance, women had been able to connect with not just Satan, but also with God. When Satan's power was discounted in favor of diagnoses of nervous disabilities, God's power also declined, and white southern women lost a major avenue of assertive self-expression and one of their few paths in this era to public moral authority.

45. John Cree et al., *Evils of the Work Now Prevailing,* 13–14.

Making the Most of Life's Opportunities

A Slave Woman and Her Family in Abingdon, Virginia

NORMA TAYLOR MITCHELL

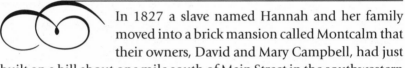 In 1827 a slave named Hannah and her family moved into a brick mansion called Montcalm that their owners, David and Mary Campbell, had just built on a hill about one mile south of Main Street in the southwestern Virginia town of Abingdon. The handsome new house included a full cellar above ground, with a kitchen, two additional rooms, two large fireplaces, and several windows. In this cellar Hannah and the Campbells' other domestic servants, numbering from twelve to twenty at any one time, would live until 1860.[1]

For assistance in the preparation of this article, I thank the staff of the Special Collections Library at the Perkins Library, Duke University, especially Robert L. Byrd and William R. Erwin; the staff of the Historical Society of Washington County, Virginia, especially Nancy E. Leasure; the Alabama Humanities Foundation; Eva Gillette Mingea Brown; Steve Galyean; Anne McLean Mingea Goodpasture; the late Ernestine Kahle Mingea; Ann Patton Malone; Anne V. Mitchell; Frank Joseph Mitchell; Stephanie J. Shaw; Sandra Gioia Treadway; David E. Whisnant; and the late Robert F. Woody.
1. Except where otherwise noted, all of the manuscripts cited are in the Campbell Family Papers, Perkins Library, Duke University, Durham, North Carolina and are written from Abingdon, Virginia. The following abbreviations are used in the notes: DC=David Campbell, MHC=Mary H. Campbell, VC (after 1849, VCS)=Virginia Campbell, and WBC=William B. Campbell. Montcalm Chain of Title, Washington County Historical Society, Abingdon, Va. DC to MHC, January 16, 1823, May 20, 1825; James Campbell to DC, May 1825, November 8, 1825; MHC to DC, May 28, 1825; DC to James Campbell, January 16, 1826, October 22, 1826; Leonidas Baugh Ledger, 1819–1829, 164, Leonidas Baugh Papers, Special Collections Department, University of Virginia Library, Charlottesville,

Above the cellar, Montcalm had two floors and a large attic. The first floor included a large drawing room and a dining room, both elegantly appointed, a library, and a center hall. Above the mantel in the drawing room hung a portrait of David Campbell painted in 1825 by the famous artist John Wesley Jarvis.[2] At the rear of the main floor, there was a room called "the wing" or "the ell." It was used for serving the formal dining room, for informal dining, and, at times, as a bedroom for relatives or for a slave. The second floor had three bedrooms, and the attic contained two additional bedrooms and several storage areas. The cellar was not connected to the Campbells' living space by a stairway, and there was no inner door. The only interior link between the two areas was a trap door, built into the ceiling of the kitchen, which could be opened from the dining room above.[3]

Thus, from the beginning, David and Mary Campbell made Montcalm a house for their slaves as well as for themselves. Even after the Campbells had a separate, one-and-a-half-story brick slave house built behind Montcalm in 1844, their slaves continued living in the cellar, using the small brick dwelling for the brief visits of their spouses and their children who lived elsewhere. Although many slaveowners housed up to six domestic slaves in the big house, the Campbells' long practice of having more than twice that number live within the mansion made their household highly unusual in the Abingdon area and the antebellum South.[4]

For more than thirty years the internal organization of Montcalm, with whites residing on the top floors and a large group of slaves on

Va.; MHC to DC, May 28, 1825; DC to VC, December 28, 1840, January 30, 1852; Margaret H. Campbell to VCS, January 6, 1854; *Abingdon (Va.) Political Prospect*, April 25, 1812, 3.

2. DC to MHC, May 20, June 6, June 13, 1825. The children of VCS and WBC presented the portrait to the Commonwealth of Virginia in 1877. It hangs on the third floor of the Virginia State Capitol. Ray O. Hummel Jr., and Katherine M. Smith, *Portraits and Statuary of Virginians* (Richmond: Virginia State Library, 1977), 20, incorrectly attributes the portrait to Flavius J. Fisher.

3. VC to Catharine Campbell, July 22, 1843; John M. Ropp to DC, November 22, 1855.

4. VC to Catharine Campbell, October 19, 1844. John Michael Vlach, *Back of the Big House: The Architecture of Plantation Slavery* (Chapel Hill: University of North Carolina Press, 1993).

the bottom, remained unaltered. The structure stood as a symbol of whites' power over blacks expressed in the paternalistic setting of a spacious and comfortable house close to town.

During this long period, however, social developments inside and outside the house gave Hannah and the other residents of the cellar significant opportunities to increase their control over not only their own lives but also the lives of their white masters. In making the most of these opportunities, the Campbells' slaves pushed hard against the limitations of slavery, prepared themselves for life after emancipation, and attained an exceptional measure of control within the big house. The record of their journey toward autonomy, documented in the Campbell family papers, shows that despite the limitations and restrictions of the system, domestic slavery could become the setting for the development of slave culture and slave power.[5]

When Hannah moved to Montcalm, she was thirty-three years old and the mother of four living children: Richard, sixteen; Eliza, eleven; Page, eight; and David, a baby named for his master.[6] She had been born in Virginia and probably had been the Campbells' slave since she was at least seventeen years old. Although the father of her four children cannot be identified, David was a mulatto. It is probable that

5. Studies of antebellum slavery and women used in this work include Catherine Clinton, *The Plantation Mistress: Woman's World in the Old South* (New York: Pantheon Books, 1982); Elizabeth Fox-Genovese, *Within the Plantation Household: Black and White Women of the Old South* (Chapel Hill: University of North Carolina Press, 1988); Eugene D. Genovese, *Roll, Jordan, Roll: The World the Slaves Made* (New York: Random House, 1972); Herbert G. Gutman, *The Black Family in Slavery and Freedom, 1750–1925* (New York: Pantheon Books, 1976); Suzanne Lebsock and Kym S. Rice, *"A Share of Honour": Virginia Women, 1600–1945* (Richmond: Virginia Women's Cultural History Project, 1984); Ann Patton Malone, *Sweet Chariot: Slave Family and Household Structure in Nineteenth-Century Louisiana* (Chapel Hill: University of North Carolina Press, 1992); Workers of the Writers' Program of the Work Projects Administration in the State of Virginia, comp., *The Negro in Virginia* (1940; reprint, Winston-Salem, N.C.: John F. Blair, 1994). My study takes exception to the conclusion of Malone and other scholars that "slaves were able to exercise more autonomy and forge more effective communities on larger holdings" than smaller ones (Malone, *Sweet Chariot*, 269).
6. "An Inventory of the Personal Estate of Ex-Gov. David Campbell Deceased, Made by His Executor, William B. Campbell, May 1859," Washington County, Va., Will Book 14, 1856–1859; MHC to DC, February 25, March 3, 1819; memorandum quoted in Frederick Johnston, comp., *Memorials of Old Virginia Clerks* (Lynchburg, 1888), 395–96.

her other children and perhaps Hannah herself were also mulattoes. From 1811 to 1827, she and her children had lived with the Campbells and their other domestic slaves in a house on the dirt road that was Abingdon's Main Street. There she did a variety of household tasks and served as Mary Campbell's personal maid.[7]

Hannah and her family were a part of Washington County's small black population, which, during the antebellum period, represented about 15 percent of the county's total population of approximately fifteen thousand. Abingdon, the county seat, contained only about fifteen hundred residents and was located three hundred miles from the state capital at Richmond. The town was more than forty years old in 1820 and was a lively political, cultural, and economic center. Its resident and transient population offered Hannah and the Campbells' other slaves an opportunity to know and be known in a world larger than their own household. They shopped and did errands at Abingdon's stores and taverns. They were sometimes hired out to work in other households or in local businesses. Now and again they went to the courthouse on Main Street, where David Campbell served as deputy county clerk for his father, John. Every day the slaves observed and interacted with wagoners, drovers, stagecoach drivers, hunters, land speculators, slave traders, mountaineers, and farm families who came up the steep Main Street hill, stopped for refreshment, and then headed off toward Cumberland Gap, one of the few easy passages through the Appalachian Mountains. Perhaps most important, Hannah and her fellow slaves had the opportunity to attend services at the town's several churches, especially the Methodist, where in the early 1820s a fervent religious revival engaged both whites and blacks.[8]

Three years before the Campbell household moved to Montcalm, forty-eight-year-old David Campbell was elected by the justices of Washington County to succeed his deceased father as the county

7. MHC to DC, February 25, March 3, 1819, Washington County, Va., Personal Property Book, 1821; "Register of Free Blacks, Washington County, Va., 1838–1863," Special Collections, University of Virginia Library; Frederick G. Bohme, *20 Censuses: Population and Housing Questions, 1790–1980* (Washington, D.C.: Bureau of the U.S. Census, 1979).

8. Lewis Preston Summers, *History of Southwest Virginia, 1746–1786 and Washington County, 1777–1870* (Richmond: J. L. Hill Printing, 1903), 137, 279–81, 621, 631–32, 634; Julia A. Tevis, *Sixty Years in a School-Room: An Autobiography of Mrs. Julia A. Tevis* (Cincinnati, 1878).

court clerk. Members of the Campbell family had been prominent in southwestern Virginia since the establishment of Washington County in 1777. David's cousin, William Campbell, had led the victorious patriot troops at the battle of King's Mountain, South Carolina, in 1780 during the American War of Independence. His uncle, Arthur Campbell, had been one of the first Washington County justices; his father, John, had been the first county court clerk, and he held the office until his death, when David succeeded him.

David Campbell himself had become a respected man, who had grown moderately wealthy from the fees of his office and the profits from his general store in Abingdon and his land investments. He had served in the United States Army on the Canadian front during the War of 1812 and had served one term in the Virginia Senate (1820–1824). As a young man, he had joined other members of his family in western Virginia and eastern Tennessee in supporting Thomas Jefferson and the Republican party. In the early nineteenth century the Campbells had forged a mutually beneficial alliance with eastern Virginia Jeffersonian Republicans such as Thomas Ritchie, editor of the *Richmond Enquirer*. David supported Andrew Jackson's election to the presidency in 1828, and he was rewarded with the appointment of his younger brother, John, as Treasurer of the United States.[9] The Campbells' prominence in southwestern Virginia meant that Hannah and their other domestic slaves had become accustomed to interacting with the area's elite whites and the slaves who served them before they moved to the impressive new house on the hill.

Hannah's mistress, Mary Campbell, was forty-four years old at the time of the move to Montcalm. She was not only David's wife; she was also his first cousin. The couple had been married in 1801 at Mary's home in eastern Tennessee, where David Campbell had gone to study law with a relative. She was then a petite girl of seventeen still in mourning for her mother, who had recently died of breast cancer. Soon after the wedding, David Campbell gave up his legal studies and took his bride home to Washington County, where he began working with his father in the clerk's office in Abingdon.

9. Norma Taylor Mitchell, "The Political Career of David Campbell of Virginia," (Ph.D. diss., Duke University, 1967); Kenneth Noe, *Southwest Virginia's Railroad: Modernization and the Sectional Crisis* (Urbana: University of Illinois Press, 1994).

At their house on muddy Main Street, Mary became a skilled and perfectionist homemaker, closely supervising several domestic slaves.[10] The Campbells longed to have children to make their home life complete, but Mary was never able to become pregnant. By the time she and David moved to Montcalm, she had given up hope of bearing a child. Not having children was a severe disappointment to the Campbells, for which they tried to compensate by their financial generosity and devotion to David's four younger brothers and his younger sister and to Mary's several nephews and nieces from Tennessee.

The Campbells paid special attention to five children of Mary's impoverished brother in Tennessee. In 1825, they brought to Abingdon his eighteen-year-old son, William Bowen Campbell, to attend the Abingdon Academy for two years before sending him at their expense to Winchester, Virginia, to study law with Judge Henry St. George Tucker. Shortly after William returned to Tennessee in 1829, his youngest sister, twelve-year-old Virginia Tabitha Jane Campbell, arrived to live at Montcalm and be educated in Abingdon. Mary and David became so devoted to this bright, lively, black-haired girl that they came to call her their "adopted daughter." From 1830 until her marriage in 1849 she spent about thirteen years with them, longer than any of their other young relatives. When Virginia was absent from Montcalm, her aunt suffered a loneliness so intense that she often made it difficult for her husband to carry on his business.[11]

Childless Mary Campbell also sought special emotional support from a slave woman named Leathy Jackson. Jackson had belonged to Mary's parents. She had been around when Mary was growing up and had come to live with Mary and David Campbell in 1818. Until she died in 1843, Leathy was a vital connection between Mary and her family in Tennessee, for whom she often longed as her relationship with her husband's side of the Campbell family became strained.[12]

---

10. DC to MHC, January 1, 1823; Mary H. R. Campbell to WBC, March 30, 1836.

11. DC to WBC, April 29, 1832, and to Margaret H. Campbell, October 4, 1847. Gay Robertson Blackford, "Reminiscences Concerning the Robertson and Blackford Families of 'The Meadows,' Washington County, Virginia, ca. 1820–70," Virginia Historical Society, Richmond, 26.

12. Archibald Roane to DC, April 29, 1809; Margaret C. Roane to MHC, October 30, 1817; MHC to DC, February 10, 1818; DC journal, July 7, 1843; DC to MHC, June 5, 1837 and to VC, November 22, 1840; MHC to DC, February 9, 1841.

Thus, when Hannah and her children moved to Montcalm in 1827, fifty-six-year-old Leathy and her seventeen-year-old daughter, Lucy, moved there, too. Although Hannah's and Leathy's families had different origins, which were never forgotten by either the Campbells or the slaves, they clearly practiced the widespread slave custom of becoming adoptive kin. The two women treated each other as sisters, and their daughters taught their children to regard one another as cousins. In the decade following the move to Montcalm, Hannah, rather than the older Leathy, became the manager of the growing black family in the cellar and of the whole Montcalm household under her mistress's supervision. Leathy performed skilled tasks such as milking cows, churning butter, and weaving cloth.[13]

About the time the household moved to Montcalm, David Campbell purchased one Michael Valentine in Richmond to become his carriage driver. Several years younger than Hannah, Michael came from a large slave family in the Richmond area. He was quickly incorporated into the cellar family, becoming Hannah's husband in a union that lasted until her death in 1860. Together the Valentines became the leaders of the black family in the cellar.[14]

When Hannah was in her late thirties, she and Michael had twin daughters named Jane and Mary; they had another daughter, also named Mary, when Hannah was forty-one. Both Hannah and Leathy became grandmothers in the 1830s as their daughters, Eliza and Lucy, respectively, bore many children and as Hannah's oldest son, Richard, began fathering children. From the 1830s to the 1860s, at least twenty-five slave children were born in Montcalm's cellar. At any one time, between twelve and twenty slaves, adults and children, lived there.[15]

The births of so many slave children caused David and Mary Campbell to long for the birth of at least one of their own kin in their

13. "An Inventory of the Personal Estate of Ex-Gov. David Campbell deceased"; VC to Frances Campbell, September 14, 1842 and Lucy Clark to Washington, April 11, 1843; VC diary, July 11, 1840; DC to MHC, January 4, 1842; VC to Catharine Campbell, March 23, 1836; Lethe Jackson to VC, April 18, 1838; DC to VC, September 10, 1840; MHC to Lethe Jackson, November 14, 1841.

14. Hannah Valentine to Eliza, November 1, 1837 and VC to DC, April 5, 1837.

15. DC to WBC, February 19, 1833 and VC to Catharine Campbell, September 5, 1835; Lucy Clarke to Washington, April 11, 1843, in which she names sixteen slaves living at Montcalm. About thirty-two different slaves are named in the Campbell Papers as residents of Montcalm.

home. Mary Campbell once begged the pregnant wife of her nephew, William, to come to Montcalm to give birth. But she did not come, and no white child was born there. None of the slave women at Montcalm ever wet-nursed or cared for white children. Instead, black children enjoyed their undivided attention and provided daily drama and entertainment for the Campbells. The children even galloped down the hill each day to greet David Campbell as he returned from his work at the courthouse.[16]

The Campbells doted on the black infants and toddlers, especially in the lonely times when no Tennessee niece or nephew was staying at Montcalm. Mary could not resist little Jackson's "flying squirrel tricks." David said that Eliza's newborn daughter was "the most beautiful colored child" he had ever seen except for the infant Eliza herself, whom he distinctly remembered at her birth in 1816. Both Mary and David delighted in the slave children who played about their house and who began to learn the tasks of kitchen and yard by the time they were three years old. They sometimes called them "our negro family." Yet David had reservations about the situation and warned his wife that she was "unwise to pet and humor the little negroes."[17]

But he never doubted that his wife knew how to work slaves. Almost every day she was out on the porches "hollering" directions to them. And there was much work to be done, even though Montcalm was a quasi-urban residence, set on a small tract of thirty-six acres. Providing food and clothing for as many as twenty-five black and white residents and guests, as well as caring for various animals, including several fine horses and dogs, kept the entire slave household busy. Throughout the year they labored under Mary's direction in the house, the kitchen, the yard, the flower and vegetable gardens, the orchard, the smokehouse, the hen house, the icehouse, the barn, the stable, and the fields. Even before the mansion was completed, David Campbell had the adjoining fields fenced and planted in corn and oats by some of

16. DC to WBC, January 31, 1845, with note inserted by MHC; DC to VC, January 1, 1834.

17. DC to VC, July 27, 1834. Among many references to slave children, see VC to Catharine Campbell, January 1, 1832; VC to Margaret H. Campbell, May 13, 1832; DC to WBC, February 19, 1833 and April 12, 1843; VC to Margaret H. Campbell, April 1, 1833; DC to Mary H. R. Campbell, August 25, 1833; DC to VC, January 1 and March 24, 1834, September 10 and 21, 1840.

his male house slaves. Later, Michael Valentine, though purchased primarily for his skill as a coachman, cultivated the small farm at Montcalm with the aid of younger male slaves.[18]

Among the male domestic slaves, only Hannah's youngest son, David, seemed to work exclusively in the house and yard. His excellent conduct and talents marked him as special among the Montcalm slave children. By the mid-1830s, when he was about ten years old, young David had become the favorite of members of the Campbell family, who praised his intelligence, his character, and his manners. His master wrote that David was developing into a "finished dining room servant."[19]

Religion played an important part in the lives of the Campbell family and their slaves. Montcalm slaves, like other Abingdon blacks, attended services at the Methodist church, where they were usually seated in the balcony. Their preference for Methodism, rather than the Presbyterian faith in which David Campbell had been raised, was encouraged by Mary Campbell and her ardently Methodist nieces from Tennessee. The Campbell slaves accompanied the white family to camp meetings in the area and interacted with the Methodist preachers who visited Montcalm during the denomination's annual conferences. When Hannah and Michael's twin daughters died from scarlet fever in 1833, a white preacher conducted their funeral at the Methodist church. While David Campbell opposed the influence of Methodist evangelical religion in his own family, which may have been the reason Mary never joined the Methodist church, he did not raise similar opposition with regard to his slaves. Whatever his views, Methodism brought drama, encouragement, and comfort to his slaves as well as

18. VC to Catharine Campbell, April 1833 and March 23, 1836; VC to Margaret H. Campbell April 1, 1833; Mary H. R. Campbell's note in DC to WBC, April 18, 1833; DC to brother-in-law, June 17, 1833, to VC, June 30, 1833, to Margaret H. Campbell, February 13, 1834; MHC to WBC March 30, 1836; Mary H. R. Campbell to Fanny Campbell, May 18, 1837; VC diary, June 18, 1840; DC to MHC, December 11, 1841, to VC, July 13, 1834, to Margaret H. Campbell, September 25, 1836; DC to MHC, January 16, 1823, to VC, September 21, 1840; Daniel M. Railey to DC, January 12, 1838; DC to VC, January 29, 1841.

19. VC to Margaret H. Campbell, November 22, 1834; DC to Mary H. R. Campbell, February, 9, 1841; MHC, Lebanon, Tenn., to Lethe Jackson, November 24, 1841; VC, Lebanon, Tenn., to DC, December 10, 1841; DC to MHC, December 11. 1841; WBC, Lebanon, Tenn., to Margaret H. Campbell, May 2, 1859.

to his wife and nieces. It also forged a strong bond between the slaves and the nieces, especially Virginia, who joined the Methodist church in 1834 while she was visiting her home in Tennessee and who returned to Montcalm filled with evangelical conviction and fervor.[20]

In 1837 David Campbell's supporters in the state legislature elected him to a three-year term as governor. His election surprised many people, including Campbell himself. He became the first man from southwestern Virginia to fill the office, and his victory set off a big celebration in Abingdon and at Montcalm. In part, Campbell's election was a reward for the important support he and his fellow western Virginians had given to the Jacksonian Democrats.[21]

Although David Campbell's election did affect the lives of the white members of the Campbell household, it had a more profound impact on the lives of the Montcalm slaves, bringing them rich new opportunities for learning about the world and about themselves. Richard, Hannah's twenty-six-year-old son, was the first to embark on the new venture, traveling to Richmond with David Campbell by stagecoach in March 1837. Once in the capital, he pleased his master with his polished conduct in the elegant executive mansion.[22]

In October of 1837 when Mary and Virginia Campbell joined the governor in Richmond, Hannah's husband, Michael, her daughter Eliza, and her son David, only eleven years old, accompanied them. "Gawky" Page, Hannah's other child, then about eighteen, was left behind. David Campbell had the mansion's separate kitchen white-washed and furnished with beds for the newly arriving slaves.[23]

20. Hannah Valentine to Eliza, November 1, 1837; DC to WBC, October 14, 1832; February 19, 1833; VC to Margaret H. Campbell, February 1, 1835, and August 29, 1843; Mary H. R. Campbell to Margaret H. Campbell, January 10, 1837; VC to Catharine Campbell, July 1, 1840, October 25, 1843, September 8, 1835, April 25, 1843; VC to Frances Campbell, September 14, 1842; DC to Mary H. R. Campbell, September 8, 1833; Virginia Campbell Shelton, *Excerpts from the Diary Written during Her Girlhood, 1835–1837*, ed. Nannie Shelton McClary (n.p., 1921), 20.

21. DC to WBC, February 7, 1837; Mitchell, "The Political Career," chapters 2 and 3.

22. DC to MHC, March 26 and April 8, 1837. See William Seale, *Virginia's Executive Mansion: A History of the Governor's House* (Richmond: Virginia State Library and Archives, 1988), 40.

23. VC to Margaret H. Campbell, October 1, 1837, February 10, 1839; DC to VC, December 28, 1840; DC to William H. Richardson, July 24, 1837, in DC's

Hannah remained at Montcalm with Page and the other slaves. Under the resident white male overseer's direction, she managed the daily routine of the house and the yard. It was Hannah who decided when a doctor should be called to a slave's bedside, Hannah who reported the death of a slave boy at Montcalm to officials in Abingdon, Hannah who got young men to pen letters to the white and the black families in Richmond, and Hannah who went to the post office. Hannah was more in charge at Montcalm while the Campbells were in Richmond than she had been when they were home.[24]

During the next three years, her husband and three of her children lived in a world vastly different from Abingdon. Richmond was a city of thirty thousand people, including about ten thousand African Americans. While there, Michael Valentine reestablished ties with his extended family, which provided him and the other Montcalm slaves immediate contacts in the black community. One of Valentine's sisters-in-law had served as a washwoman for the governor, and David Campbell reported home that he had also seen two of Michael Valentine's brothers.[25]

At the executive mansion the Montcalm slaves worked hard, helping the Campbells entertain state legislators and officials and national political leaders such as Henry Clay. Michael and David frequently drove Mary and Virginia about the city, delivering calling cards and party invitations. Whether at work in the mansion or in the carriage, the slaves had many opportunities to learn about what was going on in the city, state, and nation. In 1838 they labored for more than a week in the kitchen and dining room of the mansion alongside slaves from other households preparing for a party with more than six hundred guests. As Virginia Campbell wrote, the kitchen "resounded with the beating of eggs, pounding of sugar & last & greatest, the tongues of the slaves."[26]

Executive Papers, 1837–1840, Library of Virginia, Richmond, Va.; VC to Mary H. R. Campbell, November 20, 1837.

24. Jacob Lynch to DC, January 26, 1838, November 10, 1837, March 5, 1838; Hannah Valentine to Michael, January 30, 1838 and to MHC, May 2, 1838; Andrew Russell to DC, December 25, 1837.

25. DC to MHC, April 18, 1837 and April 21, 1837; Hannah Valentine to Eliza, November 1, 1837. Marie Tyler-McGraw and Gregg D. Kimball, *In Bondage and Freedom: Antebellum Black Life in Richmond, Virginia* (Richmond: The Valentine Museum, 1988).

26. VC to Margaret H. Campbell, February 10, 1839 and to Frances Campbell, November 23, 1839; VC to Margaret H. Campbell, February 27, 1839.

Several times during David Campbell's three-year term, Michael, Eliza, Lucy, and David accompanied their owners on trips to Abingdon and back. They usually took the carriage across southern Virginia, but on one trip, they enjoyed their first railroad ride, traveling about fifty miles. On another occasion they traveled alone while the governor and his family went to Philadelphia and New York City. When David Campbell's favorite horse died on the way to Abingdon, Michael bought a new horse for the carriage. In 1839 the entire Richmond household made an eighteen-day trip, going first to the Western Insane Asylum of Virginia at Staunton and then to the site of the projected Virginia Military Institute in Lexington. During these exciting years, Hannah was reported to be proud of her family members' excellent behavior in Richmond. She was also solicitous about their welfare, sending her husband his Bible and imploring her master not to leave them, especially David, in the city while he and his family went north.[27]

During the last year of David Campbell's gubernatorial term, serious strife developed in his family. The slaves who had taken care of them for so long had always known Mary Campbell to be demanding and temperamental, but they now witnessed her prolonged emotional and physical breakdown as she became locked in conflict with nineteen-year-old Virginia. Apparently, Mary Campbell, who had married a first cousin at the age of seventeen in frontier east Tennessee without ever experiencing life as a belle in a sophisticated urban setting, was shocked and even jealous at her niece's vivacity in the company of young men. From early January to March of 1840, Mary Campbell secluded herself in her bedroom, refusing to take meals with her family. In the spring of 1840, Mary, David, and Virginia Campbell and their slaves sadly journeyed home to Abingdon, wearied from their familial strife and disappointed that David Campbell had failed in a bid to be elected by the legislature to the United States Senate.[28]

27. VC to Catharine Campbell, June 30, 1839 and to Margaret H. Campbell, August 2, 1839; John B. Richardson to DC, June 14, 1838; VC to Frances Campbell, July 7, 1838; VC diary, July 1–9, 1839; VC to DC, April 5, 1837; Hannah Valentine to MHC, May 2, 1838.

28. WBC to VC, January 6 and February 1, 1840; VC diary, entries for January 7, 9, 13, 28 and March 19 and 24, 1840; DC to WBC, January 30 and March 24, 1840; VC to WBC, January 30, February 22, March 24, 1840 and to Ellen W. White, February 28, 1840. Mitchell, "The Political Career," 240–52.

Soon after their return home, however, David Campbell concluded that his household was "moving on in the old way—all very quiet and regular."[29] He was mistaken. Life at Montcalm would never be the same as before the Richmond years. During the next two decades, in mostly nonviolent ways, Hannah and her family would push hard against the bondage in which they lived. They would gradually achieve a high degree of individual and group autonomy, and for a time in the 1850s they would even gain mastery over Mary Campbell and Montcalm.

In their quest for autonomy, measurable by education and the free practice of their Methodist religion, the Montcalm slaves found an ally in Virginia Campbell. Now in her twenties, she had been well educated by her uncle, Abingdon tutors and schools, and her Richmond experiences, and she had remained fervently religious. With no serious prospect for marriage, she had plenty of time and energy to spend with the slaves in the cellar. Her relationship with them changed significantly from what it had been before the Richmond years. Then she had gone to the cellar to read to the slaves. Now she taught them to read. Mary Burwell, a literate, Methodist slave whom David Campbell had bought in 1840, assisted her. Several of the other slaves joined Mary Burwell and Virginia Campbell as members of the Methodist church, and they read the Bibles that Virginia purchased for them. In 1841, Leathy's daughter Lucy was married to another slave in a ceremony at the Methodist church conducted by a white Methodist minister. David and his older brother, Page, joined the Sons of Temperance in Abingdon, and David gave temperance speeches at the Methodist church.[30]

The Montcalm slaves' connections to family and friends in the Abingdon area multiplied as not only Lucy but also Eliza, Richard, Page, and David married slaves in other households and had many

29. DC to VC, January 29, 1841.

30. VC to Margaret H. Campbell, February 1, 1835; McClary, entries dated January 4, May 31, 1835, May 31, June 14, June 21, 1840; DC to VC, November 9 and December 28, 1840 and January 22, 1841; VC to Catharine Campbell, January 9, 1843; Lucy Clark to Washington, April 11, 1843; VC to Frances Campbell, November 26, 1843 and February 21, 1844 and to Margaret H. Campbell, September 19, 1844; VC to Margaret H. Campbell, August 29, 1843, and to Catharine Campbell, December 7, 1844. DC to VC, June 16, 1841; VC to MHC, July 16, 1841; DC to Margaret H. Campbell, December 27, 1844.

children.[31] No doubt that was why David and Mary Campbell built the spacious, separate brick slave house behind Montcalm in 1844. Their respect for slave marriage and family life and their enjoyment of slave children led them to provide a place of greater privacy than the Montcalm cellar offered. Yet, as the slaves at Montcalm strove to create an ever more autonomous existence, they did so primarily in the cellar of the big house. Although their culture was constructed within the house controlled by whites and was assisted by at least one white family member, it was still something apart from the whites' lives, and they could view it only as spectators, from the outside.

This independent development was never more clearly exhibited than through the rituals followed when members of the slave community died. In the 1840s and 1850s, death came often to the family in the cellar at Montcalm. Nine of Lucy's thirteen young children died, most of them from tuberculosis. Hannah's beautiful daughter Eliza died at the age of thirty-three after a terrible three-month illness, leaving several young children.[32] The slave death most fully recorded in the Campbell correspondence was that of the cherished Leathy Jackson in 1843 at the age of seventy-two. Her funeral ritual reveals clearly the slaves' elaborate communal experience of mourning, which the whites observed and appreciated but did not participate in.

Leathy's funeral began with a nighttime wake in the kitchen, marked by the slaves' "devotions & solemn singing." On this special occasion Mary and Virginia Campbell did what was apparently rare: they had the carpet in the dining room pulled back and the trap door opened so that they could sit beside it late into the night, listening to the slaves below.

The next morning, a Saturday, Leathy's funeral drew many blacks from other households. "Quite a number of coloured persons assembled in the kitchen & after singing & prayers the coffin was placed in the waggon which conveyed it to its final resting place" in the black cemetery not far from Montcalm. A Baptist slave preacher, "Mrs. White's

31. DC to WBC, July 15, 1853. In 1838 Richard's wife was moved to Mississippi; four years later Richard married Sarah McChesney. VC to DC, June 21, 1837, Hannah Valentine to Michael Valentine, January 30, 1838 and VC to Frances Campbell, September 14, 1842.
32. DC to WBC, May 1, 1854; DC, *Memorials*, 395–96.

Lace," whom Leathy had chosen to "attend at her burial," led the mourners. Mary, David, and Virginia Campbell watched the funeral procession from the house. "The procession was very large before it reached the grave," Virginia wrote, "many servants joining them in the great road. They sang all the way to the grave." Thus, Leathy's funeral became a celebration of black community and culture. Sometime later the Campbells arranged for another service to be held for Leathy, this one at the Methodist church with a white minister preaching to a white and black congregation.[33]

No evidence exists that Mary and David Campbell opposed their slaves' being taught to read or their development of an autonomous religious culture, even when the laws of Virginia prohibiting such education were violated. Living in an area with a small black population, they were not nervous about these developments and did nothing to discourage them. In addition, during the 1840s and 1850s, the Campbells further enlarged their slaves' opportunities for learning and for autonomy by making four extended visits to Tennessee. As they had done during the Richmond years, they took Michael, Eliza, Lucy, and David along on the trips. During one of the visits to Tennessee, David Campbell allowed David to return to Abingdon alone by train to visit his wife, who was ill. Once again the Campbells left Hannah, Page, and the rest of their slaves at Montcalm with renewed opportunities for autonomy.[34]

Even as they were allowing their slaves unusual opportunities, however, the Campbells were complaining about some of their actions. Soon after the return from Richmond, for instance, recurring dissatisfaction with Michael Valentine's behavior was expressed in the family correspondence. Mary Campbell and her skilled coachman were often at odds. On one occasion in the 1840s, when Michael had driven the Campbells to Tennessee, he refused to stay there under Mary's supervision when his master had to go back to Abingdon on business. By this time, Michael had become so indispensable to the Campbells

33. VC to Catharine Campbell, July 22, 1843 and to Frances Campbell, April 25, 1844.
34. John M. Ropp to DC, November 28, 1855 and DC to WBC, February 24, 1856.

that David allowed him to return to Abingdon with him. Clearly, the Campbells' relationship with their slaves was marked by both trust and suspicion.[35]

During the Campbells' absences, stealing became a problem at Montcalm. When the Campbells inventoried their belongings after their final return from Richmond, they found many things missing. Consequently, in the 1840s, before leaving home, Mary Campbell took extensive precautions, locking up her sideboard, trunks, and closets and hiding the keys. She also gave the overseer strict instructions to let no slave go to the second floor unless he was present.[36]

Lying by the slaves also became a problem. The Campbells were increasingly convinced that Hannah and Michael censored communication from the slaves. The Campbells said that they believed that David, Eliza, and Leathy wanted to tell the truth, but they were afraid of "old Hannah." They believed that Mary Burwell was quickly adopted into Hannah's family only because she became amenable to "old Hannah."[37]

During the 1850s, Mary and David Campbell themselves became more and more dependent on Hannah and on the other slaves, whom she controlled. The processes of aging and of increasing mental and physical disability rendered the Campbells more and more in need of extensive help. William and Virginia Campbell, on whom they had lavished time, affection, and money, established independent lives in Tennessee and visited Montcalm only occasionally. William Campbell's career took him to the state legislature, the United States House of Representatives, the Mexican War, the governor's mansion of Tennessee, and a circuit court judge's bench, then into the commission business and banking. At the same time he and his wife, Frances, reared a large family. Virginia disappointed her uncle and aunt's hopes that she would marry in Virginia and become mistress of Montcalm. Instead, in 1849, she returned to Tennessee to wed William

35. DC to WBC, August 3, 1840; DC to MHC, November 28, 1841; VCS to MHC and DC, October 14, 1853.

36. VC to DC, December 3, 1841; MHC to DC, December 12, 1841; DC to MHC, December 11, 1841.

37. MHC to DC, December 12, 1841. DC to WBC, November 14, 1855, and John M. Ropp to DC, November 28, 1855.

Shelton, a Baptist minister with whom she eventually had six children. During the 1850s, the only younger Campbell relative from Tennessee who would stay very long at Montcalm was William and Virginia's unmarried sister, Margaret, a school teacher.[38]

The Campbells' need for assistance continued to grow. By 1850, the emotional instability that Mary had evidenced during the Richmond years had evolved into a settled mental illness complicated by worsening eyesight. Cataract surgery restored her vision, but nothing could restore her mental health. In 1852, David Campbell wrote that his wife's only enjoyment was "to get Hannah into the wing and talk old times over with her. This she does every day."[39] Thus, Hannah continued to be of significant help to the Campbells at the same time that they came to see her as the greatest threat to their control of Montcalm.

Mary Campbell felt set upon from many directions. While the railroad, which in time connected Lynchburg, Virginia, with Bristol, Virginia/Tennessee, was being built at the foot of Montcalm hill in 1854, she was tormented by images of trespassers and pigs running wild on her property. In turn, she became a torment to her husband, who suffered from tuberculosis, a disease that also struck many of his slaves in the cellar. To make his plight worse, a cancer developed in and spread across his right eye.[40]

In this situation, the burden of caring for Mary fell on Hannah Valentine and her family. David Campbell could not manage or entertain her. It took three slaves to get her into bed at night. She often verbally assailed her servants, accusing them of stealing things that she

38. VC to MHC and DC, January 25, 1849, May 4, 1859; WBC to DC, Carthage, Tenn., May 14, 1849; DC to WBC, May 25, 1849 and October 20, 1849; William Shelton to WBC, January 29, 1866. MHC to DC, January 31, 1842; J. Milton Henry, "William Bowen Campbell," in *The Encyclopedia of Southern History,* ed. David Roller and Tobert Twyman (Baton Rouge: Louisiana State University Press, 1979), 175.

39. DC to WBC, May 25, 1849, October 26 and December 4, 1852; DC to VCS, January 1, 1852.

40. Margaret H. Campbell to WBC, May 17, 1854; DC to VCS, May 19, June 14 and 16, October 21, December 1, 1851; DC to Margaret H. Campbell, December 15, 1851; DC to WBC, February 14, 1853, August 8, 1853 and September 12, 1853; Margaret H. Campbell to WBC, February 7, 1854; DC to WBC, April 3, 1855, August 27, 1855, March 10, 1856, [May, 1858], June 17, 1858, January 26, 1859.

had mislaid. They and David Campbell had much to endure from this feebleminded, raging woman. Yet the slaves cared for her and for their frail master with patience, kindness, and faithfulness.[41]

At the same time, the slaves at Montcalm made the most of the opportunities for self-assertion that the situation offered. In his usual way, the slave David, now a handsome man almost six feet tall, gained favor and power by exemplary behavior. He became David Campbell's business assistant, going to Abingdon to pay his bills and collect debts owed him. There he evidently enjoyed respect from everyone because, his master said, he was like "a genteel white man." For the first time, he was referred to with the surname Bird, by which he would be known the rest of his life. At the big house, he often slept not in the cellar but in David Campbell's room or in the ell. Like a surrogate son, he tenderly dressed the cancerous sore on his master's face and administered his medicine. Even raging Mary Campbell recognized his position and never verbally attacked him as she did the other slaves. In fact, she trusted him enough to ask that he be the one to dress and undress her.

By all accounts David Bird never betrayed the trust placed in him. In his master's view he performed "all his duties in the best manner and always with a gravity that would become a finished gentleman." During these difficult years, David Campbell sometimes remarked appreciatively about the help he received from one of his slaves. Among the women, he especially praised Lucy and her daughter, Frances. But no one, not even Frances, so consistently fulfilled his expectations as David Bird.[42]

Some of his slaves, especially Hannah and Page, betrayed his trust as they acted in their own self-interest. In 1853, despite his and his wife's long dependence on Hannah, David Campbell risked her wrath by taking the unusual step of selling her son, Page, for "bad conduct." This was the first time since the move to Montcalm that he had violated

41. DC to WBC, March 11, 1858; DC to VCS, October 28, 1851, January 1 and January 30, 1852; John Campbell Jr. to WBC, October 20, 1852; Margaret H. Campbell to VCS, January 6, 1854 and to WBC, January 9, February 7, 1854, May 17, 1854, April 25, 1859; James K. Gibson to [WBC], February 12, 1859; WBC to Margaret H. Campbell, March 15, 1859; Margaret H. Campbell to Catharine Campbell, April 11, 1859.

42. DC to WBC, February 14 and May 14, 1853, February 24 and September 9, 1856, August 7, 1857.

the slave family by sale. But Campbell was unable to break their family unity. Two years later, while he and Mary were in Tennessee accompanied by Michael, David, and Frances, Page returned to Montcalm, where he was hidden by Hannah and the other slaves in the cellar. Since the white overseer living upstairs was hard of hearing, Page went undetected for several months. He did not remain in hiding all the time though, and finally, he was tracked to Montcalm by a trail of blood from a two-hundred-pound hog that he had allegedly stolen and killed in Abingdon. When the hog's owner and town officials reached Montcalm, Hannah and the other slaves denied knowledge of Page's whereabouts and even of the keys to unlock the back cellar room. When the men broke the door down, they found Page and the hog.

In Tennessee, David Campbell heard about what had happened, and he was furious. He declared that he was going to see that Page was sold "out of the country," thus separating him from his wife and children as well as from his mother's family. This was necessary, Campbell said, "as a matter of safety to the community." He was also furious with Hannah. He was sure that the other slaves would have told the truth about Page's misdeeds and whereabouts if they had not been afraid of "old Hannah." He held her responsible for the whole affair, and he wished he could send her off with her son. He was not surprised when Hannah, Mary Burwell (in whose room the hog had been found), and one of Hannah's grandsons, William, were tried and sentenced to whippings in Abingdon. Soon he learned that Hannah had been selling hogs, claiming that they were hers, and that other slaves were selling his firewood. When he returned from Tennessee, he found that six hundred dollars had been stolen from his library.

Clearly, David Campbell had serious problems at Montcalm. But in his weakened and dependent state, he did not act decisively against the slaves he regarded as culprits. In fact, he saw to it that Hannah was not whipped "because of her age [sixty-two]." And, for whatever reason, Page was not sold "out of the country" but was allowed to remain in the Abingdon area.[43]

In the late 1850s, life in the beautiful brick house grew intolerable for the Campbell family. Margaret Campbell wrote from Montcalm

43. John M. Ropp to DC, October 16, 1855 and to WBC, November 5 and 28, 1855; DC to WBC, November 14, 1855 and October 1, 1856, September 21, 1858.

that "Aunt nearly worries Uncle to death . . . . He is blind—The house is a ruin—Aunt says no one is going to interfere with her household & no one does." In Margaret's view, the necessity of lying to feebleminded Mary to manage her had destroyed the slaves' discipline.[44]

For the slaves, the closing years of the 1850s were a time of foreboding. They did not know what would befall them when their owners died. Since at least the late 1840s, they had speculated among themselves about the possibility that their enlightened owner might free them in his will. Apparently, in her derangement Mary Campbell assured them they would be freed. On at least one occasion, in 1848, Virginia Campbell had protested to her uncle about what her aunt was doing, eliciting from him a denial of plans to free his slaves. But the slaves apparently did not give up hope for freedom or, at least, for their home to be inherited and maintained by Virginia Campbell Shelton so that they could continue to live there.[45]

Finally, on March 19, 1859, David Campbell died and was buried in Sinking Spring Cemetery at Abingdon. His will directed his executor, William B. Campbell, to sell Montcalm and to care for Mary Campbell in Tennessee. The will instructed William to take to Tennessee only the slaves needed to tend to Mary's needs and to sell the others to compassionate owners who would not remove them from their families. But the degree of autonomy the slaves had enjoyed prior to Campbell's death remained. From March until May 1859, Margaret Campbell remained at Montcalm with her aunt, but, she wrote her brother William, "I do not take any management at all but let the servants go on as they have been doing for years. Carrying the keys using everything as they wish &c &c. I cannot do otherwise." In fact, a few days before Campbell's death, James K. Gibson wrote to William about his fear that some of the slaves who could read would find Campbell's will and "if it did not suit their notion it could be an easy matter to destroy it."[46]

When William arrived to carry out his uncle's direction to move Mary to Tennessee, he found it impossible. His aunt, who had so long

44. Margaret H. Campbell to VCS, February 25, May 4 and 26, 1859.

45. VC to Margaret H. Campbell, July 14, 1848 and Margaret H. Campbell to VCS, May 4 and May 26, 1859; John Campbell Jr. to VCS, October 10, 1859.

46. Washington County, Va., Will Book 14, 1856–1859, 402–7; MC to WBC, May 17, 1859; James K. Gibson to WBC, March 12, 1859.

doted on him, now raged against him and his wife, Frances. He became convinced that the slaves were deceitfully inciting his aunt's hatred for him to keep her and themselves at Montcalm. To his wife he wrote that the only way he could move Mary to Tennessee would be forcibly. "There never was just such a case as this that I have on hand in the person of Aunt & her servants," he declared, and he went home to Tennessee, leaving Margaret to cope with the situation.[47]

It was at this point, in the summer of 1859, that the slaves' control of Montcalm reached its height. Without consulting Margaret, Michael Valentine employed a white woman in Abingdon to come to Montcalm to help care for his mistress. On the daily carriage drives to Abingdon that Mary Campbell insisted on taking, she waged a "fight of words" with him. Finally, in August, Margaret locked valuables in a second-floor room and left Montcalm and Mary to the slaves and a lawyer in Abingdon.[48]

Two months later, Mary Campbell died at Montcalm, surrounded by some of her husband's Washington County relatives, whom she had usually disdained, and by Hannah Valentine's family. Now the long process of slave empowerment at Montcalm halted. William B. Campbell, who said the slaves' ingratitude was "unparralled," returned to Abingdon to execute his uncle's will by selling all of the property and dividing the proceeds equally between his sister Virginia and his wife, Frances. During 1860 the slave family that had lived for more than thirty years in the Montcalm cellar was divided and sold, and Montcalm was put up for sale.[49]

The disposition of fourteen slaves, aged nine to sixty-five, was not accomplished easily, except for that of Hannah's oldest child, Richard, who was willed to David Campbell's brother, John. William took care to follow his uncle's direction that the other slaves be sold only to

47. WBC to Frances Campbell, May 26 and 29, 1859; WBC to Margaret H. Campbell June 17, 1859; and Margaret H. Campbell to VCS, June 7, 1859.
48. Margaret H. Campbell to WBC, July 22, 30, 31, August 2, 1859; WBC to Margaret H. Campbell, August 7, 1859.
49. James K. Gibson to WBC, October 6 and 8, 1859; John Campbell to VCS, October 10, 1859; Eliza Gibson to Margaret H. Campbell, October 10, 1859; WBC to Margaret H. Campbell, August 7, 1859; DC's will and inventory. For the disposition of Montcalm, see James K. Gibson to WBC, April 20, 1860; John A. Campbell to WBC, April 21, 1860 and April 23, 1865; Arthur C. Cummings to WBC, September 10, 1865, October 16, 1865.

those who would pledge not to move them away from their families. Virginia Campbell Shelton, who bought Leathy's seven descendants and one young, motherless, tubercular grandson of Hannah's, argued with her brother about the value and price of the slaves. But Hannah and Michael Valentine gave William his most difficult problem. No one wanted them. Their history of self-assertion at Montcalm was well known in Abingdon; prospective buyers expected that they would mean trouble. Finally, one of David Campbell's Washington County nephews, who had already purchased one of Hannah's three grandsons, agreed to take both Hannah and Michael Valentine when William Campbell paid *him* three hundred dollars to do so.[50]

But Hannah never moved. Before she could be forced to leave Montcalm, she died in 1860 at the age of sixty-six. Her death probably spared her the news that her thieving son, Page, long known in the white community as "an infernal rascal," had been discovered with "a variety of dry goods, shoes, leather Boots, Jewelry, Pistols etc. etc." and had been shot and killed.[51]

In the midst of the disturbing changes just before her death, Hannah had learned some welcome news. Her son David Bird had been freed by Campbell's will; he had also been left the sizeable sum of five hundred dollars with which to begin his new life. Although Virginia law required freed slaves to leave the state within a year of emancipation, the Civil War may have precluded its enforcement against Bird. During the war, Bird worked briefly for a Confederate officer and then secured a job at Martha Washington College, a school for women that the Methodist church had opened at Abingdon in 1860. The literacy, household skills, manners, and religious affiliation he had gained as a slave at Montcalm served him well as a free worker. He further continued his journey to autonomy by purchasing a lot and a house.[52]

50. WBC to William Shelton, December 7, 1859; William Shelton to WBC, December 14, 1859; "List of Sales of negros [*sic*] made by WB Campbell Executor of the Will of David Campbell deceased, September 11, 1860," Washington County, Va., Will Book 15, 1860–1863; VCS to WBC, February 25 and March 16, 1860 and James K. Gibson to WBC, January 28, February 24, March 5, May 25, July 28, 1860.
51. James K. Gibson to WBC, October 14, 1861.
52. WBC to James K. Gibson, April 2, 1866 and to C. B. Fish, April 4, 1866; VCS to WBC, February 25, 1860; James K. Gibson to WBC, January 24 and October 14, 1861.

David Bird had difficulty, however, collecting from William Campbell additional discretionary funds bequeathed by David Campbell to his favored slaves. Finally, Bird sought the intervention of officials in the Freedmen's Bureau, who wrote Campbell on his behalf. This clash pitted David Campbell's two surrogate sons, white and black, against each other. Angered, William Campbell and his lawyer in Abingdon, a nephew of David Campbell's, ridiculed Bird. For the first time, members of the Campbell clan found something wrong with the former slave's behavior. Nonetheless, William Campbell assured the Freedmen's Bureau that he would pay Bird his money.[53]

During the next thirty years, David Bird and his second wife reared a family of six children, including a son named David and a daughter named Eliza after her father's beautiful young sister who had died in slavery at Montcalm in 1848. By 1900, Eliza had become a school teacher in Abingdon. In 1915, Robert A. Lancaster, author of *Historic Virginia Homes and Churches*, echoed the Abingdon oral tradition about David Bird, when he wrote:

> He belonged to a type now almost entirely extinct, loyal and faithful, indispensable to those whom he served. Not only was he thoroughly accomplished in all the craft of house life of the day, but his imposing stature, impressive dignity, and polished manners rendered him truly ornamental. He lived to ripe old age, and upon his death in recent years the funeral train was largely composed of the descendants of his white friends of earlier days.[54]

David Bird's Montcalm relatives in Washington County and in Tennessee, who had not received their freedom from their master but from Abraham Lincoln and the Thirteenth Amendment to the United States Constitution, also pursued their autonomous lives, evidencing the range of behaviors that students of the immediate post-emancipation period have identified.[55] Most of them became independent people

53. David M. Bird to WBC, February 22 and March 10, 1866; York A. Woodward to WBC, March 28, 1866; WBC to James K. Gibson, April 2, 1866 and to C. B. Fish, April 4, 1866.
54. U. S. censes for 1870, 1880, 1900; Robert A. Lancaster, *Historic Virginia Homes and Churches* (Philadelphia: J. B. Lippincott and Co., 1915), 478.
55. Especially see Leon F. Litwack, *Been in the Storm Too Long: The Aftermath of Slavery* (New York: Alfred A. Knopf, 1979).

and preserved their family connections, using the skills and the habits they had learned at Montcalm. Jackson, Hannah's grandson whose "flying squirrel tricks" Mary Campbell had found irresistible back in 1834 and who had been sold to a Campbell nephew after the Campbells' deaths, took the surname Dixon after emancipation and became a laborer, heading his own household though he was still illiterate. His step-grandfather, Hannah's husband, Michael Valentine, lived with the Dixons until his death.

Hannah's other grandson, William, who at his birth in 1835 had been named for William Bowen Campbell and in 1855 had been whipped for lying about his thieving uncle, Page, was also sold to a Campbell nephew in Washington County. After emancipation, he established an independent household in Abingdon but kept the surname of Campbell. In the 1940s, William's son, Joseph Francis Trigg Campbell, belonged to a property-owning black community at Fractionville, two miles from Abingdon. There he recalled the story of his father's birth as a slave in the cellar of Montcalm. He said his own children had gone north to make money, but he was content to remain in the land of his ancestors.[56]

In Brownsville, Tennessee, the slave Lucy, her children and grand-children, and Hannah's grandson, Charles, lived through the Civil War with the Sheltons. When freedom came, they shocked and angered Virginia by leaving her as a group, under the leadership of a former slave whom Lucy's daughter, Frances, had married in Tennessee. Virginia, who had long been a friend to the slaves in the cellar at Montcalm, declared the "Abingdon Negroes . . . the most abominable set that I am acquainted with." Like many other whites she was unable to accept the results of the slave journey to autonomy that she herself had done so much to enable. The disabled and alcoholic slave Jefferson, one of Lucy's sons, was the only former Montcalm slave still with her when she died in 1866 at forty-six.[57]

Thus, Hannah Valentine's family moved from slavery to freedom. Their experience as slaves at Montcalm had not shielded them entirely

56. Goodrich A. Wilson, "The Southwest Corner," *Roanoke Times,* 1948, and U. S. Census for 1880.
57. VCS to William Shelton, July 6 and 18, 1865; VCS to WBC, January 29, 1866.

from some of slavery's worst aspects, such as a lack of privacy, poor health, addictions, high mortality, illiteracy, a capricious mistress, whippings, and sale away from the family. But life within Mary and David Campbell's household had offered them an unusually high degree of individual and group autonomy before emancipation. Most of them had used their advantages within slavery so well that when emancipation finally came they were able to continue doing what they had learned to do under Hannah's tutelage: make the most of life's opportunities.

Her Will against Theirs

Eda Hickam and the Ambiguity of Freedom in Postbellum Missouri

KIMBERLY SCHRECK

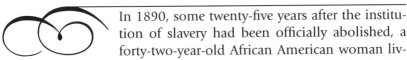 In 1890, some twenty-five years after the institution of slavery had been officially abolished, a forty-two-year-old African American woman living in Cooper County, Missouri, filed suit against the white family with whom she had lived since childhood. Eda Hickam had been a slave in the Hickam household since the age of seven, and she said that despite the abolishment of slavery in the United States, she had continued to live and work as a slave from 1865 to 1889. It was not until her master, Joseph Hickam, died in 1889, that she was informed of her freedom. In her suit, she claimed that she deserved back wages for the twenty-five years the Hickams had kept her in ignorance of her freedom. She would spend the next four years trying to gain compensation from Joseph Hickam's estate. This peculiar scenario, that a slave never heard about emancipation and that a white family concealed an event of such magnitude from her were the issues that arose in Eda Hickam's court trials. Her attorneys sought to prove that she had been fraudulently led to believe she was still a slave, while attorneys for the white Hickam family argued she had been informed of her freedom and had thrown herself on the Hickams' mercy, asking to be allowed to stay with them and continue to receive their support.[1]

The records cannot reveal whether Eda Hickam was informed of her freedom in 1865 or whether Joseph Hickam and his family intended to

---

1. *Hickam v Hickam,* Cooper County Court Records, case no. 4003. Kimberly A. Schreck, "Their Place in Freedom: African American Women in Transition from Slavery to Freedom, Cooper County, Missouri, 1865–1900" (M.A. thesis, University of Missouri, Columbia, 1993).

conceal her freed status from her. Those questions do not constitute the central theme of this study, although they were central to Eda Hickam's court battles. Court records do, however, show that Eda Hickam and the white Hickam family had divergent opinions about the meanings of the words *freedom* and *slavery*. Arguments for the two sides suggest that the definitions were not fashioned within the courtroom, but rather, had been constructed in the day-to-day relations of Eda and the Hickams. This ambiguity is revealed in Eda Hickam's understanding of her postbellum experience; it differed markedly from that of the white Hickams. These different perspectives, when examined within the context of postbellum race relations in Cooper County, Missouri, reveal the incongruent understandings of postbellum social relations that were held by Eda Hickam and her former owners. Eda Hickam defined her postbellum experience as exploitative while the Hickam family characterized their behavior toward Eda as benevolent.

As a small child, Eda lived with the Hickam family on their farm in Moniteau County. She would have been about sixteen when slavery ended in 1865. In 1876, she moved with the Hickams twelve miles north to a farm in Cooper County. Upon Joseph Hickam's death in the summer of 1889, as Joseph's children were dividing up his estate, they not only turned Eda away to fend for herself, but they did so without offering her any portion of Joseph Hickam's ample estate, which amounted to more than seven thousand dollars.[2]

Eda Hickam's awakening came as Joseph's surviving kin both literally and figuratively alienated her from their family. As they were in the process of selling and dividing up Joseph's assets, Eda stood before a judge in the Cooper County Probate Court arguing that the entire Hickam family had purposefully kept from her information about the emancipation of slaves from 1865 to 1889. She asked that the judge award her $1,440 in wages for her twenty-five years of unpaid service, which amounted to five dollars per month plus interest.[3]

As Eda sought remuneration for the years of slave labor, James Hickam, Joseph's youngest son and administrator of his estate, aggressively maintained that Eda Hickam willfully stayed with the family while knowing full well she had been freed in 1865. Eda challenged her

2. Cooper County Probate Records, estate number 2567.A.
3. *Hamilton-News Graphic*, January 3, 1890.

former owners' power to define as freedom what was a subordinate, if not legally enslaved, experience. If she had been free, Eda argued, then the white Hickams should have paid her wages.

James Hickam, however, held tight to the family inheritance. He argued that Eda Hickam had been "fully informed" of the Emancipation Proclamation and had, in 1865, been offered the choice of "remaining at her old homestead or leaving." He further argued that Eda had desired to remain with her master and did so "of her own free will and accord." No one questioned how James knew what Eda had been told, even though he had been only three years old in 1865. Nor did anyone point out the contradictions that arose when he referred to the Hickam household as Eda's "old home" or when he implied she had a "free" choice to remain or leave. Apparently James Hickam believed it was Eda's "home" so long as she lived there under the terms set by the white members, which meant living there as an unpaid, subordinate worker. The fact that James Hickam paid to the local paper a fee of eighteen dollars to publicize his arguments reveals the lengths to which he sought affirmation from the white populace during his trials with Eda Hickam. The *Boonville Weekly Advertiser* furnished James a means to portray himself and his deceased father as benevolent and generous patriarchs. The articles that appeared in local newspapers regarding Eda Hickam's case were short and inconspicuously buried among editorials and advertisements; the case was never the subject of a leading story. But on January 9, 1890, the Cooper County probate judge, who perhaps was cognizant of the discrepancy between the Hickam men's actions and their words, awarded Eda Hickam $785, about half of what she had requested.[4]

To untangle the roots of Eda and James Hickam's disparate understandings of Eda's inclusion in the Hickam family, the relationship between Eda and the Hickams must be understood within the context of institutionalized slavery. Eda Hickam's perception of her relationship to the white Hickams was certainly informed by her slave experience. She was raised in the area of Missouri known as "Little Dixie," which

4. *Boonville Weekly Advertiser*, December 27, 1889; *Boonville Weekly Advertiser*, December 27, 1889; *Hamilton-News Graphic*, January 3, 1890; *Hickam v Hickam*. James Hickam's age in 1865 is determined from the Tenth U.S. Census, Cooper County, Missouri, Saline Township, roll 683, 1880.

comprised the fertile counties in the middle of the state, bordering on the Missouri River, where slaves accounted for more than 25 percent of the total population. The 1850 Census shows the largest slave owner in Cooper County owned seventy slaves, twenty-nine of whom were older than fifteen years of age; the second largest owned thirty-two, twenty-three of whom were older than fifteen years of age. There were, of course, a great many white households that owned only one or two slaves. Farmers in this region usually owned only a small number of slaves who assisted them both in the cultivation of commercial crops and in various other tasks necessary for the homestead to run efficiently. Slaves from this region, historians have argued, were less likely to work in gangs, as did slaves in other parts of the South, and they frequently performed a wide variety of tasks for their owners, including both agricultural and domestic work. Depositions from Eda's suits against the Hickam family suggest that her work within the Hickam household was the kind that might have been performed by a family slave, even long after slavery should have ended. As Joseph Hickam's only slave, Eda was probably closely supervised, and she lacked a separate slave community that would have afforded her reprieves from the company of her white owners. She would have had difficulty developing a sense of dependence, emotional or otherwise, on any people except those who owned her.[5]

It is not difficult to imagine why Eda might have perceived herself as a member of the Hickam household, even if only a subordinate member. After all, southerners often used their slaves' supposed status as family members in defense of the institution of slavery. Joseph Hickam's son Squire revealed in his court deposition that his father had inherited Eda and a slave boy when they were young children, and except for the short time Hickam kept the slave boy, Eda was their only slave. The only black kin mentioned in any of the depositions

5. There is some discrepancy among historians as to which counties should be included in the area referred to as "Little Dixie." Douglas Hurt's definition, used for this paper, is a "Little Dixie" composed of the following counties: Howard, Boone, Saline, Callaway, Cooper, and Clay. R. Douglas Hurt, *Agriculture and Slavery in Missouri's Little Dixie* (Columbia: University of Missouri Press, 1992), 215–16; Harrison A. Trexler, *Slavery in Missouri, 1804–1865* (Baltimore: Johns Hopkins University Press, 1914), 100, 106–8. U.S. Census, 1850 Slave Schedule, Cooper County, Missouri.

was Eda's stepfather, Sam Davis, with whom, the records indicate, she was not closely associated. There is also no evidence to suggest that Eda interacted with other African Americans living in the region. In fact, court records and newpaper articles about the case imply that Eda claimed that the Hickams prevented her from doing so. Isolated from the comforts that could be cultivated in a separate slave culture, Eda grew increasingly dependent on the family that owned her, and her dependence no doubt influenced her perception of her relationship to them.[6]

If Eda had in fact considered herself a member of the family up until Joseph's death, she quickly realized that she was not to enjoy such status permanently. She was forced to reevaluate her relationship to the family in whose household she had long resided. Eda decided that if she was not going to receive any money or material possessions as a member of the family, she would seek compensation for labor she had performed as the Hickams' employee. She argued that the Hickams had exploited her unpaid labor by withholding from her the information that slaves had been freed in 1865, an idea no doubt stemming from the fact that each member of the Hickam family except her was awarded money and property from Joseph Hickam's estate. Thus, it was after her expulsion from the Hickam household that Eda Hickam began to understand her relationship to the family in market terms.

As a slave, Eda was bound via a market relationship to her owner, Joseph, and her understanding of her relationship to the Hickam family seems to have remained a non-market one so long as the family did not sever their familial ties to her. When they did, however, Eda argued before a judge that if she had not been bound to the Hickams as a family member, then she had been illegally bound to them as a slave. As she actually was not their slave after 1865, Eda Hickam wanted their acknowledgment of her transformation from slave to employee. Her demand challenged the Hickams' right as white patriarchs in the

6. Squire Hickam, deposition, July 17, 1890, Cooper County Court Records, case no. 4003 (all depositions hereinafter in Cooper County Court Records, case no. 4003 unless otherwise noted); U.S. Census, 1860 Slave Schedule, Moniteau County, Missouri; *Hamilton-News Graphic*, January 3, 1890; Mr. Cosgrove, deposition, May 5, 1890; Sam Davis, deposition, May 4, 1890. Leon Litwack, *Been in the Storm So Long: The Aftermath of Slavery* (New York: Alfred A. Knopf, 1979), 226–27.

South to define household dependents—both white and black—as family, when the family bond was extended to Eda only so long as the patriarch, who benefited from this arrangement, lived. The probate judge who awarded Eda Hickam half of the back wages for which she sued, perhaps in recognition of the different ways that the plaintiff and the defendant were located in relation to the Hickam family, compromised rather than completely validating either argument.

Dissatisfied with the award, Eda Hickam appealed the probate court's decision to the Cooper County Circuit Court. This was the second of Eda's four efforts to recover back wages. A jury of the Hickams' peers considered the depositions of at least fifteen people, taken in the six months since the probate court's ruling, before deciding that Eda was not deserving of more than $785 in back wages. During this trial, white acquaintances of the Hickam family testified that it seemed unlikely Eda could have lived with them for twenty-five years and never have been informed of her freedom. Other deponents who had known the Hickams in both Moniteau and Cooper Counties, however, admitted that they had never known Eda to correspond with other members of her race who might have informed her of her freedom in the event that her white family failed to do so. Whether Eda Hickam interacted with other members of her race was specifically asked of almost every person called upon to testify. While no one could confirm that she had interacted with other freedpeople outside the close supervision of white family members, nearly everyone doubted the probability of the white family successfully preventing Eda from speaking confidentially to other freedpeople during the twenty-five-year period in question. [7]

Attorneys for Eda sought to prove that the Hickams had, in fact, fraudulently led her to believe she was still a slave, had treated her no differently after 1865 than before, and had prevented her from interacting with other freedpeople who might have revealed her freed status to her. To that end, Eda's attorneys gathered witnesses who testified that her freedoms had been restricted. In one deposition, a Mr. Cosgrove, an African American man, testified that once while passing the Hickam farm in Cooper County he greeted Eda out by a woodpile. When Eda replied, "Good morning," James Hickam reportedly struck

7. Depositions, Circuit Court trial, *Hickam v Hickam*.

her in the face with a stick and told her she was not allowed to talk to "no dam free negro." Similarly, Sam Davis, Eda's stepfather, remembered a conversation he had with Joseph Hickam about a year prior to his death in 1889. When Davis said that it had been many years since he had seen Eda and asked to visit her at the Hickam farm in Cooper County, Joseph allegedly told him she was "getting along fine" and that he did not want Sam to "disturb her." According to Davis, Joseph Hickam then said, "I don't want no dam free niggars to come around me there, no how."[8]

It seems the Hickam men were aware of the limits they placed on Eda's freedom, even if they did not regard her as a slave. Or perhaps these testimonies indicate their awareness of the different way in which the black population calculated "freedom" and "slavery." Perhaps Joseph Hickam saw a need to isolate Eda from people who might have posed a threat to the relationship of dependence that allowed the Hickams to keep Eda in a slave-like position without considering her part of their family, an argument that is supported both by the physical punishment they meted out to her and by their omission of Eda's name from the the Hickam family household in the 1880 census. Only the white Hickam family members and the black hired field workers were listed, suggesting that Eda was correct in arguing that she fell into neither category. The fact that the Hickams employed black men to work their fields seems to contradict Eda's argument that she had been excluded from interacting with other African Americans but, again, the point of this study is not whether she knew she was free, but how she understood her relationship to the whites for whom she worked.[9]

The presence of other African American workers renders Eda's argument that the Hickams had secluded her from contact with other freedpeople problematic, though this point was not raised by the defense in the trial depositions. This seems to suggest either that census data does not necessarily reveal an accurate picture of mixed-race household structure or that rural households successfully separated field workers

8. Mr. Cosgrove, deposition, May 5, 1890; Sam Davis, deposition, May 4, 1890.
9. Tenth U.S. Census, Cooper County, Missouri, Saline Township, roll 683, 1880. This census lists the entire white Hickam family, as well as two black workers under their employ at the time, neither of whom was named or matched the description of Eda Hickam.

from household servants. Whatever the case, this census data again points out the importance of analyzing Eda Hickam's relationship to the Hickam family without centering on whether or not there is evidence to confirm or refute her knowledge of the emancipation of slaves in 1865. When Eda Hickam appealed the probate judge's decision, James Hickam's defense attorney argued that she had been fully informed of her freedom and had knowingly rejected her right to leave. The defense further contended that both sides knew Eda had chosen to remain with the Hickam family, believing them to be kind enough to permit this because she had no other options for survival. Their case was constructed on testimonies that supported this contention. Squire Hickam, for instance, recalled a conversation between himself and his father wherein Joseph asked Squire, "What am I to do with my niggers? Lincoln has freed my niggers." Squire then reminded his father, "Pa, you haven't got but one," and told him, "Notify her, Pa, of her freedom." Upon allegedly taking his son's advice, Joseph told her, "Ede, you are free, . . . and I want you to go and do for yourself; I have nursed you long enough, and took care of you." According to Squire's testimony, Eda then pleaded, "Master, I don't want to go; I want to stay with you as long as you and mistiss lives; I am not able to make a living for myself." According to Squire's rendition of the conversation, both slave and master recognized that if Eda Hickam could not succeed in the market, she could not be free.[10]

Squire Hickam portrayed his father as a benevolent slave owner who, after 1865, felt a sense of obligation to care for his erstwhile property even though he was under no legal or moral compunction to do so. In his depositions, Squire further recalled that Joseph told Eda at the time of emancipation, "Now Ede, I have nursed you long enough, you had better get out and do for yourself, I am not able to hire you." After this Eda commenced crying and expressing her desire to stay, at which point Joseph Hickam allegedly struck the deal that doomed the then-teenaged Eda to twenty-five more years of unpaid servitude. "Well Ede," he said, "if you will be a good nigger, and mind me as you have heretofore, just that long you will stay with us; but

10. Squire Hickam, deposition, July 17, 1890. Litwack, *Been in the Storm So Long,* 292–342; Jacqueline Jones, *Labor of Love, Labor of Sorrow: Black Women, Work, and the Family, from Slavery to the Present* (New York: Vintage Books, 1985), 44–78.

when you get too big to mind us, you have got to go and hunt a new home." Eda's response, according to Squire, was to implore, "Master, I am getting all the wages I ever expect to get, I don't want to go, I want to be one of the family."[11]

Squire's testimony demonstrates his anticipation of the crux of the plaintiff's accusations, particularly his argument that Eda was granted permission to remain a member of the Hickam family, even after the law no longer upheld the Hickams' right to extract labor from her in exchange for the food and shelter they provided. He testified that "she was treated just like one of the family. She had the same kind of grub, and the same kind of clothing." Yet he also referred to her as "a very intelligent, good common sense nigger."[12] By arguing that Eda was included in the Hickam family, Squire tried to deflect her accusations that she had been kept as a slave, but his evaluation of her reflects a race consciousness that prevented her being either perceived as an equal or paid for her services. Squire Hickam's definition of slavery as a familial category supports his argument that she was treated like "one of the family," yet it simultaneously renders the white family's expulsion of Eda from their household in 1889 an abridgement of traditional family bonds.

For the Hickams, the definition of a family was malleable, and they modified it to serve their purposes. They included Eda in their family until the time arrived to divide the deceased patriarch's estate. Then the Hickams no longer wanted to claim her. This reflects the difficulties white Southerners had in letting go of the assumptions inherent in the antebellum slave system in their dealings with blacks under the labor conditions of the New South. Joseph Hickam's family benefited from their father's clinging to an old system that defined a black woman as part of the family, yet when her inclusion in the family would have meant sharing their father's estate with her, they embraced the ideology that, lacking the ownership of Eda's body, they could repudiate their claim to her as a family dependent. This ambiguous definition of family persisted in the white press's reporting of the Hickam affair. The *Hamilton-News Graphic*, a newspaper from a neighboring county, for example, illustrates the tendency of whites to regard Eda Hickam

11. Squire Hickam, deposition, July 17, 1890.
12. Ibid.

as the lowest-status dependent within the Hickam household. While describing Eda as being "apparently as intelligent as any of her race," the writer of the article also sympathized with the embarrassment the Hickam family, being "one of the wealthiest and most influential in that part of the county," experienced as a result of what they described as Eda's unwillingness to leave the Hickam household twenty-five years previously.[13]

Other members of the community appeared ambivalent when testifying about Eda's relationship to the Hickams in the postbellum years, alternately supporting and rejecting her claim. Mrs. Lucy D. Moore, a longtime acquaintance and frequent visitor to the Hickam farm, testified that she could neither confirm that Eda had known of her freedom nor deny she had been fraudulently induced to continue living with the Hickams under the pretense she was still their slave. Although Lucy Moore thought she recalled Eda's interaction with other persons of color, it was possible, she admitted, that she was remembering interactions that had taken place prior to 1865. Mrs. Moore, who had been acquainted with the Hickam family between 1863 and 1873, also recalled that Eda had spent a great deal of time sick in bed, needing her white "family" to care for her.[14]

Eda's poor health increased her dependence on the Hickam family as evinced by the testimony of the Hickam family physician, Dr. Christian. He testified for the defense that Eda had suffered from "catalepsy" for most of her life. The "falling fits" from which she suffered caused her to lose consciousness for entire days at a time, according to Christian, and were due to obstructions to her monthly cycles resulting from overwork and undue stress. Christian testified that he had been present when Joseph Hickam first informed Eda of her freedom in 1865. Joseph Hickam allegedly declared in Eda's presence, "I don't want her here; I have told her that she was freed by Abe Lincoln and that she could go." According to the doctor, Eda then queried, "Where will I go? I've got no place to go to and who would take care of me?"[15] It is impossible to know whether Eda's work load in the years after 1865 was overly strenuous, or whether her daily work schedule resembled

13. *Hamilton-News Graphic*, January 3, 1890.
14. Lucy D. Moore, deposition, February 12, 1890.
15. Dr. Christian, deposition, February 14, 1890.

the conditions under which she had worked as a slave; however, there can be no doubt that Eda's dependence on the Hickams was intensified by her need for nursing and medication and her lack of other kin to take her in.

Another contributing factor to Eda Hickam's continued dependence on her white family was her youth at the time of emancipation. In the years immediately following the war, it was not uncommon for former slaves who were younger than eighteen to be detained by their former owners under apprenticeship laws. The children were not necessarily protected even if they had kin. White authority could override the wishes of freedmen and freedwomen with nothing more than testimony that the parents were unable to adequately provide for their children. This phenomenon, which pervaded the South, did not bypass Cooper County. Children who were under the age of eighteen at the time of emancipation and who lacked kin networks were especially vulnerable to getting caught in nebulous relationships with their former owners that precariously suspended them somewhere between the exploitative aspects of slavery and the actualization of a departure from it. Lacking kin and being about sixteen in 1865, Eda Hickam would have fallen through this crack.[16]

Census data from Cooper County indicate that while between 10 and 14 percent of the households in rural Cooper County townships were composed of both white and black members, the latter group was almost entirely women and children. Presumably, most of the African American children living in white households in Cooper County after emancipation were living with their former owners. The most compelling confirmation of that presumption was that they, like Eda, shared the surname of the whites living in the home. Often single freedwomen with children lived in white households, presumably because they, too, were bound by a relationship of dependence on their former owners. Without kin, single women and children probably

16. Newly freed children were particularly susceptible to exploitation by their former owners. See Ira Berlin, Steven F. Miller, Leslie S. Rowland, "Afro-American Families from Slavery to Freedom," in *Black Women in American History: From Colonial Times to the Nineteenth Century,* ed. Darlene Clark Hine (New York: Carlson Publishing, 1990), 84–117; Brenda Stevenson, "Distress and Discord in the Virginia Slave Families, 1830–1860," in *In Joy and in Sorrow,* 103–7, 116, 124; Litwack, *Been in the Storm So Long,* 229–42.

found difficult any prospect of gaining autonomy from the white families upon whom they had depended for food and shelter prior to emancipation.[17]

Even if Eda's ability to realize her freedom had not been limited by poor health and youth, few employment options outside domestic service existed for freedwomen. Between 1870 and 1920 opportunities for gainful income in Little Dixie counties changed very little. In fact, they changed only in that black women's jobs in domestic service became increasingly specialized, and black domestic workers became increasingly likely to live away from the white families who employed them. Those freedwomen who successfully escaped working in conditions that recapitulated the mistress/slave relationship of antebellum households tended to be those who were able to pool their resources with their kin and move away from isolated rural areas. Those who stayed often continued to toil in white households as they had in slavery.[18]

Eda Hickam made a third attempt to recover what she believed the Hickams owed her. This time the case was argued before the court of appeals in Kansas City, Missouri. This trial turned not on who was telling the truth but on Eda's understanding of her relationship to the rest of the Hickam family. Eda's attorney argued she had fraudulently been detained as a slave and that, if "by fraud, deceit, or duress she was kept in ignorance of her rights" and was induced to render Joseph Hickam services, she should be entitled to payment, whether or not he intended to pay her or she intended to charge him. James Hickam's defense, conversely, centered on Eda's responsibility to know of her free status, as well as to know her place within the Hickam family, arguing that there was no evidence to support her charges. Consequently, the defense argued, the white heirs were under no obligation to pay for her services. They should not be penalized for presuming that Eda knew that "under the law of the land she was a free woman," and "ignorance of the law, which every man is presumed to know, does not afford an excuse." Finally, defense attorneys cited

17. Ninth and Tenth U.S. Censes, 1870 and 1880; Jones, *Labor of Love, Labor of Sorrow*, 58–77.
18. Schreck, "Their Place in Freedom," 47–53, 76–84, 90–97; Jones, *Labor of Love, Labor of Sorrow*, 71–72.

cases affirming that according to Missouri law, there should be no compensation for labor done within the context of a family unless there was at the time an expectation of the one member to give, and the other to receive, pay for such services. Thus James Hickam's case was bolstered by a claim that Eda had indeed been considered a family member, even as he and his siblings had turned her out of their household to fend for herself.[19]

The Court of Appeals judge was persuaded that Eda's case had been too quickly dismissed in the Cooper County circuit court judgment and that sufficient evidence existed to prove she had been "fraudulently induced, by the conduct of Joseph Hickam, to render services for him under the belief that she . . . owed him such labor as his slave." Believing it possible that the Hickams had purposefully kept Eda as their slave, the judge reversed the judgment for $785 and remanded the case for retrial.[20]

Eda Hickam did not benefit from the appeals court's decision. When the case was returned to the Cooper County Circuit Court for a second trial, almost four years after Eda's first attempt to gain back wages, the jury declined to grant her anything, despite the judge's instructing them to vote that the Hickam estate owed her back wages "if they believe[d] valuable services were rendered by Eda for Joseph, regardless of a contractual agreement to pay for such services." Nonetheless, on May 4, 1893, Eda's suits against the Hickam estate ended. Not only had she lost the $785 she was originally awarded, she had also exhausted her opportunities for appeal.[21]

Throughout the four trials in the *Hickam v. Hickam* dispute, neither side could prove that Eda either had or had not ever been informed of her freedom, nor could they prove that Joseph Hickam and his family had or had not intentionally deceived her. The lack of evidence in Eda Hickam's initial suit led the jurors in the first circuit court

19. Eda Hickam's attorney also argued that during the war and until the death of her "old master," Joseph Hickam, "she was not allowed to, and never did, leave his premises except in the company of a member of the white Hickam family; that she was not allowed to visit any of her own race, and no colored person, not even her stepfather, was allowed to talk to her alone." She also, allegedly, "was never permitted to go to church . . . and lived in absolute ignorance of the fact that the Negroes had been set free," *Missouri Appeals Reports*, 501.

20. Ibid., 498–99, 505, 508.

21. *Hickam v Hickam*, May 3, 1893.

trial to maintain the probate judge's split decision over Eda's place within the white Hickam household and uphold his award of half the back wages for which she sued. By the fourth and final trial, the jury had sided completely with the defendant and deemed Eda Hickam undeserving of any back wages. Perhaps Eda's tenacity stripped the white jury of the uncertainty they may have felt four years earlier when they supported the probate judge's decision to award her $785 in back wages. Possibly the jurors also resented Eda's assertion that a respectable white family had behaved in a criminal manner. Perhaps they feared that her victory in this case might put ideas into their own servants' heads, potentially threatening their ability to employ domestic help cheaply. Eda's persistence in seeking compensation from whites whom she claimed had exploited her labor may have been regarded by whites as impudence. Early in her trials it seems that at least some whites were willing to consider the possibility that Eda's slave-like living conditions since 1865 were the result of exigencies beyond her control; at least, this was the position held by some white deponents. Yet by her fourth trial, whites seem to have resented Eda for her agency more than they pitied her for her victimization. Indeed, the longer Eda Hickam pursued her legal quest for back wages, the more she compelled the white Hickams and other community members to regard her as an assertive, rather than a submissive, member of the black populace.

The context of the trial further affected its outcome. Cooper County was in the midst of a period of virulent racism, strengthened no doubt by the fact that the African American population was becoming more self-sufficient and economically empowered with each passing year. Whites believed that African American men had regressed toward bestiality and unrestrained sexuality, but they continued to regard African American women as passive, safe, and domestic and to employ them as household servants. As one article in a Cooper County newspaper explained, African American women were regarded as "negroes" because they were industrious, respectful, and "amenable to authority," in the racial caste system whites tried to maintain. African American men, on the other hand, were often deemed to be "niggers" because they were "idol, brutal drunkards" and a "perpetual menace to public order." This dual view of former slaves reflects contradictory understandings among whites of freedom's meaning in the postbellum period. Prior to emancipation there was little ambiguity over what it meant to be a slave. Even though conditions varied widely among slaves, one constant was slaves' legal status as property of their owners and the subsequent limits to slaves' ability to control the course of their own lives. They were not free, despite the successful efforts of many slaves to carve some degree of autonomy for themselves. Historians of slave culture have argued that the same kinship networks that enabled slaves to achieve control and autonomy within the slave community were utilized by freedmen and -women in their quest to gain independence from their former owners. But if slaves lacked both a slave community and kinship ties, they would not be able to enjoy or benefit from their legal freedom, whether or not they were informed of their emancipation.[22]

The historiography of late-nineteenth-century race relations generally equates the virulent racism of whites toward blacks with the assertive behavior of black men. White attitudes toward African Americans were highly gendered in the 1890s and 1900s. African American men's access to legal, political, sexual, and economic power posed the greatest threat to the race-based social order to which whites so desperately clung. Evidence for this can be found in the plentiful suggestions in Democratic newspapers that African American men were "increasing in criminality" and "deteriorating morally" with "frightful rapidity" in the absence of the slave system's strictures to keep them in line.[23]

Such attitudes, which prompted the codification of racial segregation throughout the South in the 1890s, had implications for Eda Hickam. In her efforts to distance herself from the antiquated and restrictive system of slavery and actualize a sense of freedom, Eda Hickam altered somewhat the way she was perceived by whites. But the gendered nature of racism during this period meant her image remained

22. Patricia Morton, *Disfigured Images: The Historical Assault on African-American Women* (New York: Greenwood Press, 1991), 18–37. *Boonville Weekly Advertiser,* January 9, 1903.

23. *Boonville Weekly Advertiser,* January 29, 1904; Schreck, "Their Place in Freedom," 102–51; Joel Williamson, *The Crucible of Race: Black-White Relations in the American South since Emancipation* (New York: Oxford University Press, 1984); C. Vann Woodward, *The Strange Career of Jim Crow* (New York: Oxford University Press, 1955).

unfettered by the brutal castigations that were directed toward assertive black men in the county, despite the possibility that her persistence through three court trials against her former owners exhibited to whites an unacceptable degree of assertiveness. After emancipation, white and black residents of Cooper County were compelled to negotiate changes in the ways they interacted with one another. By the late 1880s, a new generation of whites, most of whom had not been alive during slavery but who had been raised in a society that promoted white supremacy, began to launch aggressive attacks on the black populace. They felt increasingly threatened by the new generation of African American men, many of whom refused to submit to white rules regarding racial hierarchy. White men in Cooper County were particularly vexed by black men's political power. To justify opposition to political activity among black men in the 1890s, whites dredged up arguments that African Americans were biologically inferior to whites. These arguments were directed at black men and, consequently, chastising references to black women virtually disappeared from newspaper articles, leaving the men the recipients of racial slurs.[24]

In 1889, the *Boonville Weekly Advertiser* featured prominently a diatribe penned by a Mississippi Delta newspaper editor, James K. Vardaman, that flagrantly asserted the inferiority of black men. The piece, entitled "A Southern View of the Negro," declared, "Southern people will not have negro rule. The negro is not a white man with black skin. His is a different race. He is a barbarian, and barbarians cannot rule civilized people." By the 1890s, whites in Cooper County were making distinctions between different degrees of racial inferiority. Vardaman's demagoguery reflects a transition in white attitudes toward black men. Whites saw them as having changed from compliant, obedient, trustworthy "Sambo" characters into impertinent, unintimidated, brutish "niggers."[25]

The distinction made between compliant, deferential "Negroes" and impudent, dangerous "niggers" depended on the degree of social and sexual threat black men could pose to white men's power.

24. *Boonville Weekly Advertiser*, January 29, 1904. Joel Williamson, *Rage for Order: Black-White Relations in the American South since Emancipation* (New York: Oxford University Press, 1986), 78–86.

25. *Boonville Weekly Advertiser*, October 4, 1889; Williamson, *Rage for Order*, 70–86, 147–51.

"Niggers" were defined in the *Boonville Weekly Advertiser* as "idle, brutal drunkards, with complete disregard for the 'decencies of society.' " They tended toward "vice and vagrancy" and were "a perpetual menace to public order" and a "curse to the community." Those described as "Negroes," however, were "good citizens . . . staunch Americans" who were respectful of laws, amenable to authority, good family providers, useful to their community, and showed "proper respect for appearances." However, "Negroes" were not spared all condemnation. Instead, the "Negro[s]" in Cooper County was held "responsible to a regrettable degree for the 'Nigger[s],' " and, it was said, as "decent" black people, they owed it to themselves "to cast out the vagabonds and criminals . . . who bring reproach on [them] and who keep alive the prejudice against the race."[26] According to this definition, African American women fell almost exclusively into the category of "Negroes," a necessary characterization, given that domestic servants with whom whites interacted on a daily basis were only acceptable to whites if they could be perceived as docile.

Eda Hickam's resistance against her white family took place in this gendered context; she was never characterized in newspaper articles or depositions as menacing or threatening. As a woman, she could not pose the threat to white male preeminence, even within the Hickam family, that a black man who dared to cast a vote or have sexual relations with a white woman could. After all, black women working as domestics in private white households occupied the most directly integrated sector of southern society, just as white men were taking actions in the 1890s to segregate the races in the public sector.[27] Because she was a woman, Eda Hickam was unaffected by the primary objective of Jim Crow legislation, disenfranchisement. Because she was a woman, she was able to challenge her white family's decision to sever her connection to them via a legal system from which black men were being excluded. The Hickams, their attorneys, and their white peers in the county judged Eda's resistance quite differently than they would have judged that of a black man they perceived to be overstepping his racially defined place in society. For example, approximately five years after Eda Hickam's suits ended and five miles from the Hickam farm,

26. *Boonville Weekly Advertiser,* October 4, 1889.
27. Woodward, *The Strange Career of Jim Crow,* 82, 67–109.

in neighboring Howard County, a black man by the name of Frank Embree was lynched in the presence of more than one thousand whites from the Little Dixie region for the rape of a fourteen-year-old white girl. Described in local newspapers as a "black fiend," a "devil," and a "brute," Embree was relentlessly tracked until caught and then jailed in an Audrain County jail, some twenty miles from the crime scene. A "better organized or more orderly mob was never seen," the Fayette *Democratic-Leader* reported of the crowd that carted Embree back to the area where the alleged crime had been committed. After delivering one hundred three "fearful lashes" to his nude body, they threw a noose around his neck, and pulled his body into mid-air. All concurred that the "negro rapist . . . was given no more than he deserved."[28]

This horrific event relates indirectly to the question of defining a "family." In justifying their actions on the basis of protecting white women, white mobs sought to protect their own gender identities as paternal protectors and providers of their families. But they espoused the alleged threat of rape as causal in their actions when in fact it was the actual threat of race mixing that moved them to violent extremes. Gender thus made a structural difference in racism since it was black men who could make and name families and who could become patriarchs in their own right. Most black women, on the other hand, continued to be perceived as familial dependents, so defined by whites, whether they were living in mixed-race or African American households.[29] Eda Hickam could challenge the way whites defined her position in their household, but she could not threaten the patriarchal social order. What Eda Hickam really called into question in her trials was not racial identity so much as the bounds, responsibilities, and benefits of patriarchy.

Certainly the battle Eda waged was taken quite seriously and fought quite aggressively by Joseph Hickam's white descendants. James Hickam, in fact, spent no less than $544 of his father's $7,000 estate on legal fees in his campaign to deny Eda the $1,440 for which she sued.[30] Yet throughout the ordeal, Eda was regarded by whites more as childlike and intellectually inferior than as calculating or menacing.

28. *Fayette Democratic-Leader*, June 22, 1899.
29. Jones, *Labor of Love, Labor of Sorrow*, 58–62.
30. Cooper County Probate Records, estate number 2567.A.

Perhaps because she had lived under conditions that closely resembled those she had known for so long in slavery, people in the county harkened back to an almost bygone racial conceptualization of her attempts to challenge white power over black freedoms. Although she was mocked, Eda Hickam was not accused of criminal behavior nor upheld as evidence that the black population was retrogressing into a less civilized state outside of slavery. Eda Hickam, in fact, accused whites of criminal and indecent behavior, and she called into question their reliance on an old social order—the paternalistic relationship of a master to his slaves—to justify their exploitation of her labor.

It is impossible to know whether the Hickams intended to conceal Eda's free status from her. It is clear, however, that since Eda worked without wages for the family that had previously owned her, her life did not significantly change after 1865. She continued to have her freedoms restricted by rules set by whites whose watchful eyes, oppressive demands, and physical punishments she was unable to escape. It is also evident that Eda did not regard being turned away from the Hickam household in 1889 as a liberating experience, as her long-awaited acquisition of freedom. The reality was that Eda was free only to starve by herself in a world that no longer had a place for her and was not interested in developing one. And if she was held as a slave between 1865 and 1889, then it is also true that to the extent she ever had a family, she had it under her years of uninformed freedom. Because Eda lacked a kin network that would have enabled her to escape dependence on the white family that had owned her, she was left with no choice but to define her relationship to the white Hickams as familial. They, on the other hand, could have a more malleable definition of family. They claimed Eda as a member of their household to justify not paying her wages for the work she performed. Then they rejected her when white family members became heirs to Joseph's estate. The Hickams' perception of their relationship to Eda was rooted in the antebellum ideal of a paternalistic slaveholder. This image was extended into the postbellum period only insofar as it reinforced the white Hickams' claim to the deceased patriarch's estate.

Eda Hickam's suits against the only people she had ever considered her family reveal the complicated meanings the words *slavery* and *freedom* held in the postbellum period. For Eda Hickam, slavery was defined as labor performed for a family that neither claimed her nor paid for her services. Yet for the white family to deny she was illegally held as a slave, they had to argue she was a free member of their family. Ironically, they offered this argument for the purpose of keeping her out of the will. They could do this because they were arguing for a category of family that only whites perceived, one they found increasingly difficult to maintain in the decades following the abolition of slavery.

Half My Heart in Dixie

Southern Identity and the Civil War in the Writings of Mary Virginia Terhune

KAREN MANNERS SMITH

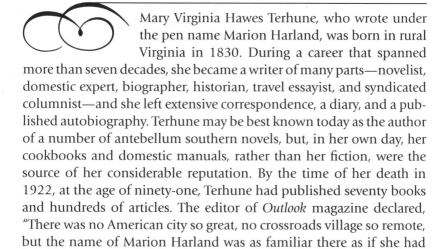 Mary Virginia Hawes Terhune, who wrote under the pen name Marion Harland, was born in rural Virginia in 1830. During a career that spanned more than seven decades, she became a writer of many parts—novelist, domestic expert, biographer, historian, travel essayist, and syndicated columnist—and she left extensive correspondence, a diary, and a published autobiography. Terhune may be best known today as the author of a number of antebellum southern novels, but, in her own day, her cookbooks and domestic manuals, rather than her fiction, were the source of her considerable reputation. By the time of her death in 1922, at the age of ninety-one, Terhune had published seventy books and hundreds of articles. The editor of *Outlook* magazine declared, "There was no American city so great, no crossroads village so remote, but the name of Marion Harland was as familiar there as if she had been a president of the United States."[1]

Terhune's extraordinary life and career inspired written reminiscences by her son and her eldest daughter and a lengthier memoir by one of her grandsons.[2] Her own fictional and prescriptive works are

I would like to thank descendants of Mary Virginia (Hawes) Terhune for their generosity in sharing family papers relevant to Terhune. Thanks, also, to Drew Gilpin Faust and Elisabeth Muhlenfeld for extensive commentary on an earlier version of this article and to the Virginia Historical Society, whose provision of a Mellon Fellowship enabled the completion of research for the larger project of which this article is a part.

1. Editorial, *Outlook* 131 (June 14, 1922): 286.

2. Albert Payson Terhune, "Two Very Real People," *Proving Nothing* (New York: Harper and Bros., 1930); Christine Terhune Herrick, "Marion Harland: A Study in

studded with nuggets of autobiography, tantalizing bits of information
about this complex figure who was both a southerner and a northerner
and who preached the doctrine of exclusive domesticity for other
women while she herself pursued a lucrative career as a writer, editor,
and lecturer. A woman who claimed to be peddling nothing more
than womanly influence through her writings, Terhune saw herself as
a creator and preserver of culture, with a mission to American women
as important as that of any minister or politician.

Terhune's legacy as an American woman writer is now being redis-
covered by scholars of women's history and literature who find her
public and private writings instructive in several areas. Terhune's work
reveals much about the lives of middle-class urban women in the
antebellum South, a subject that needs more scholarly attention. She
also represents a very small band of nineteenth-century women who
chose both career and family, pursuing powerful ambitions without
overstepping gender conventions and, in Terhune's case, without supporting women's rights. In fact, Terhune steadfastly maintained and
preached an alternative to this form of social revolution. Intriguingly,
the domestic ideology Terhune promulgated was rooted in Republican
motherhood and prewar southern gender traditions, yet it became
the cornerstone of her popularity as a writer and found enthusiastic
audiences well into the twentieth century, persisting even in the face
of changing roles for women and advances in household technology.

While Terhune's ideas about gender remained almost unchanged
throughout her lifetime, her relationship to the South and to her
southern identity altered considerably. The evolution in her outlook
depended as much upon her social and literary ambitions and her
connection to the literary marketplace as it did upon her conflicting
sectional loyalties and reaction to the devastation of the Civil War.

Endowed at birth with a legacy of sectional ambivalence and status
anxiety, Terhune was the daughter of Samuel Pierce Hawes, a transplanted Bostonian who ran a crossroads general store in rural Virginia,
and Judith Anna Smith, a Richmond belle with connections to the

---

Efficiency." This latter manuscript, now lost, is quoted extensively in Mary Hudson
Wright, "Mary Virginia Hawes Terhune ('Marion Harland'): Her Life and Works"
(Ph.D. diss., George Peabody College for Teachers, 1934); Frederic Franklyn Van
de Water, "Talented Family," typed ms. memoir in the private collection of one
of Terhune's descendants.

Virginia planter aristocracy. While Samuel Hawes struggled to build his business, he and his family rented a series of small holdings that were worked by eight or ten slaves inherited from Judith Smith Hawes's father. Terhune's early years were punctuated by visits to her mother's relatives, who had plantations in Henrico and Goochland Counties. The Hawes children—seven in all—were invited to the plantations only when they were ill or when their mother needed rest and recuperation. They seem to have been regarded as needy relations, and it is likely that Judith Hawes's relatives thought she had made a poor marriage with her Yankee shopkeeper.[3]

Young Mary Virginia, however, was as proud of her father's New England Puritan ancestry as she was of her mother's links to the settlers of Jamestown. From her youngest days, she was aware that she embodied the union of two American regional archetypes. But her social class was a source of nagging concern: her mother's family had made it clear that her relationship to the Virginia aristocracy was a distant one, and as a merchant's daughter she would never be more than middle class. Further complicating the issue of her identity, Terhune traced her intellectual abilities to her aristocratic maternal grandmother, but it was her northern father who fostered his daughter's education and her youthful literary ambitions, while her mother attempted to thwart those ambitions and turn her daughter into a southern lady.[4]

Under her father's supervision, Terhune, along with one of her sisters, was instructed by a series of tutors and governesses. "Educate them as if they were boys and preparing for college," Samuel Hawes told one tutor. The girls learned rhetoric, history, and mathematics, geography, Latin, and French. On their own they studied the Bible. They read religious essays as a matter of course and devoured novels by the score. Among Terhune's favorite European authors were Charles Dickens, Walter Scott, William Thackeray, Ann Ward Radcliffe, Maria Edgeworth, Hannah More, and the Brontë sisters. She also read William Shakespeare, John Dryden, Alexander Pope, William Cowper, John Keats, and William Wordsworth, always committing long

3. Marion Harland [Mary Virginia Hawes Terhune], *Marion Harland's Autobiography: The Story of a Long Life* (New York: Harper and Bros., 1910), 1–69.

4. Kate Sanborn, *Our Famous Women* (Hartford, Conn., 1883), 632; Mary Virginia Hawes (Terhune) diary, February 18, 1849, private collection.

sections of their work to memory. Favorites among American authors were Washington Irving, Ik Marvel, Grace Greenwood, and fellow southerners E. D. E. N. Southworth and Maria McIntosh. Terhune and her sister capped their private education with two years in a Presbyterian girls' seminary in Richmond. After she left school in 1847, Terhune continued to study foreign languages and music with private tutors for a number of years.[5]

The Hawes family had moved to Richmond in 1845, a change that delighted everyone. Richmond had a population approaching forty thousand by 1860 and was the industrial and mercantile center of the South. By some estimates, it was "the wealthiest city of its size in America and perhaps in the world." Terhune quickly became as much of a cosmopolite as her Presbyterian church and family would allow, decorously frequenting the downtown shops with sisters and girlfriends and attending concerts, picnics, parades, dauguerreotype galleries, and traveling panorama exhibitions in the company of mixed groups of young people. A favorite evening's entertainment was a theological lecture. Terhune also belonged to a musical group that met weekly for practice and private concerts. The Hawes' house on Leigh Street was open to visitors most evenings, and seldom did a day pass without a visit from a gentleman caller. The collegial atmosphere of these evenings was a source of great joy to Terhune, an opportunity to dispense with conventional flirtation and to talk freely with men about politics, religion, literature, and philosophy under the approving eye of her father. Among Terhune's male friends were young Virginians attending college in Richmond or clerking in downtown businesses and northern merchants whose work had brought them to Richmond. There were at least two young members of Richmond's prosperous German mercantile community. Caught up in this busy urban environment, Terhune thrived; her life more closely resembled the lives of northern city girls than those of her more sheltered sisters on plantations in the South.[6]

5. Harland, *Autobiography*, 97; Hawes (Terhune) diary, April 19, 1849; Elizabeth Fox-Genovese, *Within the Plantation Household: Black and White Women of the Old South* (Chapel Hill: University of North Carolina Press, 1988), 257–71; Hawes (Terhune) diary, November 7, 1849.

6. Virginius Dabney, *Richmond: The Story of a City* (Charlottesville: University of Virginia Press, 1990), 133; Hawes (Terhune) diary, 1848–1852, passim.

In 1851, Terhune made her first trip north, spending the summer with her father's relatives in Massachusetts, an adventure she recorded in detail in her diary. Initially she found her Yankee relatives lacking in the southern warmth to which she was accustomed, but she quickly discovered that they were loving, religious people, not especially citified, even though most of the uncles and cousins were Boston business and professional men. After this visit, Terhune found it impossible to subscribe to the popular southern prejudices of her era, which suspected northerners of corruption, materialism, and coldheartedness.[7] A visit to New York City in 1855, where she marveled at the sights and attended the theater, essentially cemented her attraction to the urban North.

Terhune's fondness for things northern was not unqualified, however. Her strict Presbyterianism meant that she remained hostile to northern intellectual forms of Protestantism, such as Unitarianism. Similarly, her convictions about the social and personal importance of woman's domestic role, learned through a childhood spent observing her mother and other mistresses of large southern households, made her deeply suspicious of the northern women's rights movement. As Terhune saw it, the women's rights movement equated domesticity with drudgery and utterly failed to recognize the hegemonic power of women within the home. The irony of her position—glorifying domesticity while pursuing a professional career—seems to have escaped her, much as it escaped her northern counterpart, Catherine Beecher. Finally, like many Virginians of her generation raised on stories of slave uprisings, Terhune may also have shared the southern fear of that other northern abomination, abolitionism, though she did not express opinions about abolitionist agitators in her private writings or letters of the period.[8]

Terhune began to write for publication in the late 1840s, fulfilling an ambition that had begun in childhood with the creation of poems and, later, during her adolescence, stories that she kept hidden for

7. Hawes (Terhune) diary, July–September 1851; see also William R. Taylor, *Cavalier and Yankee: The Old South and American National Character* (New York: George Braziler, 1961).

8. Hawes (Terhune) diary, July 13, 20, 27, 1851; Mary Virginia Hawes (Terhune) to Virginia Eppes Dance, October 18, 1855, Terhune Papers, Perkins Library, Duke University, Durham, N.C.; Harland, *Autobiography*, 186–95.

years in an old trunk. Proud of her work, Terhune confided to her diary that "there is that within me which should command respect, if not admiration." But she also feared her mother's contempt and was conflicted about having aspirations that ran contrary to her mother's wishes. In February of 1847, after a series of arguments with her mother about the hours she "wasted" on writing, she burned much of her accumulated work in a grand penitential fire.[9]

Fortunately, other family members—her sister and a younger brother, and, especially, her father—sympathized with her desire to publish her writings. She had their full support in 1847, when she began to publish religious essays under a male pseudonym in local papers. From this didactic material she progressed to fiction, drawing upon her country childhood, her life in the urban South, and her firsthand knowledge of Yankees and "Yankeeland." By 1854, writing as "Marion Harland," Terhune had produced several short stories for *Godey's Lady's Book* and a best-selling novel. The novel, *Alone*, was set in Richmond and on a nearby plantation sometime in the early 1840s. Three other antebellum novels, *The Hidden Path* (1855), *Moss-Side* (1857), and *Nemesis* (1860), made use of settings in Richmond, Philadelphia, New Hampshire, and New York, as well as plantations and villages in rural Virginia. Their domestic heroines and their villains were both southerners and northerners, about equally divided. The parts of *Alone* and *The Hidden Path* that were set in Richmond were based on Terhune's own experiences there. In one instance, the characters and setting of a pivotal chapter in *The Hidden Path*, a chapter involving a scheming hussy, a deadly snakebite, and a broken engagement, were taken from a picnic day that Terhune had described in a long diary entry in May 1850.[10]

Terhune's comfortable prose style and her ability to sustain dramatic tension place *Moss-Side* and *Nemesis* among the best examples of mid-nineteenth-century American woman's fiction, or "domestic fiction," as scholars have come to call the moralistic and romantic novels

9. Hawes (Terhune) diary, February 9, 1847; last entry for February 1847, dated only "Friday."

10. Terhune used the pseudonym Robert Remer for religious essays she published in the *Watchman and Observer* and the *Central Presbyterian* between 1847 and 1851; Hawes (Terhune) diary, May 23, 1850; Marion Harland [Mary Virginia Hawes Terhune], *The Hidden Path* (New York, 1855), 143–48.

about, by, and for women that proliferated throughout the middle years of the century, accounting for most of the best-selling fiction of the era. Besides romance, Terhune's early fiction deals with religion and the moral life, social class distinctions, a woman's appropriate role in her family and community, and the place of the woman artist in society. All these themes were deeply meaningful to Terhune; her engagement with them indicates her powerful ambition to become not just a popular regional domestic novelist, but a great novelist—the Charlotte Brontë of her own country and generation. The young writer had serious aspirations to artistry that far exceeded the self-conscious professionalism ascribed to so many of the domestic novelists of the period.[11]

In 1855, Richmond writer and editor John R. Thompson accused Terhune of stealing both plot structure and incident from Charlotte Brontë's *Villette* for use in *The Hidden Path*. Thompson was probably right. A few years later, in a novel titled *True as Steel*, Terhune incorporated a modified version of the incident in *Jane Eyre* in which the madwoman escapes from her attic confinement, attacks her captor, and burns down the house. Like Terhune's later interpolations of Shakespeare and Dickens quotations in her cookbooks, such borrowings were not the sign of an impoverished imagination; rather they were a form of homage to her beloved English literary models and an implicit assertion that she, too, was a member of the illustrious company, with literary concerns that were not limited to a single region of the United States.[12]

Far too shrewd merely to assert her literary worthiness within the text, Terhune also sought national and international exposure for her work on a practical level. As early as 1854, she secured a northern

11. "Domestic fiction" has been defined in Nina Baym, *Woman's Fiction: A Guide to Novels by and about Women in America 1820–1870* (Ithaca, N.Y.: Cornell University Press, 1978) and Mary Kelley, *Private Woman, Public Stage: Literary Domesticity in Nineteenth-Century America* (New York: Oxford University Press 1984). Anne Goodwyn Jones discusses the ambitions of southern novelists and their self-conscious professionalism in *Tomorrow Is Another Day: The Woman Writer in the South 1859–1936* (Baton Rouge: Louisiana State University Press, 1981), 51–55.

12. John R. Thompson, "Editorial," *Southern Literary Messenger* 21 (October 1855): 637; Marion Harland [Mary Virginia Hawes Terhune], *True as Steel* (New York, 1872), 320–26.

publisher for the second edition of her first book and a contract
for a second book. Shortly thereafter, she signed contracts for the
publication of *Alone* in England and France and for the novel's trans-
lation into German by the same Leipzig house that published Bryant,
Longfellow, and Hawthorne.[13] In the decades that followed, Terhune's
arrangements with a succession of New York publishers kept about a
dozen of her novels in print and selling well for over half a century.

Critics gave Terhune's early novels serious consideration, the southerners among them hailing her as the "New Star of the South" and
claiming for her a role as a regional propagandist. Somewhat more
astutely, George Bagby reviewed *Nemesis* for the *Southern Literary Messenger* and was delighted with what he perceived to be Terhune's lack
of regional partisanship, her "desire to avoid the common error of
heaping praise upon Virginia." (In a separate editorial note chiding
southern critics and reviewers, Bagby pointed out that "Virginia has
buttered her novelists with flattery until respiration is impossible.")[14]

Terhune's first novels contain none of the overt propaganda that
had characterized the writings of earlier southern domestic novelists
such as Caroline Howard Gilman, Maria McIntosh, and Caroline
Lee Hentz, all of whom used fiction to counter abolitionism and to
explain southern institutions in the hope of creating intersectional
understanding. Nor can Terhune be classed with the fiercely dedicated
southern propagandist Augusta Evans, whom she befriended in the
years before the Civil War. It can only be said that Terhune made
use of southern materials in her early novels: that she celebrated
the southern landscape and climate and the genial lifestyles of the
southern gentry, that she emphasized the importance of women's emotions and domestic role in a way that was characteristically southern,
that she employed slave characters as Greek chorus or comic relief
(without overtly defending the institution of slavery), and that she
did not anathematize the North or northerners. Her ambitions were
too extensive and her allegiances too evenly divided to make her a true
southern partisan. Raised from childhood to take sectional rivalry for

13. A notice from the end pages of Terhune's novel *Sunnybank* (New York,
1866).
14. Newspaper clipping in Terhune Papers; George William Bagby, "Editorial,"
Southern Literary Messenger 31 (November 1860): 398; George William Bagby,
"Editorial," *Southern Literary Messenger* 31 (September 1860): 238.

granted, and accustomed all her life to her dual identity as both a northerner and a southerner, Terhune did not perceive any particular or present danger as the sectional crisis worsened after 1860.[15] Her circumstances at the outset of the Civil War, however, compelled her to make a choice.

In 1856, Terhune had married a northern minister, Edward Payson Terhune, whom she had met and fallen in love with two years earlier in Richmond. By 1859, she and her husband and growing family were living in Newark, New Jersey, and she was earning an excellent income from her writing. Although she had been initially reluctant to leave her native state, Terhune had grown fond of Newark and her northern neighbors. She justified her relatively easy adaptation to northern life by claiming that New Jersey was a mid-Atlantic, not a Yankee state and therefore a more comfortable place for a displaced Virginian than New England would have been. She was genuinely happy about her proximity to New York City. While many of her loved ones and all of the sunny scenes of her youth remained in Virginia, New York represented access to theater, music, and higher culture, and it was the center of American literary circles she hungered to join.[16]

The Terhunes happened to be visiting Richmond during the final days of the Virginia secession convention in mid-April 1861. The Hawes family, all staunch Whig unionists, were appalled that Virginia had, as they saw it, capitulated to the demands of the deep South secessionists. They invited their daughter and her children to remain in Richmond through the crisis they were certain would be of short duration. Terhune felt her duty was to her husband. The Terhunes and their children caught what would be the last through train to the North for four years.[17]

Terhune spent the war in New Jersey while her parents remained in the Confederate capital and her brothers reluctantly fought in the Confederate army. Day after day, trembling with anxiety, Terhune read newspaper lists of the Confederate dead, searching for the names

15. Harland, *Autobiography*, 360–69. For an alternate interpretation of Terhune's antebellum southern novels, see Elizabeth Moss, *Domestic Novelists in the Old South: Defenders of Southern Culture* (Baton Rouge: Louisiana State University Press, 1992), chaps. 4, 5.

16. Harland, *Autobiography*, 356–57.

17. Ibid., 382–88.

of her brothers and cousins. She could gain almost no news from her beleaguered parents and did not learn of her sister's death from smallpox until many months after the event. Even in Newark, funerals of friends and acquaintances became a weekly occurrence. Terhune's own firstborn son died of diptheria in 1861.[18]

Despite these personal tragedies, Terhune prospered. Her early novels continued to sell in northern markets, and, in 1864, solidifying their commitment to continued residence in the North, she and her husband built a summer home on twenty-four lakeside acres in the New Jersey hinterland. (In her 1910 autobiography, Terhune deliberately falsified the date of the land purchase and construction, so as to minimize the crass materialism of mansion-building during the national conflict).[19]

During the war, Terhune published four books. Two were set in New York and two in the border states of Kentucky and Maryland, at some unspecified time before the war. It was in the Maryland novel, Colonel Floyd's Wards (1863), that Terhune deepened her exploration of what she had long considered the seamy underside of southern society. Earlier, in Alone (1854) and Moss-Side (1857), she had attacked the code duello and the absurdities of southern chivalry in the name of religious righteousness and sensible middle-class morality. In Colonel Floyd's Wards, she exposed the corruption of a powerful southern planter and traced his descent into depravity and lawlessness. The novel also hinted at the vitiation of historic bloodlines in aristocratic southern families and discussed a condition Terhune called "hereditary insanity," which she attributed to the persistence of kin marriage among the first families of the South.[20] Depravity, insanity, and the decay of famous families had been staples of village gossip in Terhune's childhood—gossip fueled by envy of the upper classes and a fundamentalist Protestant sense of moral superiority to the rich. It would be difficult to see Colonel Floyd's Wards as anything other than an attack on southern culture. It was one of Terhune's darkest novels and an appropriate production for her wartime northern audiences.

18. Ibid., 380, 394, 397.
19. Harland, Autobiography, 406–7; Passaic County, New Jersey, Registry of Deeds, Register B3, 47.
20. Other southern novelists explored similar themes. See, for example, Caroline Lee Hentz, Planter's Northern Bride: A Novel (Philadelphia, 1854).

When Terhune's erstwhile friend Augusta Evans heard "with painful emotions of mingled shame and indignation" that Terhune had sided with her husband and remained in the North during the war, she was shocked at the betrayal of sectional loyalties by one whom so many had considered the "boast and ornament of Virginia literature" and a loyal daughter of the South. (Evans always claimed that she herself had renounced her northern fiancé at the outbreak of hostilities.) Evans's outrage seems ironic, given that unswerving loyalty to one's husband was a prime component of southern gender ideology. But Evans was wrong to assume that Terhune's decision was based solely on wifely compunction. During the war Terhune was working out her own position with regard to the South and writing about the flaws in southern society. She was also reviewing the pro-Union politics she had learned from her father, apportioning blame for the war among greedy politicians and hotheaded rabble-rousers from the deep South and lamenting the failure of the Virginia legislature to hold fast against the rising tide of sectional madness. Eventually, she reached a position that allowed her to express her strong Union sympathies, sympathies that would echo those of the majority of her readers then and in the future, and at the same time permit her to remain, at heart, a southern woman. The guns had scarcely stopped firing when Terhune rushed her Civil War novel into print.[21]

Sunnybank (1866) is set on a Virginia plantation belonging to Union loyalists whose daughter is engaged to a northern merchant and whose two sons enter the Confederate army solely for the purpose of defending their native state. Their dilemmas resemble those of the members of the Hawes family, except that their home is in the middle of the war zone and subject to repeated raids and visitations by both armies. (Terhune's one noncombatant brother, a minister, had lived under these conditions throughout the war.) In this book, the loyal Unionists appear to best advantage, but the invading Yankee army is depicted as drunken and rapacious, and the Confederates, as either foolish and blind or corrupt and treacherous. The plantation

21. Augusta Evans to Janie Tyler, March 14, 1862, quoted in William P. Fidler, *Augusta Evans Wilson 1835–1909* (Tuscaloosa: University of Alabama Press 1951), 88. Terhune and her family, as Virginians and Unionists, were not alone in blaming the deep South. See Daniel W. Crofts, *Reluctant Confederates: Upper South Unionists in the Secession Crisis* (Chapel Hill: University of North Carolina Press, 1989).

master is repeatedly persecuted for his failure to become a Confederate sympathizer. A few of the slaves run off; others remain in residence, loyal to the white family even after the planter has informed them of their emancipation. The slaves' attitude in *Sunnybank* reflects the antebellum conventions of most southern novels with regard to slave loyalty and the integrity of the plantation community, an attitude Terhune simply reiterated without comment at this stage of her career. Although perfectly willing to discuss the relationships of northerners and southerners and the internecine political strife among southerners themselves, she was not ready to examine the issue of slavery.[22]

Sunnybank is structured as an epistolary novel, except that it uses diaries instead of letters. Each chapter is an entry in the diary of either Elinor, the Unionist daughter of the household, or Agatha, a family ward and Confederate sympathizer. The device allowed Terhune to enact her own Civil War on the domestic level, to record everyday privations, illnesses, and heartbreaks, while the larger conflict raged all around, mostly unseen. Notwithstanding this attempt at a balanced account, the author's Unionist sentiments are clear. As far as she is concerned, justice is on the side of the victors. Simultaneously, she mourns the passing of a beloved way of life and cherishes a vague hope that something might be saved from the ashes of the South: the novel's northern romantic hero decides to live in Virginia after his marriage to Elinor, hoping he will be able to help restore Sunnybank, not to its former glory, but to respectable usefulness.

Sunnybank was excoriated in the southern press, while northern critics grudgingly acknowledged that it would probably appeal to a very large class of women readers. Thomas Nelson Page, a prominent southern novelist, later hailed it as the "first work to utilize the romantic material of the war without gross partisanry." Terhune had used *Sunnybank* to work through her anguish about the war. She had also produced a highly marketable book, a novel in her old style with politics that would appeal to the majority of her readers. Although the war soon became a rich and enduring subject for fictional exploitation, Terhune never wrote about it in that vein again.[23]

22. William R. Taylor traces the literary conventions of slave loyalty, kindness, affection, and cooperativeness to the "rapid growth of sentimental modes of expression" during the 1830s and 1840s in *Cavalier and Yankee*, 304–7.

23. Mary T. Tardy, *Living Female Writers of the South* (Philadelphia, 1872), 435; Review of *Sunnybank, New York Roundtable*, 1866, quoted in Tardy, *Living*

As emotionally devastating as the war had been for Terhune, it had altered the fortunes of her southern family and friends forever. Within eight years after the war, both her parents were dead, and as late as 1880, her oldest brother, a rural minister, was still struggling against poverty. His children were much despised by Terhune's son, Albert, who considered his cousins to be raw yokels. At least one relative did rebuild his life successfully: Terhune's brother Horace Hawes became a wealthy businessman and a pillar of Richmond society. But the postwar impoverishment of other planter relatives and old friends continued to trouble Terhune, who felt she ought to share something of her own good fortune with them. While it is not clear how much financial help she gave her Virginia relatives, and she did refuse an urgent request for funds from her closest childhood friend, Terhune invited her nieces and nephews and her brother for extended summer visits at her New Jersey estate. Albert rather spitefully remembered that these cousins had to be deloused before they were allowed to enter the house, and that his uncle, the rural minister, spat tobacco juice all over his mother's lavender guest bedroom.[24]

Terhune resolutely rose above any such intimate signs of New South degradation, inventing instead a fantasy of her life and status in the Old South to console herself and indoctrinate her children. Somewhere she unearthed a genealogy that proved her noble English ancestry, and she had a family coat of arms made to hang in the front hall. Recounting stories of her youth, she earnestly tried to convince her son, and later her grandson, that the Lees, the Randolphs, the Marshalls, and all the other First Families of Virginia used to stand aside in the dusty road when Samuel and Judith Anna Hawes drove past.[25]

In her postwar northern incarnation, Terhune became increasingly well-to-do. By 1871 she had turned her attention to writing the cookbooks, domestic manuals, and etiquette books that were her

---

Female Writers, 435; Thomas Nelson Page, "Literature in the South since the War," Lippincott's Magazine 48 (December 1891): 743.

24. Albert Payson Terhune to Frederic Van de Water, December 17, 1936, December 5, 1939, Albert Payson Terhune papers, Alexander Library, Rutgers University, New Brunswick, New Jersey; Mary Virginia Hawes Terhune to Virginia Eppes (Dance) Campbell, May 28, 1880, Terhune Papers; Profile of Horace Hawes, in William H. Blanton, The Making of a Downtown Church: The History of the Second Presbyterian Church, Richmond, Virginia, 1845–1945 (Richmond: John Knox Press, [1945]), 377–79.

25. Van de Water, "Talented Family," 2.

contribution to the emerging "culture of gentility" of the postwar
United States. Her first and always best-loved cookbook, *Common
Sense in the Household*, remained in print for fifty years, earning in its
first decade the phenomenal sum of thirty thousand dollars. Terhune
wrote for an audience of middle-class housewives who had little or no
domestic help, though she herself never had fewer than three servants
and, in her own upwardly mobile trajectory, always managed to stay
at least one social level ahead of her readers. Writing for them, like
caring for her nieces and nephews, was a form of noblesse oblige
reminiscent of her own treatment at the hands of her mother's planter
relatives during her childhood. After 1875, Terhune was able to afford
to travel to Europe every few years. In the 1890s, she began to speculate
successfully in real estate. She spent the last thirty-five years of her
life living in her beloved New York City, a member of a select and
congenial circle of writers, editors, publishers, musicians, and theater
people.[26]

Terhune approached the matter of regional literary settings very
cautiously in the years after the Civil War. The majority of her postwar
novels were set in northern states, and her travel books and biographies
dealt with European subjects. And all of this literature was outweighed
by her vast output of domestic manuals. The 1880s witnessed the birth
of a national literature of reconciliation and initiated three decades
of retrospective glorification of plantation life, and Terhune found
a new opportunity to use the materials of her southern childhood.
Her writings of this period reveal her eagerness to participate in the
reconciliation process. Late in the 1880s, after surveying the remains
of wartime damage to a colonial Tidewater mansion, she wrote, "Upon
those whose political rancor and greed brought on the fratricidal strife,
let the odium rest of these and other calamities which a united people
is anxious to forget."[27]

26. Ibid., 60; Christine Terhune Herrick, *Like Mother Used to Make* (Boston,
1912), Mary Virginia Hawes Terhune to Charles Scribner, Charles S. Scribner
Papers, Princeton University Library, Princeton, N.J.; J. C. Derby, *Fifty Years among
Authors, Books, and Publishers* (New York, 1884), 567; Patricia Hill,"Writing out
the War: Harriet Beecher Stowe's Averted Gaze," in *Divided Houses: Gender and the
Civil War*, ed. Catherine Clinton and Nina Silber (New York: Oxford University
Press, 1992), 264.
27. Marion Harland [Mary Virginia Hawes Terhune], *Some Colonial Homesteads
and Their Stories* (New York, 1897), 12; Francis Pendleton Gaines, *The Southern*

In 1884 Terhune published *Judith,* the most celebratory of all her southern novels. Based on Terhune's experiences as a guest at the plantations of her mother's kin, *Judith* is a detailed evocation of Virginia planter life in the early 1830s. It features a southern ghost story, a revival sermon, and two tragic romances. *Judith* also recounts the stories of two Virginia slave insurrections, Gabriel Prosser's uprising in 1800 and Nat Turner's Rebellion in Southampton County in 1831. *Judith* contains Terhune's only major disquisition on slavery, a long section articulating the argument that had been standard among liberal southerners of the 1830s: slavery was an evil not of their making, a corrupt legacy, but one that was not susceptible to radical overhaul in any future they cared to foresee. Responsible stewardship of what she believed to be the inferior race was, to Terhune, the only option open to enlightened Virginians of the period.[28]

Terhune's view of African Americans was never reconstructed; in her 1910 autobiography she reiterated virtually the same ideas about their limited capacities that she had held in 1884 and all her life before that. In domestic manuals she shamelessly lamented the passing of the slave cook and butler, whose skill and dedication no modern hired servant could be expected to emulate. As disfranchisement and racial hatred hardened throughout the South during the late nineteenth century, it became all the easier for popular writers like Terhune to turn out entertainments glorifying the lost days of prosperity and racial subjugation.[29]

Ironically, *Judith* was first published in serial form by Albion Tourgee, the Radical Reconstructionist judge turned novelist and editor. In the 1880s, Tourgee became the publisher of an elegant weekly magazine, *Our Continent.* How he reconciled Terhune's glorification of antebellum southern institutions with his own politics is difficult

---

Plantation: A Study in the Development and Accuracy of a Tradition (New York: Columbia University Press, 1924), 62–63, 74–89.

28. Moss, *Domestic Novelists,* 116 n. Terhune's reproduction of the liberal slaveholder's attitude is accurate for the 1830s and is likely to have been the one that survived in her own family.

29. Marion Harland [Mary Virginia Hawes Terhune], *The Housekeeper's Week* (Indianapolis, Ind.: Bobbs-Merrill, 1908). For the northern perspective on African Americans, see Nina Silber, *The Romance of Reunion: Northerners and the South 1865–1900* (Chapel Hill: University of North Carolina Press, 1993), 124–25, 141.

to imagine. Perhaps the answer lies in the fact that *Our Continent* was in
deep financial trouble by 1883. Terhune was a nationally acclaimed
author and the southern plantation a subject of increasing popular
interest. The need to raise circulation and the need to respond to the
tastes of the reading public took precedence over the exigencies of
conscience.[30]

Terhune never wrote about the New South or about the deep South.
Except in *Sunnybank*, written much earlier, she avoided the Civil War as
a topic and refrained from writing any southern stories that took place
after 1840. Nevertheless, she had a strong interest in being identified,
once again, as a southern writer. In the 1890s, when Terhune, in her sixties, was at her most productive and the demand for nostalgic southern
literature was at its height, she produced three books for young girls
and a book of short stories, all based on incidents and legends from her
Virginia childhood. According to her son and grandson, these reminiscences were highly mythologized, and the Hawes family's social status
elevated by several notches.[31] Four-fifths of Terhune's autobiography,
written at the age of eighty, were devoted to the story of her life in
the South. She was so old that she had convinced her publisher and
several reviewers that she was the only living writer qualified to tell the
story of the Old South. "Of all the authors still on active professional
duty in our country," she wrote in 1909,

> I am the only one whose memory runs back to the stage of
> national history that preceeded the Civil War by a quarter century.
> I, alone, am left to tell, of my own knowledge and experience, what
> the Old South was in deed and truth . . . . It was my lot to know
> the Old South in her prime, and to see her downfall. Mine to
> witness the throes that racked her during four black and bitter
> years. Mine to watch the dawn of a new and vigorous life and the
> full glory of a restored Union.[32]

30. Otto H. Olsen, *Carpetbagger's Crusade: The Life of Albion Winegar Tourgee*
(Baltimore: Johns Hopkins University Press, 1965), 252–64.

31. Marion Harland [Mary Virginia Hawes Terhune], *An Old-Field School-Girl*
(New York, 1897); *When Grandmamma Was New: The Story of a Virginia Childhood*
(Boston, 1899); *In Our County: Stories of Old Virginia Life* (New York: G.P. Putnam's
Sons, 1901); *When Grandmamma Was Fourteen;* Van de Water, "Talented Family,"
25.

32. Harland, *Autobiography,* ix–x.

In general, Terhune preferred to write about colonial Virginia, or Virginia of the early Republic, when the Old Dominion's noblest statesmen were alive and Virginia was the queen of the young nation. It was a safe South to write about, acceptable to a wide audience and untainted by sectional rivalry or the horrors of civil war. Writing about colonial Virginia did not require Terhune to review her own prewar ambivalence about southern identity or her deep suspicions of the aims of the Confederacy. She published a historical novel about William Byrd II of Westover, a series of articles on colonial Virginia plantations, and a biography of George Washington's mother. On the basis of these works, and her leadership in a fund drive to erect a monument to Mary Ball Washington, Terhune was elected to the august Virginia Historical Society, one of the first women ever to be admitted.[33]

Terhune was by no means alone in her efforts to focus attention on colonial Virginia. The outpouring of her works about early Virginia coincided with similar works by Thomas Nelson Page and other novelists and with the birth of the Association for the Preservation of Virginia Antiquities (APVA). The association was organized by elite white conservatives not only to preserve colonial buildings, but also to control and shape the public perception of American history and to claim the Old Dominion as the rightful birthplace of the nation. By evoking past memories, elite Virginians of the 1880s and 1890s could avoid dwelling on the troubling present; they could also use the colonial past as a way to control the state's cultural future. Terhune herself joined the APVA in 1893, and her writings helped to foster the rapid growth of the "Old Virginia Mystique" after 1900.[34]

By the second decade of the twentieth century Terhune had settled the matter of her regional identity. She had decided that she was an American of the upper class, with links to the dominant literary establishment and roots in the grand Old Dominion of Virginia. Any sense of a broader southern identity had been shattered by the Civil War and its aftermath. She saw herself as a Virginian, as distinct from a southerner, the possessor of a set of glorious traditions but

33. Wright, "Mary Virginia Hawes Terhune," 377.
34. James M. Lindgren, *Preserving the Old Dominion: Historic Preservation and Virginia Traditionalism* (Charlottesville: University Press of Virginia, 1993) 20–23.

no relation to the Confederate warmongers and memorializers of the deep South states. Terhune was never to participate in the grand turn-of-the-century Confederate celebrations or to become a supporter of the Lost Cause. Significantly, she did not join the United Daughters of the Confederacy, though there were several active chapters in her old hometown of Richmond. She was, however, a proud Daughter of Pocahontas and a member of the Daughters of the American Revolution. Half her heart was in the North, where she had found a city to call home and a public that rewarded her literary efforts with fame and fortune; but half her heart was in Dixie—that is, in the Virginia of her memory and imagination, a Virginia she had helped to create and sustain in the minds of the American reading public.[35]

Mary Virginia Hawes Terhune never lost her powerful ability to transform experience, especially where it related to unpleasant aspects of the New South. In 1921, the last year of her life, almost totally blind and rather frail but mentally as sound as she had ever been, Terhune paid a farewell visit to Richmond in the company of her son and daughter-in-law. She insisted that they take her to visit her girlhood home on Leigh Street. Her son knew the neighborhood had decayed and the house had become a rundown Salvation Army shelter. He tipped the janitor to keep people away for a few moments and, very reluctantly, took his mother inside.

The structure had been altered drastically since the Hawes family lived there, the first floor divided up into small, dirty cubicles. Unable to see her surroundings, Terhune paused and told her son, "This was our drawing room, when I was a girl. It fills the whole side of the house, you see." In response to her query about the room's condition, her son and daughter-in-law assured her that it was well maintained.

"It was harder for us to keep our voices politely enthusiastic," Albert Payson Terhune later wrote, "when she pointed out of a window to a ghastly expanse strewn with muck and garbage." He went on to describe his mother's poignant recollection:

35. Wright, "Mary Virginia Hawes Terhune," 377. For the UDC in Virginia, see Angie Parrott, " 'Love Makes Memory Eternal': The United Daughters of the Confederacy in Richmond, Virginia, 1897–1920," in *The Edge of the South: Life in Nineteenth-Century Virginia*, ed. Edward Ayres and John C. Willis (Charlottesville: University Press of Virginia, 1991), 219–38.

I'm so glad the people who live here keep the dear old garden as lovely as it used to be. My mother took such pains in laying it out and in tending it. I know how happy she would be to know it hasn't been changed. You'll see how all the paths with their box borders and flower beds converge toward that summerhouse in the center. In another month the jasmine blossoms will cover every inch of it. In that jasmine summerhouse, back in 1855, your father asked me to marry him.

At the time, Albert Terhune was disturbed and saddened by his mother's condition, but he later came to understand the meaning of that visit. "No, it wasn't funny. It wasn't even pathetic," he reflected. "Her eager blank eyes were seeing the whole place far more accurately than we were. We saw only the squalor and filth and desolation of it. She saw it with the clearness of a hundred golden memories."[36]

36. Albert Payson Terhune, *The Book of Sunnybank* (New York: Harper and Bros., 1934), 78–79.

Making the Connection

Public Health Policy and Black Women's Volunteer Work

SUSAN L. SMITH

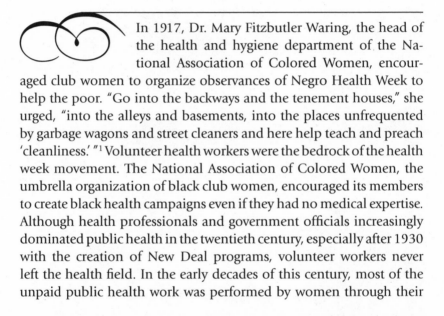

In 1917, Dr. Mary Fitzbutler Waring, the head of the health and hygiene department of the National Association of Colored Women, encouraged club women to organize observances of Negro Health Week to help the poor. "Go into the backways and the tenement houses," she urged, "into the alleys and basements, into the places unfrequented by garbage wagons and street cleaners and here help teach and preach 'cleanliness.' "[1] Volunteer health workers were the bedrock of the health week movement. The National Association of Colored Women, the umbrella organization of black club women, encouraged its members to create black health campaigns even if they had no medical expertise. Although health professionals and government officials increasingly dominated public health in the twentieth century, especially after 1930 with the creation of New Deal programs, volunteer workers never left the health field. In the early decades of this century, most of the unpaid public health work was performed by women through their

My thanks to the commentators and audience at the 1994 Third Southern Conference on Women's History and the following people for their comments on earlier drafts: Andrea Friedman, Linda Gordon, Judith Walzer Leavitt, Gerda Lerner, Leslie Reagan, Leslie Schwalm, and Martha Swain. This research was funded by a Woodrow Wilson National Fellowship Foundation Rural Policy Fellowship and a Woodrow Wilson National Fellowship Foundation Women's Studies Research Grant. This article is based on material from a larger work entitled *Sick and Tired of Being Sick and Tired: Black Women's Health Activism in America, 1890–1950* (Philadelphia: University of Pennsylvania Press, 1995).

1. Mary Fitzbutler Waring, M.D., "Sanitation," *National Association Notes* (April–May 1917): 8–9.

voluntary associations. The history of volunteer health work among African American women in the South demonstrates that the labor of community volunteers was maintained rather than replaced by government public health programs.[2] The significance of such volunteerism has often been underestimated. In fact, women's unpaid labor was a critical component in the creation of community health care in the twentieth century.[3]

In the early twentieth century, many African Americans living in the South struggled against poverty and poor health. In rural areas many worked as sharecroppers on white-owned plantations and lived in small cabins, usually with no plumbing and only an outdoor privy or toilet. Malnutrition was a serious problem because most food had to be purchased at the plantation store, which offered a limited selection of items, mostly salt, sugar, grits, cornmeal, molasses, and fatback. Rural southerners faced a range of health problems, including malaria, typhoid fever, hookworm disease, pellagra (caused by a vitamin deficiency), and venereal disease. The mortality rates for infants and mothers were high.[4]

2. On white women's health reform, see Judith Walzer Leavitt, *The Healthiest City: Milwaukee and the Politics of Health Reform* (Princeton: Princeton University Press, 1982), chap. 6. The literature on black women's community activism is growing rapidly. See Gerda Lerner, *The Majority Finds Its Past* (New York: Oxford University Press, 1979), chap. 6; Paula Giddings, *When and Where I Enter: The Impact of Black Women on Race and Sex in America* (New York: William Morrow, 1984); Kathleen C. Berkeley, " 'Colored Ladies Also Contributed': Black Women's Activities from Benevolence to Social Welfare, 1866–1896," in *The Web of Southern Social Relations: Women, Family and Education*, ed. Walter J. Fraser, R. Frank Saunders Jr., and Jon Wakelyn (Athens: University of Georgia Press, 1985), 181–203; Cynthia Neverdon-Morton, *Afro-American Women of the South and the Advancement of the Race, 1895–1925* (Knoxville: University of Tennessee Press, 1989); Anne F. Scott, "Most Invisible of All: Black Women's Voluntary Associations," *Journal of Southern History* 41 (February 1990): 3–22; Linda Gordon, *Pitied but Not Entitled: Single Mothers and the History of Welfare, 1890–1935* (New York: Free Press, 1994), chap. 5.

3. George Rosen, *A History of Public Health* (New York: MD Publications, 1958), 382; Anne Firor Scott, *Natural Allies: Women's Associations in American History* (Urbana: University of Illinois Press, 1993); Nancy Hewitt and Suzanne Lebsock, eds., *Visible Women: New Essays on American Activism* (Urbana: University of Illinois Press, 1993).

4. Hildrus A. Poindexter, M.D., "Special Health Problems of Negroes in Rural Areas," *Journal of Negro Education* 6 (July 1937): 400, 403, 412; Pete Daniel, *Standing at the Crossroads: Southern Life since 1900* (New York: Hill & Wang, 1986).

Despite these health needs, southern public health provisions were severely limited. Racial politics, along with economic constraints, had a powerful impact on the development of public health in the South, whose history of slavery and tradition of white supremacy shaped public health policy. Most notably, white determination to maintain economic and political power over black people fueled resistance to any public welfare programs that might inadvertently benefit them. White southern fears of black progress and racial equality significantly slowed the development of state-funded public health campaigns, to the detriment of all southerners.[5]

During the so-called Progressive Era, white health officials often justified neglect of black health needs on the grounds that African Americans would soon become extinct. Many shared the views of prominent health statistician Frederick L. Hoffman, who argued in 1896 that black people would eventually die out because of "racial degeneration." Hoffman argued that black decline was due to the physical and moral deterioration of former slaves released from the "civilizing" influence of whites.[6] Even after World War I, when most officials acknowledged that African Americans would not become extinct, many southerners still attributed high black morbidity and mortality rates to inherent racial inferiority rather than unhealthy environments, extreme poverty, and inadequate health care.

Black women in the South, where most black people resided until World War II, carried out health work because of the historical neglect and denial of health services to African Americans.[7] Over time, black reformers, much like white health reformers, turned to government and charity organizations to ensure the permanency of their volunteer efforts. Unlike their white counterparts, however, black activists found only limited government resources available for their communities.

Black women did not work in isolation but within a community network of female health advocates, including midwives, teachers,

5. Howard N. Rabinowitz, *Race Relations in the Urban South, 1865–1890* (New York: Oxford University Press, 1978), xv, 31, 333.
6. Frederick L. Hoffman, *Race Traits and Tendencies of the American Negro* (New York, 1896), 310–11, 329.
7. Edward H. Beardsley, *A History of Neglect: Health Care for Blacks and Mill Workers in the Twentieth-Century South* (Knoxville: University of Tennessee Press, 1987), chaps. 1, 6.

home demonstration agents, sorority and club women, and a few public health nurses and doctors. Layworkers played an important role in black health work because segregation and racism severely limited the number of black health professionals. For example, in 1910 there were only about three thousand black doctors and an equal number of black nurses in the United States, scarcely an adequate number to meet the health needs of the ten million African Americans, most of whom relied on black workers for health care.[8]

Middle-class black women were unwilling to resign themselves to the state of ill health among black people. They believed that their class and gender made them uniquely fitted to bring about the salvation of the race. As members of women's clubs they were among the first public health volunteers. Club women believed that health work was distinctly women's work. According to one black club woman in Jackson, Mississippi, club women were active in health work because "the responsibility for the health of the family is largely upon the women."[9]

Club women promoted public health work by mobilizing their communities to support National Negro Health Week, an annual nationwide observance. Launched by Booker T. Washington in 1915, National Negro Health Week focused community involvement on preventive medicine through clean-up projects, health awareness programs, and medical examinations. These black health campaigns combined the strategies of the nineteenth-century sanitation movement, which focused on cleaning up the environment, with the twentieth-century emphasis on personal hygiene and germs.[10]

8. Herbert Morais, *The History of the Negro in Medicine* (New York: Publishers Company under the auspices of the Association for the Study of Negro Life and History, 1969), chap. 5. On black doctors, see Beardsley, *A History of Neglect*, chap. 4; David McBride, *From TB to AIDS: Epidemics among Urban Blacks since 1900* (Albany: State University of New York Press, 1991); and Vanessa Northington Gamble, *Making a Place for Ourselves: The Black Hospital Movement, 1920–1945* (New York: Oxford University Press, 1995). On black nurses, see Darlene Clark Hine, *Black Women in White: Racial Conflict and Cooperation in the Nursing Profession, 1890–1950* (Bloomington: Indiana University Press, 1989).

9. Mrs. M. M. Hubert, "Club Women's View of National Negro Health Week," *National Negro Health News* 3 (April–June 1935): 3.

10. Smith, *Sick and Tired of Being Sick and Tired*, chap. 2; Paul Starr, *The Social Transformation of American Medicine* (New York: Basic Books, 1982), pt. 1, chap. 5.

As local government provisions developed, black women used the observance of National Negro Health Week to make claims for black entitlement to a share of community resources. Given the constant shortage of funds and health care personnel, much of the energy of volunteers went into soliciting financial aid, especially from local governments and charity associations. The Community Chest, a philanthropic organization that dispersed funds to worthy civic projects, was often a target.

Black women's health activity followed the general pattern of early-twentieth-century public health reform. Their emphasis on education and cooperation between private organizations and government health departments were hallmarks of the "new public health" after 1910.[11] Black women health reformers faced an added burden. They had to convince health department officials that black health could and should be improved. They had to counter white beliefs about apathy among poor blacks and demonstrate that blacks cared enough about their health to participate in health programs.

A significant proportion of black women's volunteer efforts centered on creating community health clinics to implement public health policies. Such clinics were part of the wider neighborhood health center movement that took place from about 1910 to the 1930s, in which medical and social services were provided within specific neighborhoods.[12] For example, in Georgia, the Savannah Federation of Colored Women's Clubs, representing over one hundred separate clubs, established the Cuyler Children's Free Clinic. Throughout the 1920s and 1930s the clinic provided free health care to about four hundred poor children each month and offered a Tuesday clinic for adults, mostly domestics, laborers, and the unemployed. Volunteers staffed the clinic, which was under the full control and financial responsibility of the federated women's clubs. The Georgia club women convinced black and white physicians to donate their medical services,

11. Leavitt, *The Healthiest City,* 204, 228; and Barbara Gutmann Rosenkrantz, *Public Health and the State: Changing Views in Massachusetts, 1842–1936* (Cambridge: Harvard University Press, 1972), 130.

12. George Rosen, "The First Neighborhood Health Center Movement: Its Rise and Fall," in *Sickness and Health in America: Readings in the History of Medicine and Public Health,* ed. Judith Walzer Leavitt and Ronald L. Numbers (Madison: University of Wisconsin Press, 1985), 475–89.

and they lobbied city and county commissioners to cover the costs of the Cuyler clinic and the salary of a nurse.[13]

From Atlanta to Detroit, black women's participation in community health programs led to the establishment of permanent health councils. In 1930, for example, two hundred black women formed the Daniel Hale Williams' Health Guild in Detroit. This guild, named after a famous black surgeon, organized an observance of Negro Health Week by soliciting assistance from the city department of health, black physicians, teachers, and ministers. The guild members started a number of health projects, including an eight-week health clinic held in black churches that immunized over five thousand children against diphtheria. They also divided the city into fourteen districts, each with a chair and twenty assistants, to arrange health education lectures and health examinations at local black schools, churches, and women's clubs. Finally, members oversaw neighborhood clean-up campaigns and visited all the homes in their districts, handing out literature on family health to mothers.[14]

Rural African Americans were as eager as urban residents to support public health work. Twenty-three men and women of Saint Mary's County in Maryland assisted with their sixth observance of Negro Health Week, and according to the authors of the health week report, "what we have accomplished has been done entirely through the country people themselves, working in cooperation with the Chairman and Secretary of this organization. There were no trained workers, other than these two. The work was done after school hours, at night, and on Sundays."[15]

Elsewhere, residents of East Carroll Parish, a small delta county in Louisiana, created their own health week campaign. According to the director of the county health department, Negro Health Week "was 100 percent in the hands of the colored people and the accomplishments

13. William George Tyson, "The Incidence of Syphilis in Negroes," *Journal of the National Medical Association* 27 (February 1935): 8–9.

14. Detroit Health Week Report, April 28, 1930, Department of Records and Research Collection, Hollis Burke Frissell Library, Tuskegee University, Tuskegee, Ala.

15. Cardinal Gibbons Institute, Saint Mary's County, Maryland, Health Week Report, 1930, submitted by Victor H. Daniel, chairman, and Constance E. H. Daniel, secretary, to Tuskegee Institute, April 21, 1930, Department of Records and Research Collection, Tuskegee University.

recorded represent what they did under their own leadership and initiative." Assisted by the county's black public health nurse, community workers provided information on the benefits of "washing teeth, taking baths, cleaning homes, sunning beddings, killing bed bugs, repairing privies, cleaning up yards and papering houses." Furthermore, they secured previously unavailable garbage removal services from a local town, thus beginning the extension of government services to black neighborhoods.[16]

The impressive growth in the observance of Negro Health Week demonstrates that African Americans were receptive to the messages of the growing black health movement. According to reports of health week activities, campaigns existed in every state where African Americans lived, in rural counties and major metropolitan areas. This activity even spread beyond the United States to Montreal, Canada, the Virgin Islands, and British colonies in West Africa. The number of people involved in health week activities dramatically increased from five hundred thousand in 1933 to five million in 1942, suggesting that it was, in fact, a mass movement.[17]

Furthermore, in 1932 leaders of the black health movement convinced the federal government to open an Office of Negro Health Work in the United States Public Health Service to coordinate Negro Health Week activities. This office marked the first time since the creation of the Freedman's Bureau in the post–Civil War era that the United States government had institutionalized black public health work within the federal bureaucracy. However, the government office proved to be more a clearinghouse for community-based efforts than a source of government funding. Unpaid community workers remained the backbone of black public health work.[18]

One of the most impressive health programs undertaken by a volunteer group was the Alpha Kappa Alpha Mississippi Health Project.

16. M. V. Hargett, M.D., Director of East Carroll Parish Health Unit, May 3, 1930, and East Carroll Parish, Louisiana, Health Week Report, 1930, Department of Records and Research Collection, Tuskegee University.

17. Chart, "Negro Health Week Observance for the six years 1925–1930," Department of Records and Research Collection, Tuskegee University; *Southern Letter* 43 (March 1927): 4; *Southern Letter* 45 (March–April 1929): 3; Roscoe C. Brown, "The National Negro Health Week Movement," reprint from *Health Officer* 1 (September–October 1936): 146–51, 206–12; *National Negro Health News*, 1933–1950.

18. Smith, *Sick and Tired of Being Sick and Tired*, chap. 3.

Members of the Alpha Kappa Alpha (AKA) Sorority designed and financed the project, and from 1935 to 1942, sorority volunteers worked for several weeks each summer in the Mississippi Delta. Volunteers tried to address the problems of black sharecroppers who received little of the New Deal government relief during the Great Depression. AKA sought to create a model of the type of social welfare program that the local and federal government ought to provide to neglected African Americans.

The Mississippi Health Project typified the way in which black women's volunteer health work tried to connect public health policy to black health needs in an environment that necessitated careful negotiation. To improve health conditions for sharecroppers in the Mississippi Delta, AKA leaders had to do more than establish health clinics. They had to secure at least tacit approval, if not full cooperation, from the predominantly white federal, state, and county health officials. They also had to overcome resistance from plantation owners who feared that the women were little more than "outside agitators" interfering in southern labor relations. In an attempt to placate the necessary players, AKA leaders consciously censored criticism of white authorities in their annual reports on the health project. At the same time, they had to reassure black sharecroppers that there was no risk involved in participating in the clinics.

Although sorority members shared a history of racial oppression with those they aided, they did not share similar class positions. Alpha Kappa Alpha, the oldest black sorority in the United States, was founded by black female students at Howard University in Washington, D.C., in 1908. AKA recruited black college leaders and academic achievers from historically black colleges and predominantly white colleges across the country. Many of the college sorority members continued their affiliation after graduation. At the time of the health project, the sorority had over two thousand members in one hundred twenty-five chapters, including both undergraduate and alumnae chapters.[19]

19. Marjorie H. Parker, *Alpha Kappa Alpha: 60 Years of Service* (n.p.: Alpha Kappa Alpha Sorority, 1966); J. D. Ratcliff, "Cotton Field Clinic," *Survey Graphic* 29 (September 1940): 464–67; *Alpha Kappa Alpha Mississippi Health Project, Annual Report* (hereinafter *AKAMHP, Annual Report*) (1935–1942), Howard University, Moorland-Spingarn Research Center, Washington, D.C.

The educational background, urban residences, and moderate economic security of the middle-class sorority women differed dramatically from the circumstances of the sharecroppers who lived and worked in the Delta. The flat delta was settled through levee construction and railroads at the turn of the century and was part of the Mississippi River floodplain in the northwestern part of the state. By 1910 Delta cotton plantations had produced prosperity for planters and poverty for sharecroppers.[20]

Alpha Kappa Alpha's work in Mississippi began in 1934 with a teacher-education program directed by Ida Louise Jackson, the president of the sorority from 1933 to 1937. Jackson, a native of Mississippi, moved to Oakland, California, in 1918 with her family. Resisting racial barriers, in the mid–1920s she fought successfully to become the first black teacher hired in the Oakland public schools. She was a highly educated woman and earned a bachelor's degree in education in 1922 and master's degree in 1923 from the University of California at Berkeley, where she helped to start a chapter of AKA. She also did doctoral work at Columbia Teachers College.[21]

Jackson launched an education program in Mississippi after she discovered the desperate situation of the black poor in the Delta. In 1933 Jackson attended a fund-raising concert in Oakland by girls from the Saints Industrial and Literary School of Lexington, Mississippi, a religious school headed by Dr. Arenia C. Mallory. Jackson was dismayed at Mallory's descriptions of the bleak conditions in Mississippi. She could not understand why the government did not send assistance and thought it was time that the nation's black leaders helped those who could not help themselves. Jackson decided to return to her home state and see the situation firsthand. She was appalled by the extreme poverty and inadequate educational facilities in rural Mississippi. It seemed to her that the situation had worsened since her childhood. In 1934 she garnered sorority support and launched the AKA Summer School for Rural Teachers as a way to improve the quality of education

20. Ratcliff, "Cotton Field Clinic," 464–67; *AKAMHP, Annual Report* (1935); and Daniel, *Standing at the Crossroads*, 84.

21. "Ida Louise Jackson," *Ivy Leaf* 57 (spring 1980): 10; Marianna Davis, ed., *Contributions of Black Women to America*, (Columbia, S.C.: Kenday Press, 1982), 2:406; "Ida L. Jackson," in *There Was Light: Autobiography of a University, Berkeley: 1868–1968*, ed. Irving Stone (New York: Doubleday & Co., 1970), 249–66.

for black children. Jackson selected six teachers to serve as instructors from among the AKA volunteers and paid them from her own pocket, supplemented by funds from the sorority.[22]

Although Jackson initially saw education as the key to improving conditions for southern African Americans, she soon changed her mind after traveling around the plantations. She concluded that malnutrition, decayed teeth, eye problems, and the effects of syphilis and tuberculosis had to be addressed before educational opportunities would be meaningful.[23]

Jackson approached Dr. Dorothy Boulding Ferebee (1898–1980) and asked her to direct an AKA health project in Mississippi. Ferebee accepted the invitation and became medical director, in addition to performing her job at Howard University, conducting her private medical practice, and raising her young twins. Born in Virginia, Ferebee grew up in Boston. She earned degrees at Simmons College in 1920 and Tufts Medical College in 1924. At Tufts she was 1 of 5 women in a class of 137 medical students. According to Ferebee, "we women were always the last to get assignments in amphitheaters and clinics. And I? I was the last of the last because not only was I a woman, but a Negro, too." Despite these obstacles, Ferebee graduated as one of the top five students in her class, and after repeated rejections by white hospitals, secured an internship at Freedmen's Hospital, a black institution in Washington, D.C. When she completed her internship in 1927, Howard University hired her as an instructor of obstetrics at the medical school.[24]

22. Arenia C. Mallory King headed the school, later Saints Junior College, from 1926 to 1983. "Ida Louise Jackson," 10; Davis, *Contributions of Black Women*, 406; Stone, "Ida L. Jackson," 249–66.

23. Ratcliff, "Cotton Field Clinic," 465; Ida L. Jackson, "My Reflections on Alpha Kappa Alpha's Summer School for Rural Teachers and the Mississippi Health Project," *Ivy Leaf* 52 (summer 1976): 11; Parker, *Alpha Kappa Alpha*, 101–2; "Lexington: A Noble Task," *Ivy Leaf* 13 (March 1935): 12.

24. Carolyn Lewis, interview with Dr. Ferebee, "Hard Work Can Topple the Barriers," *Washington Post*, n.d., folder on Dr. Dorothy Ferebee, Howardiana Collection, Howard University Archives, Moorland-Spingarn Research Center, Howard University, Washington, D.C.; Davis, *Contributions of Black Women*, 407; "A Thumbnail Sketch of Our Supreme Basileus Dorothy Boulding Ferebee," *Ivy Leaf* 18 (March 1940): 4; and "Dorothy Boulding Ferebee," *Tufts Medical Alumni Bulletin* 27 (March 1968), folder on Dr. Dorothy Ferebee, Health Sciences Library, Howard University, Washington, D.C.

Ferebee began her social reform work in Washington, where for thirteen years she served as president of the Southeast Settlement House. This institution, which she founded in 1929, provided day care and recreational opportunities to black children. She had first seen the need for social services while performing ambulance duty in the poor black section of the city. The final impetus came when she rescued a nine-year-old boy from the police station. He had been taken in for stealing milk from his neighbor's porch for the younger brother he was babysitting. After hearing this, Ferebee explained, "I went down and got him and paid for the milk and right then decided we needed a place for black children of working mothers."[25]

Ferebee's interests in health and welfare continued throughout her lifetime, but her service as medical director of the Alpha Kappa Alpha Mississippi Health Project led to her national reputation in the field. She took charge of the AKA project and selected assistants from among the sorority volunteers on the basis of previous relevant experience. She chose twelve AKA members to participate in Mississippi that first summer, including one doctor, two nurses, and several teachers and social workers. AKA workers were not paid but AKA used membership dues to reimburse the volunteers for their expenses in laundry and room and board. There were, of course, other costs. Some women found it difficult to be away from their jobs for so long. For example, Dr. Zenobia Gilpin had to withdraw at the last moment because of the demands of her practice.[26]

The sorority volunteers encountered many difficulties in carrying out their plans for the health project, yet they demonstrated resiliency and creativity in the face of white resistance. Because the volunteers came from across the nation, they decided to meet at Ferebee's home in Washington and take the train down to Mississippi together. When a white railway agent refused to sell train tickets to Ferebee, due to

25. Jacqueline Trescott, "Making a Practice of Persistence," *Washington Post,* May 5, 1978.
26. Dorothy Boulding Ferebee to Ida Louise Jackson, June 30, 1935, Dorothy Ferebee Papers, Manuscripts Division, Moorland-Spingarn Research Center, Howard University, Washington, D.C.; K. E. Miller to Dr. J. A. O'Hara, March 19, 1937, General Files Group 9, 1936–1944, Record Group 90, United States Public Health Service (USPHS), National Archives, Washington, D.C.; and "Negro College Women Conduct Health Project in Delta," *National Negro Health News* 8 (October–December 1940): 26.

the limited seating for African Americans in segregated trains, the sorority women decided to borrow cars and drive to Mississippi. They had to take along a load of medical supplies and face the many travel difficulties segregation created for black Americans. As Ferebee recalled, it was "a 2,000 mile run over unknown roads, many without restroom facilities, or over night accommodations, or even gas stations willing to serve black travellers."[27]

The AKA participants faced more difficulties upon reaching Mississippi. They set up their headquarters at the Saints Industrial and Literary School in Holmes County, where it would be easier for African Americans to obtain food and lodging. The plan was to hold the health clinics from 9:00 A.M. to 4:00 P.M. six days per week for six weeks at the Saints School, with lectures for adults in the evening. The clinic opened as planned in a boys' dormitory at the school, but after their first few days of clinic operation, attendance was very low. The women tried to find out why and learned that white plantation owners, wary of outsiders, refused to allow "their" sharecroppers to leave the plantations and attend the clinics. Undaunted, the AKA women agreed among themselves that they had not come all this way for nothing. The women decided to turn their cars into mobile health clinics and drive out to each plantation. The result was that the health project reached far more people than any centralized clinic ever would have.

Despite the dusty country roads and inadequate facilities, the sorority volunteers ran their clinics professionally, with as much order and efficiency as possible. They set up clinic tables with crisp, white linens and put on matching white uniforms to "give an air of healthfulness and cleanliness." Teachers, such as Marion Carter from St. Louis, Missouri, and nurses, such as Mary E. Williams from Tuskegee Institute in Alabama, took patients' health histories and prepared children for immunizations, while Ferebee gave the injections.[28]

AKA reports indicate that the sorority women tried creative approaches to persuade the sharecroppers to attend the clinics. Knowing that sharecroppers were also wary of outsiders, clinic staff went to local

27. Dr. Dorothy Ferebee, "The Alpha Kappa Alpha Mississippi Health Project," *Ivy Leaf* 52 (summer 1976): 14.
28. Parker, *Alpha Kappa Alpha*, 106; Ida L. Jackson, "A Message from Our Supreme Basileus," *Ivy Leaf* 13 (September 1935): 3–4.

church services, where they advertised their clinics and attempted to allay fears about white retaliation for clinic participation. The sorority women emphasized that their clinics were created by black women health workers for black sharecroppers in the hope that this fact would encourage participation. Aware of the illiteracy of much of the rural population, the volunteers used visual materials and lined up colorful posters to attract attention and explain the health messages. They also encouraged attendance by providing gifts for the children, including toothbrushes and clothing. By 1939 they had begun giving nutrition lectures and introducing new food items by offering free meals at the end of the day when people were most hungry. Ferebee remembered that "thousands of tenant families came at first timidly as many had never seen a doctor or a nurse. But soon they came in droves." These various strategies helped the health project to reach thousands of children and adults.[29]

The conditions under which the AKA women worked in the Delta were not ideal. Jackson reported to the sorority members after the first year that if any member was "desirous of doing missionary work—'See America First' before going to Africa." The women found that the most accessible places to hold clinics were in small black churches, often the only black-controlled institutions. Jackson remembered that "many of these churches served also as the only school in the area. At other times we set up our equipment under the trees. On one occasion we had to use the porch of a plantation owner's house (under close supervision of the owner)."[30]

The white planters of the Mississippi Delta apparently feared that the sorority women were promoting unrest and civil rights activity, so they kept close watch on the women at the clinics. According to Ferebee, the planters employed " 'riders' with guns in their belts and whipping prods in their boots; riders who weaved their horses incessantly, close to the clinics, straining their ears to hear what the

29. Ella Payne Moran, "A Project Conducted in Mississippi, Alpha Kappa Alpha Sorority Health Project, Mississippi, 1935–1942," August 1942, Ferebee Papers; Dr. Dorothy Ferebee, "Proposed Plan for a Demonstrational Dietotherapy Project by the Alpha Kappa Alpha Sorority Health Unit," Ferebee Papers; *AKAMHP, Annual Report* (1939); Ferebee, "The Alpha Kappa Alpha Mississippi Health Project," 15.
30. Jackson, "Message from Our Supreme Basileus," 4; Jackson, "My Reflections," 13.

staff interviewers were asking of the sharecroppers." In later years she recalled that the project was "labelled by those racist Mississippians, as a program organized by meddlesome, communist black women, coming into their Delta to stir up trouble and to incite tenant farmers."[31]

Although the annual AKA health reports never explicitly stated that sorority volunteers regarded their health work as civil rights activity, they walked a precarious political line. AKA leaders never spelled out their intentions in official records because they regularly submitted their reports to local government authorities. As Ida Jackson explained, they had to be careful about what they wrote because antagonizing "white power" would be counterproductive to helping sharecroppers.[32] In retrospect, both Jackson and Ferebee felt thankful that no violence against the AKA staff ever resulted.

Despite the fact that state public health work expanded in Mississippi during the 1920s and 1930s, the AKA project reached people that government workers did not. The AKA clinics supplied sharecroppers with physical examinations, vaccinations, nutrition and personal hygiene information, clothing, food items, and treatments for malaria and venereal disease. Dr. Mary C. Wright (Thompson) of Boston provided dental services, including instructions in dental hygiene, and extracted as many as sixty unhealthy teeth per day.[33] These unpaid health workers cared for 150 to 300 people daily at the clinics, for a total clinic attendance each summer of 2,500 to over 4,000 people. The effect on the health of children was perhaps most significant. AKA health staff provided well over 15,000 children with immunizations against smallpox and diphtheria.[34]

The greatest impact of the Mississippi Health Project may have been on the more than forty AKA members who volunteered over the years. As noted in an annual report, "each worker emerged from the field of service with a deeper insight and a richer understanding of the life, the needs, and the outlook of the agrarian worker of the South." Ruth A.

31. Ferebee, "The Alpha Kappa Alpha Mississippi Health Project," 15; Dr. Dorothy Ferebee, "A Brief Review of the Mississippi Health Project of the Alpha Kappa Alpha Sorority" (paper presented at the sixty-fifth anniversary of Alpha Kappa Alpha sorority, February 10, 1973), Ferebee Papers.
32. Ida Jackson to Dorothy Ferebee, June 2, 1936, Ferebee Papers.
33. Ruth A. Scott, "Life's Blood in Mississippi," *Ivy Leaf* 18 (September 1940): 5.
34. Parker, *Alpha Kappa Alpha*, 104–7; AKAMHP, *Annual Report* (1935–1942).

Scott described her first day with the health clinic in 1940 as "nothing short of staggering" as she saw the hundreds of people lined up outside the clinic door awaiting the arrival of the sorority women. The annual reports indicated that the women developed a critique of the southern economic system in their analysis of how to improve health conditions. They came to believe that real change required altering the entire living and working environment of the sharecroppers. In 1941, Ferebee, who was by then president of AKA, reported that "the Health Project has revealed many significant findings, but none more important than the fact the standard of health is indissolubly linked to all the socioeconomic factors of living." The AKA members saw firsthand those factors, especially poverty, that constrained the lives of sharecroppers.[35]

AKA analysis of the root causes of poor health had an effect on both the programs of the clinics and the direction of future AKA projects. From 1939 to 1941, Ferebee widely publicized the importance of the health project through numerous public lectures and a 1941 CBS radio broadcast. She reported in her broadcast that the desperate situation of the depression had motivated the sorority women to take action on behalf of the poor:

> Recognizing the distressing problems of the masses of our people, especially at the lowest economic levels, and recognizing the fact that health is one of the primary needs of all underprivileged people, we set out to offer something beyond an academic discussion of the deplorable conditions of this group.[36]

Over the years, AKA volunteers tried to address conditions that they could help change, such as inadequate diet and lavatory and recreational facilities. The approach of the health project became a combination of clinical operation, health education, and research on socioeconomic conditions.

At a time when the New Deal expanded federal responsibility for the welfare of citizens, AKA leaders turned to government officials to provide endorsements and funding for the health project. Ida Jackson

35. *AKAMHP, Annual Report* (1937), 16–17; Scott, "Life's Blood in Mississippi," 5; *AKAMHP, Annual Report* (1937); *AKAMHP, Annual Report* (1941), foreword.
36. *AKAMHP, Annual Report* (1941).

and Dorothy Ferebee tried to turn AKA's limited voluntary effort into a permanent, government-run program. From the very beginning, AKA leaders had informed federal government officials, including Surgeon General Hugh Cumming and Dr. Roscoe C. Brown, head of the Office of Negro Health Work at the U.S. Public Health Service, of the progress of the health project. AKA approached Dr. Martha Eliot of the Children's Bureau, Secretary of Labor Frances Perkins, and Alfred Edgar Smith of the Works Progress Administration (WPA) for funding from federal relief programs and the Social Security Act. Through these contacts Ferebee was able to get a few black nurses and clerks employed through WPA to assist with the project. Ferebee and Jackson also contacted officials at the Mississippi State Board of Health and received the endorsement of Mississippi politicians.[37]

AKA efforts to gain federal support even reached into the White House, where, on behalf of their sorority, Jackson and Ferebee explained the purpose of the Mississippi Health Project. In 1935 Eleanor Roosevelt invited them to meet with her to discuss the first summer's health work as well as problems that black women faced.[38] The AKA leaders hoped Roosevelt's support would aid them in securing financial assistance. Jackson reported of the meeting:

> First of all, we felt safe in saying that in spite of Federal provisions for relief, this relief program was not reaching the rural Negro. Secondly, if the Negro is to profit by the measures introduced by this Administration, it meant that Negroes would have to be given supervisory and other places of responsibility with "Federal Protection."[39]

Jackson indicated that Eleanor Roosevelt responded with the suggestion that "possibly our Health Project might become a Federal Project

37. Some of this correspondence is reproduced in *AKAMHP, Annual Report* (1935). See also Roscoe C. Brown to Dorothy Boulding Ferebee, February 27, 1935, Ferebee Papers; AKA folder, Organizations, Group 9, 1936–1944, General Files, Record Group 90, USPHS; and Mississippi folder, Correspondence and Reports, 1917–1952, Record Group 102, Children's Bureau, National Archives, Washington, D.C.
38. "Ida Louise Jackson," 10; Jackson, "My Reflections," 13; *Ivy Leaf* 14 (March 1936): 23; Stone, "Ida L. Jackson," 201.
39. Ida L. Jackson, "The Conference with Mrs. Roosevelt," *Ivy Leaf* 14 (June 1936): 4.

with AKA Supervision—with the proviso that we could find trained persons on relief who could operate or conduct the Project."[40]

AKA leaders tried to shape federal and state public policy through the Mississippi Health Project. The annual reports of the project continually referred to the program as a model to be emulated by the government, as merely a demonstration of the possibilities for reaching those people often missed by relief programs. The 1937 health report observed that "certainly a limited project in a single Southern State could not pretend to have quantitative value." Yet, "the final achievement of the Mississippi Health Project will be realized only when Federal, State, or County governments adopt the fundamental principles of its technique and expand this service to large-scale proportions."[41]

Although AKA leaders tried to convince the federal and state governments to take over the work, by and large their requests went unheeded. Despite the fact that about half the population of Mississippi was black, black sharecroppers simply were not a priority. Other than endorsements, the federal government offered the sorority little more than surplus food items and a few WPA workers. Support at the state level also proved to be disappointing, even though the Mississippi State Board of Health was well informed about the sorority's health program. Jackson and Ferebee repeatedly tried to arrange a meeting with the executive officer of the state health board, Dr. Felix J. Underwood, but he refused.[42]

Underwood's resistance at first seems puzzling. Here was a dedicated public health officer who had led the Mississippi State Board of Health since 1924. He had achieved national recognition for his public health work as he attempted to improve the state's backward image as "the unhealthiest State in the Union."[43] During the early 1930s he

40. Jackson, "The Conference with Mrs. Roosevelt," 4.
41. *AKAMHP Annual Report* (1937), 9; *AKAMHP, Annual Report* (1938), foreword.
42. Ida Louise Jackson to Dr. Martha Eliot, May 17, 1943, Dr. Van Riper to Dr. Martha Eliot, May 24, 1943, and Dr. Beach to Dr. Van Riper, July 19, 1943, Central File, 1941–1944, RG 102, Children's Bureau.
43. Allen Rankin, "Mississippi's Medical Giant," *Coronet* (October 1954): 149. See also Lucie Robertson Bridgforth, "The Politics of Public Health Reform: Felix J. Underwood and the Mississippi State Board of Health, 1924–1958," *Public Historian* 6 (summer 1984): 5–26.

served as public health adviser to President Franklin D. Roosevelt's Committee on Economic Security, which produced the 1935 Social Security Act. His efforts helped to ensure that health programs were among the provisions of the act.

Certainly Underwood was in a difficult political position in the economically underdeveloped, segregated South. He was an advocate of government funding for community health care at a time when many white politicians, business leaders, and physicians staunchly resisted universal social programs as attacks upon the status quo and signs of socialism. As a public health professional, he was convinced that an aggressive campaign of immunization and health education for the general public could lower morbidity and mortality rates. In particular, he pioneered the promotion of maternal and child health work, which focused on health education in the schools, mother and baby clinics, and regulation of midwifery. He even appealed to economic arguments and white self-interest to justify state health programs for African Americans. Compared to his successor, Archie Lee Gray, a staunch segregationist who became executive health officer in 1958, Underwood was progressive in his support for universal, yet segregated, public health programs.

However, as his response to the sorority leaders demonstrates, he was not interested in offering state resources to a health program that he did not control. He might tolerate such volunteer health work in his state, but he certainly would not validate a project by rewarding it with state resources when it was not official government activity.

After investing twenty thousand dollars, in 1942 the sorority decided that the Mississippi Health Project had to come to an end. World War II gas rationing had restricted travel, and the sorority chose to invest most of its money in war bonds. However, the sorority's involvement in health work did not end. Ida Jackson continued for at least two more years to run a smaller-scale health program in Holmes County, Mississippi. In 1945 the sorority opened a National Health Office in New York City under Estelle Massey Riddle (Osborne), a professor of nursing education at New York University, to coordinate the work of a nationwide network of local AKA health committees.[44]

44. Parker, *Alpha Kappa Alpha*, 111–12; Ferebee, "The Alpha Kappa Alpha Mississippi Health Project," 15; Flora B. Chisholm, "Full-time Health Education

Finally, the sorority attempted to shape public policy through the AKA Non-Partisan Council on Public Affairs, which it established in 1938 and continued for ten years. The council, which grew directly out of AKA's public health work, lobbied Congress and government departments to promote antidiscrimination legislation and ensure that the federal government responded to the health and welfare needs of all Americans. While organizations like the National Association for the Advancement of Colored People (NAACP) fought for civil rights in the courts, AKA lobbied Congress. The council, headed by sorority member Norma Boyd, was guided by the words of nineteenth-century black reformer Frederick Douglass, who argued, "Power concedes nothing without a demand." The sorority needed to work toward both long-term legislative solutions and immediate survival needs, explained AKA member Portia Nickens. "One phase of the work cannot gain results without the other." Finally, in 1948 AKA joined with six sororities and fraternities to form the American Council on Human Rights, a similar lobbying group.[45]

As the history of the Alpha Kappa Alpha Mississippi Health Project shows, volunteers helped to carry out public health policy in conjunction with, and at times despite, government officials. In countless ways, middle-class black women used their volunteer health work to try to stimulate government interest in the plight of black America. However, despite black women's lobbying efforts, African Americans were not a priority for government officials, and most health departments failed to demonstrate a serious commitment to improving black health. Even the federal government's so-called rescue of the southern public health system in the 1930s did not have a significant impact on black

Program of the Alpha Kappa Alpha Sorority," *National Negro Health News* 15 (October–December 1947): 11–13; and Ida L. Jackson to Dr. Martha Eliot, April 24, 1944, Central File, 1941–1944, RG 102, Children's Bureau.

45. Photo album with text by Portia Nickens, Ferebee Papers; Dorothy Ferebee, "A Message from Our Supreme Basileus," *Ivy Leaf*, 18 (December 1940): 3; quote from Frederick Douglass in "The Alpha Kappa Alpha Sorority Continues Health Project and Establishes National Non-Partisan Council," *Aframerican Woman's Journal* 1 (1941): 38. The other organizations were Alpha Phi Alpha, Delta Sigma Theta, Phi Beta Sigma, Sigma Gamma Rho, and Zeta Phi Beta. "American Council on Human Rights," National Association for the Advancement of Colored People, Washington D.C., Branch Collection, Manuscripts Division, Moorland-Spingarn Research Center, Howard University, Washington, D.C.

southerners. State-level administration of federally funded programs meant that black Americans did not receive an equal share of the benefits of relief.[46]

The history of black women's volunteer activity in the South shows that women's health work not only preceded government work, it remained a constant presence even as the role of government expanded. Government programs in the South benefited from, and often merely supplemented, the ongoing labor of women. Black women's labor shaped the implementation of public health policy in black communities. Public health work involved complex interactions among black and white men and women, both paid and unpaid health workers. Without a doubt, women's volunteer work underpinned the development of public health throughout the South and across the nation.

46. Here I differ from Edward Beardsley, who overemphasizes the positive impact of the federal government on the health of black southerners in *A History of Neglect*, chap. 7. See also Harvard Sitkoff, "The Impact of the New Deal on Black Southerners," in *The New Deal and the South*, ed. James C. Cobb and Michael V. Namorato (Jackson: University Press of Mississippi, 1984), 117–34.

Sarah Patton Boyle's
Desegregated Heart

JOANNA BOWEN GILLESPIE

 If churches in the United States were in the habit of honoring their female lay elders for gifts other than financial, Sarah Patton Boyle (1906–1994) would be a candidate for Episcopal veneration. She was a unique witness in that denomination's history, one of a handful of white "mainline" Christians who wrote and acted against racism in the years preceding the civil rights movement of the 1960s.[1] Her style of racial rebellion—existential self-examination that issued in conscience- and societal-challenging activism—produced "living waters" in a church peopled with moderate, well-educated, spiritually reserved white Americans, in a denomination that had long since rationalized, religiously, the legal and cultural segregation of black Americans.

Sarah Patton Boyle began her racial reeducation in the year 1950. During the succeeding decade she wrote many articles promoting white attitude change, the most visible titled "Southerners Will *Like* Desegregation" in the *Saturday Evening Post* (1955). A lifelong Episcopalian, she was the only woman appointed in 1960 to that

I am grateful that the Episcopal Women's History Project gave me an excuse to contact Patty Boyle in 1992 (I wasn't even sure she was alive), that our friendship had a chance to ripen before her death in 1994, and that she entrusted letters describing the religious aspects of her pilgrimage toward a desegregated heart to me. Ultimately, they will be deposited in her file at the National Archives of the Episcopal Church in Austin, Texas.

1. Page numbers cited parenthetically in the text are from Sarah Patton Boyle, *The Desegregated Heart* (New York: William Morrow & Co., 1962). "Mainline Protestant" refers to historically prominent denominations: Episcopal, Presbyterian, Methodist, Baptist, Congregational, etc. See Wade Clark Roof and William McKinney, *American Mainline Religion* (New Brunswick, N.J.: Rutgers University Press, 1987).

denomination's Advisory Committee on Intergroup Relations; in October 1962 she delivered a position paper, "Witness of a Lone Layman," to the church's National Council that indicted its inaction at the national and local levels. She cited its halfhearted gestures in the direction of racial equality and the negligible support she had found in her own congregation—the seedbed of her reform actions. During the 1950s, being a race reformer implied such transgressions against the social order as "disturbing the peace, trespassing on forbidden ground, and committing assault and battery on human complacency."[2] Sarah Patton Boyle was made to feel that she, a cradle Episcopalian, exemplified these ultimate offenses in her own home terrritory. Although a trueborn southern lady, she had gone beyond the conventions of her era and dared to challenge both her region and her church to honor its own highest rhetorical standards.

In 1962, she also published a book about the process of "unlearning" her region's moral practices; she gave it the arresting title *The Desegregated Heart*. It was an autobiographical account of her painful induction as an adolescent into the racial etiquette (and rationalizations) deemed essential to a white Virginian of her background and, when she awakened in her forties to the truth about segregation, of scraping away the resultant blinders. The bedrock ideal she had to relinquish was the carefully cultivated belief that southern paternalism toward the "Negro" was "the noblest outreaching of the human spirit," an image with which many white Christians like establishment Episcopalians soothed their collective conscience. Racial reeducation enabled Sarah Patton Boyle to see that icon in its true light, as a social design intended to "humiliate and reinforce inferior social status" (106) rather than an expression of high-minded, Christian noblesse oblige. When *The Desegregated Heart* was published, one reviewer skeptically observed that Boyle had somehow managed to "end up

2. The aggressive word *inaction* was only implied in the paper, her written style being direct instead of blunt. Her chosen autobiographical persona was "ladylike" but to our late-twentieth-century eyes is too forceful to be fully masked by a disingenuous voice. See Sidonie Smith, *A Poetics of Women's Autobiography: Marginality and the Fictions of Self-Representation* (Bloomington: Indiana University Press, 1987); Arthur M. Schlesinger, *The American as Reformer* (New York: Atheneum, 1968), 66.

as naive as she went in," but another noted that she had made this "essentially inward and spiritual adventure as exciting to read as a detective story."[3]

Although a few other white Americans, in the early 1960s, were also beginning to expose the dehumanizing results of racial segregation, Sarah Patton Boyle's story was uniquely situated in the distinctive culture of Virginia Episcopalianism. When *The Desegregated Heart* received a Dr. Martin Luther King Jr. Award in 1963, at the Seventh Annual Meeting of the Southern Christian Leadership Conference (September 24–27, Richmond, Virginia), Patty Boyle (she deplored and refused to use the name Sarah) took her place among the "tiny minority" of white southerners who were willing to risk actions that actively undermined the structures of segregation. A burning cross on her Charlottesville, Virginia, lawn in 1956 was vivid testimony to her effectiveness; she was one of a handful of Episcopalians, lay or clergy, to be thus "honored."[4]

Yet today, many in her denomination do not know her name or her writings. Several Episcopal seminaries do not have *The Desegregated Heart* on their library shelves. In a relatively small denomination, how can a work of this moral significance be unknown to its own future leaders? Should her historical invisibility be attributed to academic dismissal of lay theologians or to her being from the South, instead of the intellectually dominant Northeast? Is it because she was female rather than male? Or could such institutional amnesia arise from the

3. Her other books were *For Human Beings Only* (New York City: Seabury Press, 1964) and *The Desert Blooms* (Nashville, Tenn.: Abingdon, 1983); Anne Firor Scott, *Journal of Southern History* 29, (August 1963): 424–25; *Virginia Quarterly Review* 39 (winter 1963): xxvii.
4. David Chappell, *Inside Agitators: White Southerners in the Civil Rights Movement* (Baltimore: Johns Hopkins University Press, 1994), xxiv; Sarah Patton Boyle, telephone interview with author, July 1, 1993. *Desegregated Heart* was chosen for a series called *Signal Lives*, exemplifying the "persuasive power of the autobiographical voice" (New York: Arno Press, 1980). Sarah Patton Boyle File, Episcopal Women's History Project Collection, National Archives of the Episcopal Church, Austin, Tex. (hereinafter cited as SPB File D). [Jane Schutt], "A Flaming Cross for Christmas," *Church Woman* 31 (December 1965). See also Sheryl Spradling Summe, "Alive to the Cause of Justice: Julia Hampton Morgan and the Montgomery Bus Boycott," in *Stepping out of the Shadows: Alabama Women 1819–1990*, ed. Mary Martha Thomas (Tuscaloosa: University of Alabama Press, 1995), 176–90.

unacknowledged ambivalence of a church that often in its history served as "chaplain to the oppressors"—Episcopal bishop Barbara Harris's characterization?[5]

Sarah Patton Boyle's local church affiliation provides an important key to her identity and an interpretive thread in the first-person narrative that gives form to *The Desegregated Heart*.[6] She had grown up hearing the scriptural standards of justice in the elegant cadences of the King James Bible; liturgical rhythms—kneeling and standing, singing hymns, and joining in formal, corporate prayers—were in her bones. A rational, ordered internal piety bespoke her psychic membership in the Anglican elite of white Virginia. What wellspring of her racial rebellion can we today view as denominational?

Religion, the bedrock of her identity, furnished the language of Boyle's awakening to the inequities of the Southern Code, as she came to call it; yet when she took her "stand with Negroes against the white South," as she wrote in her author's note, she found herself isolated in the midst of her local congregation (xi). Generally speaking, Episcopalians in the 1950s—known for their principled tolerance and avoidance of absolutisms such as teetotaling—occupied a relatively liberal position in terms of morality and social activism among Protestants. In fact, novelist Louis Auchincloss, urbane chronicler of late-twentieth-century Eastern WASP elite culture, had one of his fictional characters observe that opposition to racial and ethnic discrimination was among the few major moral values still prevalent among white upper-class Americans.[7]

But when Sarah Patton Boyle began to denounce the inherent injustice of southern racial mores, white Virginia Episcopalians chose to barricade themselves behind the "nobility of the Southern Cause"—

5. The most visible Episcopal Civil Rights hero is martyred seminarian Jonathan Daniels, recently added to the Calendar of Lesser Feasts and Fasts. Charles W. Eagles, *Outside Agitator: Jon Daniels and the Civil Rights Movement in Alabama* (Chapel Hill: University of North Carolina Press, 1993); The Right Reverend Barbara Harris, Keynote Address given at "Unlearning Racism," Conference, Province I of the Episcopal Church, Holyoke, Mass., November 19, 1993.

6. J. B. Gillespie, "Gender and Generations in Congregations" in *Episcopal Women: Gender, Spirituality and Commitment in a Mainline Denomination*, ed. Catherine M. Prelinger (New York: Oxford University Press, 1992), 167–221.

7. Bruce Bawer, "Requiem for the Upper Crust," *New York Times Book Review*, December 4, 1994, 62.

a "dogma [that] was the true religion of many of us whether or not we called ourselves Christians," she summarized. "The South and what we thought of her . . . were more precious to us than anything we learned in church" (8).[8] Only the exceptional white churchgoer, one deeply exposed to a Social Gospel consciousness on such issues, could respond openly to the crescendo of race awareness during the 1950s.[9] Undoubtedly Patty Boyle's internal religious heritage helped her survive the crucible in which she found herself after desegregating her heart, but its external congregational manifestations offered largely negative spiritual sustenance.

The influence of another daughter of the south, Lillian Smith (1897–1967), was a direct and concrete model for Patty, providing a template against which to compare female racial rebels of the period. Having started in the 1930s, Smith was an outspoken advocate of equality between races by World War II—one of a few white liberals giving public voice to pro-desegregation sympathies in that era. Her 1942 "Portrait of the Deep South Speaking to Negroes on Morale" satirized a "democracy" that contradictorily excluded its own "colored folks," revealing how totally she was "at odds with most of the whites in her region." In that same year Sarah Patton Boyle, almost a decade younger and several levels of southern white culture distant, was still unawakened to her complicity in the myths of white superiority.[10]

During the 1940s, the Young Men's and Young Women's Christian Associations (YMCA/YWCA) were the major national formerly

8. Charles Reagan Wilson, *Baptized in Blood: The Religion of the Lost Cause 1865–1920* (Athens: University of Georgia Press, 1980).

9. Wade Clark Roof, *Community and Commitment: Religious Plausibility in a Liberal Protestant Church* (New York: Elsevier, 1978); Gardiner H. Shattuck Jr., "Serving God in the World: Theology and Civil Rights Activism in the Episcopal Church, 1958–1973" in *Anglican and Episcopal History* (forthcoming); "The Strange Career of Tollie Caution: Black Clergy and the Dilemma of Racial Integration in the Episcopal Church, 1943–1973" (paper presented at the Conference of National Episcopal Historiographers and Archivists, Austin, Tex., June 1995).

10. Anne C. Loveland, *Lillian Smith: A Southerner Confronting the South* (Baton Rouge: Louisiana State University Press, 1986) 36–37. See also Roseanne V. Camacho, "Race, Region and Gender in a Reassessment of Lillian Smith" in *Southern Women: Histories and Identities,* ed. Virginia Bernhard et al. (Columbia: University of Missouri Press, 1992), 157–76; John Egerton, *Speak Now against the Day: The Generation before the Civil Rights Movement in the South* (New York: Alfred A. Knopf, 1994), 74, 128.

all-white organizations actively promoting racial integration. The women's group was particularly active, and Lillian Smith, aligned with them, also joined the first interracial organizations to coalesce in her part of the South: the Commission on Interracial Cooperation, and its successor, the Southern Regional Council, both founded in Atlanta. Her best-known book, *Strange Fruit*, a novel about an interracial couple in a small Georgia town, was published in 1944, and her autobiographical indictment of southern culture, *Killers of the Dream*, in 1949.[11]

Smith's public literary stature made it possible for her to organize (among other things) a 1957 television forum of white ministers willing to speak out against segregation. She, of Protestant background turned agnostic as an adult, was the southern female reformer who could invite the Dean of the Episcopal Cathedral of St. John the Divine in New York City (the Reverend Dr. James Pike, himself the host of a regular Sunday morning television program)—not the lifelong Episcopalian Patty Boyle.[12]

Building on her national recognition after 1944, Lillian Smith's articles often appeared on the editorial pages of the *New York Times* and other major publications, chastising white liberals for "not really putting up a fight for human rights in the South." She agonized in print over the Little Rock school desegregation crisis while Boyle was one of the lonely whites defending school integration in her native Charlottesville. In 1956, Smith received a Franklin Roosevelt citation from the Americans for Democratic Action (presented by Eleanor Roosevelt) for a speech titled "The Right Way Is Not a Moderate Way," of which fifty thousand copies were printed and distributed. Modeling her print campaign for attitude change on Smith's, Boyle directed her efforts at her own state and social class—civic spokesmen and leaders, often denominationally Presbyterian and Episcopalian. For a time she clung to the hope that "moderation" was a possible stance. Both Boyle and Smith subscribed to the article of faith empowering them to

11. Susan Lynn, *Progressive Women in Conservative Times* (New Brunswick, N.J.: Rutgers University Press, 1994); Margaret Rose Gladney, ed., *How Am I to Be Heard? Letters of Lillian Smith* (Chapel Hill: University of North Carolina Press, 1993), 110, 209; Lillian Smith, *Killers of the Dream* (New York: W. W. Norton, 1944); Lillian Smith, *Strange Fruit* (New York: Reynal & Hitchcock, 1949).

12. Gladney, *How Am I to Be Heard?*, 220.

become prophets of change because they were writers: "Good words [need to be] spoken before good acts are done." They intended to alter the fact that "few good words against segregation and for human rights had yet been said in public."[13]

Within the segregated South, these two (and a few other) white women, fought the same war from the same high-minded principle—a belief that blacks and whites would both benefit from desegregation—with the same weapons: words and authorial voice.[14] Directing her print arrows at the "respectable church folk" in her own backyard, Boyle addressed an "in-house" readership; Smith aimed at intellectuals and media-gurus at the apex of the publishing world. Boyle's birthright churchfolk occupied a very specialized subculture in southern religion: Episcopalians were the self-designated upper crust in a self-designated upper-crust state, Virginia. Irrefutably born and bred of it, she was the rare person secure enough to challenge it. At the same time, as its product-turned-prophet, she was culturally constrained in a way that Lillian Smith was not.

In her incisive analysis of Virginia Episcopal culture, the first point Boyle acknowledged was that she had assumed her psyche was deeply steeped in Episcopal spirituality. In reality, she came to see, that was only a superficial aspect of her cultural whole. More symbolically, she wrote, "My religion [had been vaguely] humanist, my denomination Southern, and my church Virginia" (29). With that pithy aphorism she captured the religious function of Lost Cause mythology in her upbringing, and illuminated the self-serving cloak of dignified supe-riority with which Virginia aristocrats like her forebears had armed themselves. As a dutiful child, she had embraced that belief system wholeheartedly: "Among all the nations of the world, the South shone forth as God's best creation" (7), one that opted for "inner glory" and valued "culture above prosperity . . . fairness above profit, . . . courtesy above triumph" (8–9). Boyle cast her reflections almost entirely in

13. E. Culpepper Clark, *The Schoolhouse Door: Segregation's Last Stand at the University of Alabama* (New York: Oxford University Press, 1993), 108; Loveland, *Lillian Smith*, 119, 214; Gladney, *How Am I to Be Heard?*, 203 n.; Loveland, *Lillian Smith*, 96.

14. See also Virginia Foster Durr, *Outside the Magic Circle* (Birmingham: University of Alabama Press, 1985), and Anne Braden, *The Wall Between* (New York: Monthly Review Press, 1985).

the language of social class, colloquial religion, and psychological insight, sometimes imitating and other times contrasting with the sharper philosophical, sociological, and political arguments employed by Lillian Smith. Both women could count on shocking, or at least surprising, their readers since females, in general, were expected to write in a more flowery mode and about nontroublesome themes.

The young Patty Boyle was born and raised, with one sister six years older, in a gracious, cultivated, if not wealthy, home on Virginia land that was still part of the original crown-grant plantation to her great-grandfather. Both parents were descended from First Families of Virginia, her father having become an Episcopal clergyman.[15] Thus, her budding self was nurtured in a "setting of twisted genetic and historical facts, of snobbery and exclusiveness" (8), which she was taught to regard as a superior "if intangible" asset. In succeeding quotes, her usage of the word *Negro* (which I preserve) is intended to allow the reader access to her mindset. Such terminology, an artifact of her time and mental world, has been retained here for coloration of her chosen autobiographical voice. Throughout her writing she employed both a confiding, personal tone that made it palatable for a reader to treat it as merely one female's story, and a direct, earnest prose style to signal her high seriousness. Anyone open to her message could not miss its import.

Virginia Episcopalians epitomized a unique English-country-house way of life, in her mother's worldview. Even in a relatively low-salaried clergy household, Patty was surrounded by adoring "Negro servants" (as she was raised to think), "a sort of semislavery arrangement, but nobody—that is, no white Southerner—thought it so at the time" (14). From the minuscule daily interchanges through which a child breathes in the attitudes permeating its home—what things were to be smiled at, what denied, what worthy of outrage, where one could seek comfort—Boyle became "saturated with the assumption that Negroes," however indispensable in the household, irrevocably "belonged to a lower order of man" (14). Although she depended on

15. For her use of "Lost Cause" imagery, see *Desegregated Heart*, 6, 9, 261; The Reverend Robert W. Patton, *An Inspiring Record in Negro Education: Historic Summary of Work of the American Church Institute for Negroes*, delivered to the National Council of the Episcopal Church, February 14, 1940 (n.p.: National Council, 1940).

the companionship of servants and their children to fill her lonely days
(she was schooled at home), she also accepted the southern aristocrat's
shield of detached superiority. "Negroes" were not to be held to or
judged by "our standards," because the higher morality expected of
whites like the Boyles would have been too demanding. "Negroes"
were expected to behave, ultimately, like small children "with ideas
that were cute and funny" (19) and to be evaluated "by a segregated,
separate standard" (14). Above all they were to stay in their place. She
came to call these ideas the "Southern Code" (21).

As she later discerned, the nostalgic emotional bonds, "tender
looks," and "softened voices" (11) of white southerners recalling the
"Negro" caretakers of their childhood were the product of careful
survival strategies on the part of black southerners. "Colored supervisors . . . kept Southern white children out of mischief," the adult
Patty realized, "by a combination of moral force and the strategy of
keeping them entertained. The typical upper-class white child's relationship with Negroes presented a kind of Utopia of entertainment,
protection, and care," free from the otherwise inescapable disciplines
and punishments that normally constrain relations between child and
adult. She wrote, "No wonder our eyes and mouths soften when we
recall their faces" (15).

When Boyle turned twelve, however, the Southern Code became a
rigid curriculum, her mother its instructor and catechiser. Her book
recorded each deliberate learning of racial distance and superiority,
which was often emotionally confusing or painful. "When my training
period was over, I was as close to a typical Southern lady as anyone ever
is to a typical anything . . . a mixture of high idealism and contradictory practice, of rigid snobbery and genuine human warmth." She had
learned that virtue itself was Anglo-Saxon, which, ipso facto, justified
the inequities of privilege meted out to blacks and whites. "I [always]
thought my relationship with Negroes altogether beautiful" (29).

Racial reeducation in the 1950s revealed the "serious malignancy"
in that romantic delusion. While we white folk "loved 'our Negroes'
downward," she wrote, because of their quaint ways, childish mental-
ities, and petty thieveries, Negroes were expected to "love us upward,"
not "despite any insignificant faults we might have had, but as though
we had none" (34). The white Virginian's internalized superiority of
lineage, historical status, and "rights," Boyle came to see, required daily,

unqualified affirmation from the Negroes who created the backdrop of everyday existence. When those Negroes exceeded the unarticulated but nevertheless inviolate boundaries of "place," however, they had to be fired. On several occasions, Boyle was thus summarily deprived of those who gave her true emotional nurturance in her early life. Further, she incorporated the female's sense of responsibility for enforcing those invisible barriers: "She [a maid who was also an art student] must suffer because I had permitted familiarity!" the "sort of thing [Mother had warned] must be stopped at once. It would be WRONG not to stop it—WRONG for her, as well as for me and the South," although just why was unclear. And at that point she was unable to analyze it. What she remembered was feeling like a child "caught in some enormous breach of the family's moral code"(40).

Her father, the Reverend Robert Williams Patton, a graduate of Virginia Theological Seminary, Alexandria, Virginia, was absent a great deal. As an ordained Episcopal clergyman, he administered the American Church Institute. This organization of nine church-supported schools was the only Episcopal agency "providing for the Negro Episcopalian." His retirement in 1940 brought him many national church accolades; he published a documentary history of the institute.[16] Most unusual for one of his time and social background, the Reverend Patton was a Virginia Episcopalian who knew that Negroes were victims of poverty and lack of access to education, rather than inherently limited in intellect—a stance implicitly challenged by Patty's mother. (This made him a significant element in his daughter's mid-life reeducation, a theme to which *The Desegregated Heart* alludes several times.) Since young Patty was educated in the pattern approved for daughters of the landed gentry, by tutor at home, she was sheltered from anything as productive of social conformity as a school experience, public or private. As a solitary girl, her only "companion" was writing, but apparently she moved successfully into southern-style courtship, counting up "beaux" and garnering many marriage proposals.

Unlike other white women awakening to racial injustice in the 1940s, Boyle was denied the experience of attending college, which, according to Susan Lynn, was the common experience freeing females

16. Robert E. Hood, *Social Teachings in the Episcopal Church* (Harrisburg, Pa: Morehouse Publishing, 1990), 115; Patton, *An Inspiring Record*.

to become racially progressive in the conservative social world of privileged whites during the 1930s and 1940s. In other ways, however, she was similarly privileged because of her social class background. She too had daytime hours to fill; she too was comfortable with words, ideas, and debate; she too took for granted the right to express her opinions publicly (when she chose to, as a middle-aged woman), first in print and then speaking in public forums. Boyle's conversion to social activism was also similar to that of the women who attended college in that interwar era because it was fostered not so much through church membership as through reinterpretation of the values of a religious commitment implanted through her lifelong church involvement.[17] Generations of white churchfolk had managed to avoid thinking about the racial inequities that progressive daughters like Boyle in elitist Virginia were about to challenge.

In 1939, Boyle married a young drama professor and settled into domesticity, leaving home in one sense but still essentially rooted in childhood attitudes and customs. Even on his minuscule salary, she took for granted "a Negro maid." She also began, perhaps by rote, weekly attendance at "the university church," the Episcopal church in Charlottesville that drew its congregation from the nearby University of Virginia. Not content with dabbling in oil painting and caring for her two young sons, born in the early 40s, she secretly wrote and sold pulp fiction—giving herself a kind of closet career.[18] At some level, however, none of the more typical white matron activities sufficed. A deep spiritual yearning began to surface, perhaps in unconscious reference to the concerns that had animated her father's unusual work. What she expressed initially was the awareness that she had no commitment to anything larger than herself, a consciousness that there must exist, somewhere, a serious channel into which she could pour her total moral energy.

Boyle first articulated this longing in a letter that was part of a lengthy spiritual correspondence with the godfather to one of her sons, the Reverend Chad Walsh. Since she was a woman who loved words

17. Lynn, *Progressive Women in Conservative Times*, 28, 1.
18. Myra Dinnerstein, *Women between Two Worlds* (Philadelphia: Temple University Press, 1992), 41; Brett Harvey, *The Fifties, A Women's Oral History* (New York: Harper, 1994), 128–29, cites an unconscious need among educated women for "something to fall back on"—work as a footnote to the rest of their lives.

and found identity through writing, she had always been one who "thought things out" in letters; she herself labeled this particular letter "the most significant of the 'who am I?' statements" from her early forties. Also she was seeing a psychotherapist for help with childrearing—a fairly unusual step at the time, except among the highly educated and some urban sophisticates. In 1948, Boyle typed the following sentences to Walsh. "[I've begun to realize that] I've never been confronted with one full-size job that I thought was worth doing with my full strength," she wrote. Intensity leaps from the page. "I'm not being used, my energy is not fully consumed. I feel the constant pressure of repressed power." Then she joked self-deprecatingly: "Doesn't this all add up? I'm a potential fanatic who has not yet found my cause." Prophetically, she continued, "Nothing could stand between me and my objective if I were fired with faith and conviction."[19] Nineteenth-century women would have recognized this desire as readiness for a "call" or vocation, but such words were no part of Patty Boyle's Episcopal vocabulary. Like Harriet Beecher Stowe a century earlier, she harbored the conviction that only religion could provide "an all-redeeming" kind of "reason for absolutely condemning slavery." In Boyle's era, this meant addressing and discarding Jim Crow living and the sin of white supremacy.[20]

Her first awareness of "racism" as a concept emerged during World War II, in connection with anti-Semitism. "Perceptions of our own iniquities almost always come, first, through the shocked discovery of . . . [those same] sins in others"(47), she noted. Her personal "Ask Not for Whom the Bell Tolls" summons arrived in July 1950, when African American Gregory Swanson sued for admittance to the University of Virginia Law School in Charlottesville, the first nonwhite to successfully challenge the 125 years of whites-only at "Jefferson's university." As she read the newspaper story, Boyle recalled "clearly hearing the voice of Justice ring out above the clamoring of my well-learned Southern code" (50). She realized she was both exhilarated and terrified: here was one white Episcopalian who would welcome this brave pioneer. But what if he were lynched? "I felt as men must

19. Sarah Patton Boyle to Chad Walsh, December 28, 1948, in author's possession.
20. Alfred Kazin, "Her Holiness," *New York Review of Books*, December 1, 1994, 39–40.

have felt when wartime armies were manned by volunteers. . . . My inner land of shining ideals and eternal principles was calling for an army to fight the tyrant [known as] propriety and custom" (52).

Among churchgoing southern whites, Boyle was unusually hopeful about the possibility of harmony between the races, thanks to her father's sympathies and her as-yet-untested belief that Christian standards of justice could be achieved if people just admitted how much better that would make everything. In the religious "boom" after the Second World War, segregated mainline churches expanded into the suburbs and built large parish halls known as "education wings" but did not confront their racial exclusiveness. Meanwhile Swedish sociologist Gunnar Myrdal and a distinguished team of researchers published the first major study of race in all aspects of national life, *The American Dilemma: The Negro Problem and Modern Democracy*, and Lillian Smith, her two bestsellers.[21] Though Boyle registered them, events in the larger society such as baseball player Jackie Robinson finally breaching the color barrier in 1947 made little impact on her. She read the first bestseller to name prejudice (anti-Semitism) in American institutions and social life, *Gentleman's Agreement* by Laura Z. Hobson, that same year. And there was a new white author, James Michener, who dramatized examples of racial attitudes on the Asian front during the recent war in *Tales of the South Pacific*.

White churchgoers in all mainline denominations continued to ignore both the separate and unequal lives of their black fellow Christians, and the concurrent buildup of the legal precedents that would undergird the 1954 Supreme Court decision outlawing segregated schools. In her sheltered Virginia world, Boyle continued to believe that "the majority of educated Southerners were ready to throw off the yoke of injustice to 'Negroes' [when finally] it was called to their attention" (56). The welcoming letter she "just naturally" dashed off to Mr. Swanson—offering him any help he might need at the University—was the gesture of a gracious Episcopal lady, certainly not intended as a battle cry.

Hurt by Swanson's total lack of response to her generous if unconsciously patronizing letter, Boyle felt impelled to try to meet him in

---

21. Gunnar Myrdal, *An American Dilemma: The Negro Problem and Modern Democracy* (New York: Harper & Row, 1944).

person, to understand his rebuff. In some ways still an unsophisticated country girl despite her inborn "social security" (5), Boyle possessed the ability to construct a course of self-education when something became really important to her. Combining diligent library research and interviews, she began to seek out people who could interpret "the Southern Code" from the African American point of view. The mechanism that finally freed her from her white Episcopal blinders was the series of "lessons" to which she, a middle-aged churchgoing matron, submitted herself, a pragmatic "school" in which she faced up to, evaluated, and cast off the racist lenses she had worn since adolescence.

She came to know many black Virginians for the first time, most importantly the man who became her "tutor." T. J. Sellers was the local manager of a black insurance company and the Charlottesville editor of the black weekly newspaper *The Tribune.* Boyle's "lessons" commenced when, unsuspecting, she sent Mr. Sellers the article with which she proposed to launch her print campaign for better race relations. A well-written newspaper essay, it presented her idealistic thesis that white southerners, by which she, of course, meant the best educated and the highest-minded, genuinely desired an end to segregation. She expected to receive his admiration and congratulations, possibly even an expression of gratitude. But in a long, detailed letter, "point by point Mr. Sellers laid my Southernisms bare" (83).

She was utterly astonished. Her magnanimity had been totally misunderstood by this man, the first African American ever to speak to her as an equal, one who dared presume to instruct her, a white lady, about race. "No greater dislocation of my thought and emotion could have resulted if I had been catapulted to another planet" (84–85), she recalled. The points she learned in the succeeding weekly tutorials, as she consulted him about her writings, "knocked down my segregation walls" (102) and outlined the Southern Code in stark realism. "I learned new attitudes by becoming conscious of the faulty content of old ones" (104), such as her learned inability to address Negroes with the courtesy titles of Mr., Mrs., and Miss. Hitherto she had thought nothing of demanding private information, such as "how can you afford" some particular thing (113). Also, she recognized the flaw in paternalism: "If you feel obliged to whitewash Negroes," Sellers warned, "it's because you secretly think of them as not being good enough as they really are" (114). Confronted with the realization that she had never truly thought of blacks as "*full* Americans," she wrote, "Large as are the economic and civic wrongs of the South against her colored citizens, the tallest of our wrongs is our failure to see them as native sons" (116).

By spring 1951, Boyle had begun to realize that championing deseg-regation would be far more demanding than she had even imagined. To reassure herself that she was capable of engaging in this noble crusade, she compiled a list of her qualifications. First, signaling un-examined confidence in her social status (characteristically, she later saw), came her membership in the First Families of Virginia—self-affirmation of her ultimate "insider-dom" instead being a dreaded "outside agitator." Second came her genetically "low quota of fear . . . I felt disgustingly secure," recalling her kin relationship with "Old Blood-and-Guts," General George Patton of World War II fame (4). Third, she listed her "considerable energy and persistence," the po-tential fanaticism she had earlier noted. Fourth, she was already "an experienced, even mildly successful . . . popular-type writer . . . I knew I had a knack for [verbal] presentation." Fifth was her religious iden-tification and faith, though had she been confronted at the time for listing it last, she would have insisted that she always put it first when mentally summarizing what she thought of as her assets (119–20).

Boyle's list and its ranking is a time-capsule that reveals mid-twentieth-century white America's lack of realism about the evils of segregation. It is almost a credal statement of the romantic belief, to which Patty herself subscribed, that if a person did "what was right" to the best of one's ability, "all necessary help from Above" would just naturally bring good out of it. Her guileless plan? "As I lived out the St. Francis prayer in the South ["Lord, make me an instrument of thy peace,"], hatred and evil would dissolve" (121).

Boyle's summary of her "strengths" captured both the psychic blind-ness inherent in her elite Anglo-Protestant religious self-understanding and its inescapable limitations. She never doubted her "right" or abil-ity, even though she fancied herself a docile wife and daughter, to tackle any problem on which she might focus her full intelligence and will. Daughters of American Protestant clergy historically enjoyed a degree of intellectual and personal authority unavailable to other women, especially well-brought-up white southern females of the 1940s. What she lacked, and could only gain through painful experience, was the reality of evil—the complex truths in the experience of whites and blacks living in the same town and worshiping the same God in very different style and circumstance. She was still mired in "blinkered Victorianism," the caustic phrase her fellow regionalist W. J. Cash used to describe his clearsighted view of southern religion. Like Sarah Patton Boyle after the scales fell from her eyes, he characterized southern politics as the true religion, "the temple wherein men participated in the mysteries of the common brotherhood of white males," and partook of "the holy sacrament of Southern loyalty and hate." Cash caricatured southern Episcopalians as worshippers of "a God without body, parts, or passion," their religion "an abstraction for intellectuals . . . [one] that politely ignores hell and talks mellifluously of a God of Love." They invest, he said, in "understatement" and regard "emotion as a kind of moral smallpox." [22]

The Sunday after her self-evaluative list-making (early May 1951), Boyle went to church "stiff with anxiety, " the Southern Code ringing in her head. But the words of the opening hymn directly assured her soul about the oneness of humanity: "Earth shall be fair and all her people one; / Nor till that hour shall God's whole will be done." Another hymn just before the sermon contained a second sign: "Once to every man and nation / Comes the moment to decide, / In the strife of truth with falsehood / For the good or evil side." Even the sermon seemed personally affirming, however euphemistic in discourse. Its assurance was that by following "what seems to you the highest course, you have made the right decision" and need not fear that "later developments" will devalue or destroy it (134). Here were mysterious but apt leadings of the Divine, identifiable to one who knew the code, oblique to an outsider. Kneeling among her unsuspecting fellow worshippers that morning, Boyle felt her enlistment in the cause of desegregation confirmed, even sanctified. She had made a life commitment in the presence of God and her congregation, however unaware of her vow they might have been.

Boyle began to pour her energies primarily into writing for publication, following Lillian Smith's lead. Like other progressive women

22. W. J. Cash, *The Mind of the South* (New York: Alfred A. Knopf, 1941), 81–82, 55–56.

in the pre–Civil Rights era she had total confidence in the power of rhetoric; she organized a campaign of letters to the editors of southern newspapers.[23] Quoting Smith in an explanatory letter to her spiritual advisor Walsh, Boyle announced that her reason for undertaking this effort was to provide southern whites with a "new vocabulary" of positive ways to think about race. She had learned from Mr. Sellers that blacks were far more careful readers of editorial pages, far better informed about the opinions of whites than whites were about those of "Negroes." To that end she also wrote reviews of books by and about African Americans, articles for church magazines, and a column for the local newspaper edited by Mr. Sellers. Her intention was "to sow love" and new understanding in imitation of St. Francis (136). Also in her new internal identification with blacks, she pushed her way past "stony-faced whites" to try a seat in the back of the bus. "No day now passed without my suffering humiliations 'because of color,' " was the way she described her adopted consciousness (144).

Among American denominations, the Episcopal church remains an anomaly, thanks to its historic blending of Catholic ritual and liturgy with Protestant organization and emphasis on the authority of the Word, the Holy Bible. In the 1950s, it was also the quintessence of white, classist, social conformity. Her parish was dominated by a white male hierarchy, as were all mainline churches then, its pews filled with educated and devout women. The majority of Episcopal women in the 1950s did not become "professionals" but created careers of volunteerism and community good works, using their energies in the secular world of art museums or city planning boards. Boyle's awareness that she needed some kind of religiously sanctioned outlet for her "calling" was atypical. But a few other women with the same determination were entering the then new professional church role for laywomen as directors of religious education in large, multistaff parishes. It was the only leadership role open to church women, other than presiding over their own separate church organization, Woman's Auxiliary. Females of Boyle's background rarely thought of holding paid jobs. They expected to wear hats and white gloves to Woman's Auxiliary teas, and evidenced no awareness that

23. Lynn, *Progressive Women in Conservative Times,* 1.

their status in their religious institution was one of "privileged subordination."[24]

Boyle directed her print weapons at the churchfolk in her world, undoubtedly based on a preacher's daughter's instinct about the kinds of authority, formal and informal, that people unconsciously vested in the rector of a congregation. A deeply internalized formality governed gesture and thought for 1950s Episcopalians—giving rise to self-mocking stereotypes such as "God's Frozen People," "Whiskeypalians," "The Republican Party at Prayer," or even "Wall St. at Prayer." Members, fearful of spontaneity and "standing out," expected rational, orderly worship that was free of spontaneous exclamations or unprogrammed interruptions. Such self-protective unanimity helped determine what issues a congregation would or would not treat as "social causes," problems worthy of rector-sanctioned attention.

Unsurprisingly, when Boyle "went public" with her analysis of Episcopal and white-southern self-understanding in the mid-1950s, she created an earthquake. Fellow parishioners unabashedly recalled thinking that she must be "crazy."[25] "The average white American [of the kind she knew] never thinks about the innate dignity of man because he has never had his dignity challenged," Boyle wrote in *The Desegregated Heart*, "it cannot be for him a living issue" (174). Her characterization of white liberal self-protection was expanded a decade later by Jonathan Daniels, a New England Episcopal seminarian participating in the voter registration drive in Selma, Alabama, who wrote, "Liberalism [for Episcopalians] seems to mean not hating—and not doing anything to rock the boat."[26] Boyle's targeted readership, white mainstream-Protestant moderates, was still trying to avoid

24. A fictional portrait of the era is Frances Gray Patton's *Good Morning, Miss Dove* (New York: Dodd, Mead, 1954); Mary S. Donovan, *A Different Call: Women's Ministries in the Episcopal Church 1850–1920* (Wilton, Conn.: Morehouse Barlow, 1986); Margaret M. Miles, "Theory, Theology, and Episcopal Churchwomen" in *Episcopal Women: Gender, Spirituality and Commitment in a Mainline Denomination,* ed. Catherine M. Prelinger, 330–44.

25. An anonymous, contemporary telephone interview with the author, May 12, 1994.

26. Eagles, *Outside Agitator,* 70; F. Jonathan Bass, "Not Time Yet: Alabama's Episcopal Bishop and the End of Segregation 1955–69," *Anglican and Episcopal History* 63 (June 1994): 235–59.

the collision of its way of life with a consciousness aroused to its own racism.

By autumn of 1954, Boyle had published some five dozen articles "in Negro newspapers, and six dozen aimed specifically at Southern whites, book reviews, articles, and letters to the editor, [primarily] in the *Richmond Times-Dispatch* and the *Norfolk Virginian-Pilot*" (189). But after the Supreme Court decree that schools must desegregate, albeit with all deliberate speed, she realized that she must speak as well as write. Lillian Smith's slogan, "segregation is spiritual lynching," helped impel Boyle to conquer her southern-lady shrinking from the public platform.[27] For the public hearing about desegregating Charlottesville schools, one hundred forty-three people registered to speak. The hearing lasted fourteen hours. During the time she was there, Boyle heard sixty-eight segregationists; she was one of only seven white integrationists to speak (193). Then, in the February 19, 1955, issue of the *Saturday Evening Post*, her pro-desegregation article appeared. Wanting to attract the maximum number of readers, the editor had replaced the title Boyle submitted (Episcopalian in its quiet understatement), "We Southerners Are Readier than We Think," with the inflammatory "Southerners Will *Like* Integration."

What followed was "an abrupt change in the social climate." It became, in her words, "a chain of small wounds" (221). The boy at the newsstand where she bought her copy of the magazine refused to meet her eyes; friends crossed the street to avoid her. Telephone calls from the white citizens councils contained overt threats. Boyle believed in her heart that many among her social circle really "wanted to rally to the call of the highest that they knew," but their words conveyed uncertainty rather than conviction. They raised questions about what was "fair," "open-minded," and "looking at all sides;" they seemed mortally afraid of taking "an *extreme* stand," an abiding Episcopalian concern (215). "At church, at parties and chance gatherings, I found symptoms of embarrassment . . . people avoided looking at me, talked faster than normal . . . [would] feverishly steer conversation along impersonal lines, and at the first opportunity latched onto someone else to talk to" (220). A few who admired her desegregationist stand came to see her in private but were nowhere near her in public. No

27. Lillian Smith, "Addressed to White Liberals," in Loveland, *Lillian Smith*, 58.

one in her own congregation would "discuss" the topic at all, though she did receive letters of support from strangers and from three elderly women at St. Paul's.

The cross-burning on Boyle's front lawn in 1956 was both an expression of outrage at her betrayal of the Southern Code, and acknowledgment of her success. When she peered out the window at a six-foot cross of flames, she recalled basking in its irony: tormentors were trying to punish her with the cardinal symbol of redemptive Christian love. Newspapers in Norfolk and Charlottesville, Virginia, carried the story with her photo (taken by her teenage son) and the caption "Mrs. S. P. Boyle Not Frightened by Mobster"; it was subsequently picked up by the *Washington Post*.[28] This was the same year in which the state of Virginia initiated a program of "massive resistance," testing the theory that desegregation could not be enforced if the entire state government opposed it. Compulsory public-school attendance laws were repealed, whites-only "private" schools sprang up, and the state vowed to close any public schools actually targeted for desegregation by the federal courts.[29] Boyle was horrified at the fundamental bigotry revealed by her beloved South; she recalled Jesus' vocabulary of despair over his contemporaries' blindness: "Jerusalem, Jerusalem, ye would not!" (224).

The mechanisms used by whites to avoid desegregation, recounted in *The Desegregated Heart*, are a profile of liberal mid-twentieth-century Americans in general, not just Episcopalians.[30] Friends would press cash into her hand rather than sign anything, Boyle recalled (266). Invited to speak at churchwomen's meetings, she saw them listen politely and then heard their subsequent disparagements whispered

28. Kathleen Murphy Dierenfield, "One 'Desegregated Heart'—Sarah Patton Boyle and the Crusade for Civil Rights in Virginia," *Virginia Magazine of History and Biography* 104 (spring 1996): 251–84.

29. Philip A. Gibbs, "Virginia School Closing Experiment," in *Encyclopedia of African-American Civil Rights*, ed. Charles D. Lowery and John F. Marszalek (New York: Greenwood Press, 1992), 556; Robbins L. Gates, *The Making of Massive Resistance: Virginia's Politics of School Desegregation 1954–1956* (Chapel Hill: University of North Carolina Press, 1964); Neil R. McMillen, *The Citizens' Council: Organized Resistance to the Second Reconstruction* (Urbana: University of Illinois Press, 1971); and Robert C. Smith, *They Closed Their Schools: Prince Edward County, Virginia 1951–1964* (Chapel Hill: University of North Carolina Press, 1965).

30. Lillian Smith, *How Am I to Be Heard?*, 203; Calvin Trillin, "State Secrets," *New Yorker*, May 29, 1995, 55.

to the hostess. Her name had become anathema, the kiss of death to any petition she endorsed (277).

Gradually, Charlottesville parents and businessmen came to the realization that Virginia's lack of public education was doing them more economic damage than desegregation would. In September 1959, the public schools reopened, desegregated, and the world did not come to an end. "Quietly but quickly, white society opened its gates to me again. . . . Daily woundings ceased, daily pleasantries took their place" (290). A former friend seized her hand on the church steps and said, "I've thought of you and prayed about you so often in these months. Can't we get together?" (291). All this turnaround made Boyle feel "homeless in a vast sense" (299). She was dazed when another congregant whispered, "You'll never know what you meant to me, through all this. You saved my faith in the South" (292). She had survived this racial milestone of change, thanks to support from the National Association for the Advancement of Colored People, the American Friends Service Committee, the Virginia Council on Human Relations, and a few other southern voices willing to speak in favor of racial equality. But the bitter denominational truth—that real support had come to her only from outside rather than inside her own church—had taken both psychic and spiritual tolls.

Sarah Patton Boyle does not detail the profound depression into which she fell after this stressful time. She skips, rather, to recovery, where she found that a revitalized language of biblical images and childhood faith alone was capable of expressing her new understandings of racial justice and equality. The last six chapters of her book analyze, in theological terms, the "death" of her own "Golden Calf" [the idol of the Southern White Myth] (317) and of her being "resurrected" into a state of "salvation" that reconnected her with the blessed oneness of humanity. Having endured the depths of disillusionment, she discovered "the emptiness" of the euphemism on which she and her generation of liberal churchmembers had relied, "the highest that one knows." To her surprise she found that only orthodox, old-fashioned Christian words and concepts now became living realities to her— God, Love, service to one's fellow human beings, and an actual "saving" person, divine and human, Jesus Christ—could fill that emptiness (303). Religion and words from her childhood faith furnished the only language that could elevate her experience of despair to cosmic meaning and significance.[31]

Boyle's "conversion" illustrates the individualist nature of the Episcopal faith experience: she had to work it out by and for herself. Embedded within the deep spiritual nurture to be found in Anglican piety was a twofold path. It presented her with both the freedom to determine the form of her own personal discipleship and the spiritual mandate to define it on her own. As with her church's interpretation of scripture, she was constrained by what she had absorbed of its theology, but at the same time she was required to use her own powers of reason. In contrast with the views of other denominations, particularly the Quakers (Friends), corporate stands on an issue of conscience, to say nothing of unified action, were simply "un-Episcopalian."[32] Corporate Sunday morning worship in her kind of congregation provided a canopy of unity (language, gesture, and prayer) that paradoxically nurtured the inner autonomy of individual worshippers by giving them wide latitude for working out their personal meanings and commitments.

Beyond the congregational culture itself, the larger society also promulgated a "lone warrior" view of heroic isolation. Neither the concept of "support group" nor the soon-to-appear women's movement were available to Boyle. She had to find internal solace within corporate worship. Congregational individualism had not yet been mitigated by the "Exchange of the Peace" ritual that would be adopted in the 1960s, a liturgical innovation prescribing direct touch and eye contact that might have helped breach her physical solitude.[33] From the age of forty-four, the awakening moment when Boyle discovered that blacks did not "automatically" love her, her criticism of the Southern Code "excluded [her] from a corporateness of which I had once been wholeheartedly a part" (90). Painfully she came to see that her Episcopal heritage would not in itself be a source of public affirmation; her survival was testament primarily to the internal spiritual strength

---

31. Joanna B. Gillespie, "Racial Desegregation and the Conversion of Sarah Patton Boyle," Episcopal Women's History Conference, Raleigh, N.C. (June 1995).

32. Hood, *Social Teachings*, 106.

33. Joanna B. Gillespie, *Women Speak of God, Congregations and Change* (Valley Forge, Pa.: Trinity Press International, 1994).

derived from it. Among the "large slice of the White South [that had] stood at the crossroads in its attitude toward its colored citizens," and in her own local congregation, Boyle was the rarity who did not succumb to the self-protective rationalization "that each [of us] was too isolated to make an effective stand" (77).

The only overt criticism Boyle leveled at her church was expressed in an invited paper, "The Witness of a Lone Layman." She delivered it at the national office in New York on October 9, 1962, to the Christian Social Relations Department of the Executive Council of the Episcopal Church—one of four papers submitted by the Intergroup Committee on which she was the only woman.[34] She used that presentation to address, in her own direct but polite way, the bankruptcy of the moderate white Episcopal position as one that fell far short of even secular humanist pro-civil rights advocacy.

Boyle's opening trumpet call employed the standard 1950s euphemisms. "In regard to the brotherhood of man," she wrote, "the position of the Christian Church as a whole and of the Episcopal Church specifically, is without equivocation." Today the polite indirectness of that diction makes us impatient, but she and her listeners both understood it as elevated code for the blatant term *race*. Employing poetic and biblical imagery, she named "separation from others by elevation of self"—another euphemism, this for white superiority— as the "serpent in the garden" of earthly society. None are "so angry, bitter, and ruthless as a society whose sense of superiority is being assailed," she wrote. Therefore, white southerners who "fight *for* the brotherhood of man," aware of its contrasting meanings for black and white Americans, are "a tiny band of pioneers . . . so threatened with martyrdom and tempted toward apostasy that most of us hide in caves and catacombs of silence."[35]

Boyle's use of male pronouns and imagery in her witness is jarring to modern feminist ears but to Boyle, the use of her voice about race and justice as a woman, and for the cause of feminism itself, was secondary. In that she was typical of many women in her church. Episcopal

34. Minutes of the National Council, 1962, National Archives of the Episcopal Church, Austin, Tex. Throughout the 1950s and 1960s, "Intergroup" was the euphemism for interracial work.
35. Boyle, "The Witness of a Lone Layman."

women, in general, publicly eschewed feminism; it was considered extreme and beneath the attention of educated and refined females until the 1970s.[36] Additionally her confident use of generic male language may well have signified an easy, familial identification with the white male church establishment—an unquestioned assumption that she, a well-connected daughter of the church, was, of course, included in concepts such as *mankind* and *brotherhood*. The audience to which she addressed this print sermon was largely male: ordained Episcopal priests and bishops in top leadership posts. Ultimately, her high-toned language that struggled to remain dispassionate would be understood by all sophisticated males and females in that Episcopal era.

Few, if any, white Episcopalians had been so openly accusatory of their denomination's racial equivocation to that point, although some African American laymen, such as Benjamin Wright, at St. Paul's Episcopal Church, in Englewood, New Jersey, were voicing similar observations. In the eyes of many white "and even more colored Americans," Boyle summarized, "the Church's ineffectuality in this crisis is sufficient proof that she is out of date and can no longer lead man to his highest expression." She continued, less in apocalyptic warning than in dignified grief, "If our Church had a vital response" to the challenge of desegregation, it might indeed lose those "unwilling to live according to [the church's highest] precepts," but it would "gain" those "who wished so to live," the many humanist, semi-Christian, and uncommitted Episcopalians yearning for a note of sterling Christian leadership on racial justice. Instead, the institutional church was "lagging behind." Strugglers for a more just society are "in *very great* need of our Church's sympathetic ear and special backing," she pleaded. Fighting racism (a word that did not appear in this essay) was not just one among many "commendable activities" the church should undertake, but the crucial one, "the right of the bleeding," should give Brotherhood Fighters first claim on the church's attention. "The whole Christian Church is failing her white and colored members"—and "failing her Lord, to the degree that we are part of His Body." Since Patty herself remained a faithful, if now openly critical, daughter of

36. See Gillespie, *Women Speak;* also Pamela Darling, *New Wine: The Story of Women Transforming Leadership and Power in the Episcopal Church* (Cambridge, Mass.: Cowley Publications, 1994).

the church, she personally would be heartsick if "victory [was won] for the brotherhood of man . . . [by] the humanists, not the Christians."[37]

The mental portrait of a petite, middle-aged Virginia housewife chastising a roomful of somber white males in clerical garb is a vivid image to serve as a capstone for this section of her biography.[38] That she was in the company of leading national civil rights spokesmen may have offered some comfort, but it could not heal the disillusion with her beloved church. This solitary female's "in-house" challenge to her denomination's hierarchy presaged the other confrontations that would emerge in the 1970s, as women challenged the church's males-only ordination policy. Boyle spoke here not as someone's wife or mother, not as a licensed educator or professional theologian, not even as the embodiment of the special institutional relationship a clergyman's daughter could once claim—but rather as a serious lay member demanding righteousness in her own church.

Throughout history, prophets have stood alone and unrewarded in their home territory. The civil rights drama in which Sarah Patton Boyle played an important precursor role continued to "unfold on television in serial snippets at the dinner hour" over the next ten years.[39] In the end, the moral rightness of southern African American Christians wordlessly compelled Christians of other races to respond to their dignity and strength. Mediated through the heritage of her father's unconventional openness to race but carrying it a generational step further, Sarah Patton Boyle fashioned her own activism toward racial justice out of her church's liturgy and habits of worship, with personal encouragement from her rector but little affirmation or support from fellow churchmembers.

Boyle was divorced at the age of sixty, moved to Arlington, Virginia, and eventually published another autobiographical report—what she learned through "creative aging" while having to start life over again.

37. Boyle, "The Witness of a Lone Layman."
38. Minutes of the National Council, October 9, 1962, recorded her presentation as "peripheral to the interest of the Church," treating her paper as a merely "personal" statement. I am grateful to Gardiner Shattuck for this reference.
39. Arthur P. Kempton, "How Far from Canaan?" *New York Review of Books*, April 21, 1994, 59–65; James F. Findlay, "Religion and Politics in the Sixties: The Churches and the Civil Rights Act of 1964," *Journal of American History* 77 (June 1990): 66–92.

She died quietly in her apartment in 1994. In March 1994, the Episcopal House of Bishops, for the first time ever, issued an eight-page pastoral letter titled "The Sin of Racism" to be read in every parish during May 1994. A current emphasis in workshops on contemporary racism addresses the invisible systems of unacknowledged advantage for whites.[40] Today, although her church has a high evaluation of its own racial tolerance, Boyle's *The Desegregated Heart* still constitutes a useful text for unlearning the "lessons" of unacknowledged white privilege.[41]

40. Sarah Patton Boyle, *The Desert Blooms: Adventures in Creative Aging* (Nashville: Abingdon Press, 1983).

41. Roof and McKinney, in *American Mainline Religion*, list Episcopalians as one of the denominations foremost in acknowledging (at least rhetorically) racial minorities' rights. Quoted in David Holmes, *A Brief History of the American Episcopal Church* (Valley Forge, Pa.: Trinity Press International, 1993), 176. Peggy McIntosh, "White Privilege and Male Privilege: A Personal Account of Coming to See Correspondences through Work in Women's Studies," 1988 (Working Paper #189, Wellesley College Center for Research on Women, Wellesley, Mass.).

Alice Norwood Spearman Wright

Civil Rights Apostle to South Carolinians

MARCIA G. SYNNOTT

In August 1955, Alice Norwood Spearman, the executive director of the South Carolina Council on Human Relations, commented tellingly in her report to the Southern Regional Council on "an 'all-time low'" in interracial understanding caused by a widely publicized resolution of the "Committee of 52" South Carolinians. These "influential and highly respected" attorneys, bankers, businessmen, ministers, and politically well-connected whites denounced the United States Supreme Court's 1954 decision in *Brown* v. *Board of Education of Topeka*. The Court nullified states' rights and disrupted South Carolina's presumed "harmonious" race relations, they alleged, by following the advice of sociologists and psychologists "tainted" by Communist propaganda. The "revolt in high places," as Spearman called it, spurred massive resistance in South Carolina by encouraging the activities of the Citizens' Councils, States' Rights Leagues, and the Ku Klux Klan. Although Spearman's lineage included a maternal great-grandfather who had been one of the state's largest slave owners, her egalitarian outlook and commitment to racial justice drove her to work for desegregation. In contrast to her social peers, this unusual woman served as one of the state's most dedicated civil rights apostles.[1]

I would like to thank the following repositories for allowing me to use their manuscripts and/or oral histories: the South Caroliniana Library, Columbia; the Southern Historical Collection, Library of the University of North Carolina at Chapel Hill; the South Carolina Historical Society, Charleston; and Archives and Special Collections, Dacus Library, Winthrop University, Rock Hill, South Carolina.

1. Alice N. Spearman (hereinafter ANS), executive director, South Carolina Council on Human Relations (hereinafter cited as SCCHR), August 1955 Report, Southern Regional Council Papers Microfilm Edition, Reel 146, Harvard

Alice Norwood Spearman thought differently from other upper-middle-class southern whites. Her life story encourages a reconceptualization of some of the events that shaped twentieth-century South Carolina history, particularly its civil rights movement. Through her work on the South Carolina Council on Human Relations, as executive secretary in the late 1940s, and then as executive director from 1954 to 1967, Spearman (her last name during those years) endeavored to promote an interracial dialogue that would facilitate South Carolinians' acceptance of desegregation. Believing that women could be key participants, she recruited white clubwomen and their allies, those who were active in organizations such as the South Carolina Federation of Women's Clubs, the League of Women Voters, the American Association of University Women, the Young Women's Christian Association, and churchwomen's groups to work in the South Carolina Council.

Although Spearman failed to win over more than a few individual white clubwomen in support of the Supreme Court's decision, her campaign, nevertheless, helped convince the African American community that some white South Carolinians were committed to racial justice. In addition, the resistance that her campaign encountered among prominent white clubwomen clearly defined the parameters of the moderate-conservative position on racial issues in South Carolina. White women, no less than white men, knew just how far and how fast they were willing to be pushed to accept change in racial relationships. While at interracial meetings, white women discussed ways of bettering the status of African Americans, but they really did not want desegregation in the public schools. Based on her previous experiences at Converse College, in the Young Women's Christian Association (YWCA), and in the South Carolina Federation of Women's Clubs, Spearman, however, had come to believe that women, when told the truth, could be persuaded, perhaps sooner than men, to deal justly with the issues. Ultimately, she was proved wrong, despite her compelling message. Yet, her actions showed how much she, a white elite southern woman, had personally liberated herself from the South's racial prejudices and gender conventions.

University Library, Cambridge, Mass.; Charles Joyner, *Down by the Riverside: A South Carolina Slave Community* (Urbana: University of Illinois Press, 1984), 28–30.

From Spearman's educational, travel, and work experiences, wrote one interviewer, "the South Carolina banker's daughter developed a sense of compassion, a rejection of race as a measure of individual worth, and a desire 'to teach people to raise hell and do something.' "[2] She came to believe in the welfare state, an independent labor movement, strong civil liberties, the goal of racial equality, and the peaceful resolution of international disputes. As an individual whose activities spanned the decades from the 1920s to the late 1960s, she served as a bridge between two generations of white women activists, those who came of age between 1910 and 1930 and those who joined civil rights protests in the 1960s. Thus, Spearman should be included in that small group of southern white women who, in the 1940s and 1950s, transcended class conditioning to oppose segregation: Virginia Durr in Alabama; Anne Braden in Kentucky; Lillian Smith and Paula Snelling in Georgia, Sarah Patton Boyle in Virginia, and Katharine Du Pre Lumpkin, a Georgian transplanted to South Carolina.[3]

Spearman was born in 1902 in Marion, South Carolina, a small town located between the Great and Little Pee Dee Rivers, to Samuel Wilkins Norwood and Albertine Buck Norwood. The Norwoods were a prominent banking and business family. Young Alice Buck Norwood was in awe of her logical, austere father, and she admired the intuition and aesthetic appreciation of her lovely, dainty mother. Her parents shaped her nascent feminism, however, both by their restrictions and encouragement. Her father took an authoritarian approach to child rearing, and he once used a buggy whip on her when she came home

2. ANS quoted in Jack Bass, "South Carolinian Doesn't Pussy-Foot about Life," *Charlotte Observer,* January 3, 1967.
3. Susan Lynn, *Progressive Women in Conservative Times: Racial Justice, Peace, and Feminism, 1945 to the 1960s* (New Brunswick, N.J.: Rutgers University Press, 1992), 2, 28, 45, 65–66; Sara Evans, *Personal Politics: The Roots of Women's Liberation in the Civil Rights Movement and the New Left* (New York: Vintage Books, 1980), 26–29. In a biographical sketch of Alice Spearman Wright (hereinafter ASW), July 10, 1978, Jacquelyn Dowd Hall noted that Spearman had been described as an uncommon blend of a " 'Southern Lady' and a progressive woman." To Modjeska Simkins, an African American civil rights activist who belonged to the South Carolina Division of the Southern Regional Council, Spearman had "always been a vigilent [*sic*] and almost radical spirit." She was "a type of person like I am; she just doesn't give a damn" (Modjeska Simkins, interview by Jacquelyn Dowd Hall, Columbia, S.C., July 28–31, 1976, Southern Oral History Program Collection [hereinafter SOHPC], Manuscripts Department, Southern Historical Collection, University of North Carolina at Chapel Hill, Chapel Hill, N.C. [hereinafter SHC], 125–28).

late. If his manner made her resist male domination, his democratic leanings, independent thinking, and sense of social responsibility— he made bank loans to struggling farmers when he could—shaped her egalitarianism.[4]

On the one hand, her mother's restrictive social code and efforts to mold her into a lady, like her two younger sisters, also developed Spearman's resistance. She felt that trying to be Albertine Buck Norwood's type of lady had, as she put it in a 1981 interview, a "price that came too high." But on the other hand, Spearman understood that the role of a southern lady had its advantages; she used her charm and femininity to win over both men and women to her causes. Her mother also made her academically competitive by insisting that she take elocution lessons and excel in her Marion public school class. Spearman recognized that her mother's pushing her "may have unconsciously been in search for her own fuller self-realization, and in part a feminist answer to my father too." Her father admired her mother's physical appearance and social graces, but he never plumbed her intellectual depths. In retrospect, Spearman felt that she and her mother had teamed together to show her father that girls could be as good as boys. Compelled as an evolving liberal feminist "to see what was across the fence," she strove to develop her talents to the fullest, unfettered by gender, race, or social class.[5]

Spearman's views broadened significantly from 1919 to 1923 in the single-sex educational environment of Converse College, where she majored in history and literature and participated in YWCA activities, athletics, and student government. The senior class yearbook aptly described her as "one of those persons who seem ten people in one.

4. Spearman died on March 12, 1989. ASW, interview by Jacquelyn Dowd Hall, February 28, 1976, SOHPC; ASW, interview by Marcia G. Synnott (hereinafter MGS), July 10–11, 1983.

5. Spearman also had three younger brothers and an older half-brother from her father's first marriage. ASW, interview by Ann Y. Evans, July 3, 1981, in *Women Leaders in South Carolina: An Oral History*, ed. Ronald J. Chepesiuk, Ann Y. Evans, and Dr. Thomas S. Morgan, 42, 43 (televised by South Carolina ETV and funded in part by the South Carolina Committee for the Humanities and the Corporation for Public Broadcasting), Rock Hill, S.C.: Winthrop University Archives and Special Collections, 1984; ASW, interview by Hall, February 28, 1976; ASW, interview by MGS, July 10, 1983. See also Sara Alpern et al., eds., *The Challenge of Feminist Biography: Writing the Lives of Modern American Women* (Chicago: University of Illinois Press, 1992), 7–8; and Josephine Donovan, *Feminist Theory: The Intellectual Traditions of American Feminism* (New York: Continuum, 1992), 25–26.

188 MARCIA G. SYNNOTT

She has charm of personality and, best of all, ability—executive as well as scholastic." She served on both the student YWCA's interracial committee and its industrial commission; the latter's membership included equal representation of college students and women textile workers. Once an evangelical religious group, the student YWCAs had evolved into radical social gospel organizations; however, southern YWCAs would not integrate until World War II.[6]

Elected by Converse students to represent them at the southeast regional summer conferences that the National Student YWCA held at Blue Ridge, North Carolina, Spearman met African American YWCA secretaries and then "enjoyed telling my family that there were blacks who were so superior to us intellectually, culturally and spiritually." She also met YWCA secretary Katharine Du Pre Lumpkin. During a YWCA's six-week summer experiment, in 1922, Spearman and eleven other southern female students worked in industrial jobs in Atlanta; Spearman worked at the Fulton Bag and Cotton Mill. One of a small number of college-educated southern women, Spearman had become independent, self-confident, vocal, and enfranchised.[7]

Moving to New York City, she expanded her circle of acquaintances to include liberal, even politically radical, thinkers. Spearman took courses at the resident YWCA National Training School and earned a master's degree in religious education from Columbia Teachers College, where she was intellectually influenced by the democratic educational ideas of John Dewey and William Heard Kilpatrick. She also took a course at the Union Theological Seminary, rejected Bible fundamentalism and urged others to shed their provincialism.[8]

6. Alice Buck Norwood, *Y's and Other Y's, 1923* (Spartanburg, S.C.: Converse College, 1923), 26:66; Anne F. Scott, *Natural Allies: Women's Associations in American History* (Chicago: University of Illinois Press, 1991), 108, 180–81, 215 n. 68; Marion W. Roydhouse, "Bridging Chasms: Community and the Southern YWCA," in *Visible Women: New Essays on American Activism*, ed. Nancy A. Hewitt and Suzanne Lebsock (Chicago: University of Illinois Press, 1993), 270–95.
7. Prior to college, Spearman had known only black servants. ASW, interview by Evans, July 3, 1981; ASW, interview by Hall, February 28, 1976. Roydhouse, "Bridging Chasms," 273–74, 280–83; Lynn, *Progressive Women*, 28; Katharine Du Pre Lumpkin, *The Making of a Southerner* (Athens: University of Georgia Press, 1991).
8. ASW, interview by Evans, July 3, 1981; ASW, interview by Hall, February 28, 1976, and August 8, 1976, SOHPC; [ANS] to Dr. E. A. McDowell, September 10, 1947, SCCHR, South Caroliniana Library (hereinafter SCL), Columbia,

Bursting with ideas and enthusiasm, Spearman began work, in March 1927, at the YWCA in Germantown, Pennsylvania, and joined the Philadelphia race relations committee. Focusing on adult education and community organization, she developed skills in the YWCA's technique of involving people in discussions; she perfected them through her later work with the South Carolina Federation of Women's Clubs and the South Carolina Council on Human Relations.[9]

In 1930, after attending an international students' conference at Oxford, England, Spearman extended her trip into a three-year journey around the world. Traveling with a knapsack, she learned " 'offen a tin can,' " as she put it, referring to picking up information as she went, when she visited Sweden, joined a student group on a six-week trip to the Soviet Union, and journeyed through parts of the Middle East and India. At Lahore, she attended two conferences: the Fifth All-Indian Woman's Conference on Educational and Social Reform and the First All-Asian Woman's Conference. She subsequently visited the Philippines and attended the Institute for Pacific Relations Conference in Shanghai, China. Her travels taught her that contact with new people and new ideas was profoundly educational. That realization required a reorganization of her thinking. She returned to South Carolina in 1932; her father had died, and most of his assets were lost in the depression. Despite the family's reduced circumstances, "it was, as far as in my life[time] the perfect economic democracy," Spearman recalled: "nobody had money."[10]

Her outlook on life was thus shaped by her family background, Baptist upbringing, leadership activities at Converse College, student and adult YWCA work, international travels, and depression-era experience. To her liberal feminist perspective, Spearman added a socialist feminist insight about the nature of the white male power structure, sustained by class, gender, and race. Although it was unusual for someone with roots in a small provincial town to become a socialist, she was attracted to the Socialist Party while living in New York City.

S.C. William A. Link, *The Paradox of Southern Progressivism, 1880–1930* (Chapel Hill: University of North Carolina Press, 1992), 84, 203.

9. ASW, interview by Hall, August 8, 1976, 5–6.

10. ANS, notes for speech, undated, "Asia as I Saw It," 1–3, Alice Norwood Spearman Wright Personal Papers, SCL; ASW, interview by Hall, August 8, 1976; Bass, "South Carolinian," 8A; ASW, Interview by Evans, July 3, 1981.

During the 1930s, however, she gravitated to the New Deal. Although she proposed neither sweeping economic reforms, nor developed a sustained analysis of the socioeconomic class structure, she expressed strong commitment to a more equitable distribution of economic resources. And she was quite comfortable locating herself within the social action programs of the Christian Left.[11]

Because of her family's prominence and her own drive, Spearman was appointed director of the Social Service Department of the Marion County Emergency Relief Administration (ERA); she was the first South Carolina woman to administer a county relief program. To prevent her "material goods" from setting her apart from the relief families she visited, Spearman borrowed her brother's old, broken-down Ford and bought at a fire sale several dresses for herself for twenty-five cents each. She also encouraged people on relief to participate in decision making about the future.[12]

Her socialist views made trouble for her. She was shifted to a supervisory position, then, following her conversation with a textile worker about one of the seven pro-union men killed by special deputies or non-unionists during a general strike in September 1934, was recalled to Columbia. But Spearman, like other white southern women reformers of impeccable family lineage, was able to escape the consequences of a radical label. Indeed, social position would later protect her from harassment for civil rights activities during the 1950s and 1960s.[13]

Promoted to direct the statewide rural rehabilitation survey for the Works Progress Administration (WPA), Spearman determined which families should be transferred from relief to the rural resettlement program. In May 1935, she became state director of Workers' Education, an adult education effort jointly sponsored by the WPA and the South Carolina Department of Education. Invited to the White House for meetings of the directors of Workers' Education, Spearman

11. Eugene H. Spearman Jr., telephone conversation with MGS, September 20, 1990; Lynn, *Progressive Women*, 17–24, 3; Donovan, *Feminist Theory*, 65–69, 72–76, 82–85, 90.

12. ASW, interview by Hall, August 8, 1976; ASW, interview by MGS, July 11, 1983.

13. ASW, interview by Hall, August 8, 1976. David Robertson, *Sly and Able: A Political Biography of James F. Byrnes* (New York: W. W. Norton & Co., 1994), 177–79; Dewey W. Grantham, *Southern Progressivism: The Reconciliation of Progress and Tradition* (Knoxville: University of Tennessee Press, 1983), 200–217.

met Eleanor Roosevelt, who served, she thought, as "a perfect porter at the gate," quickly grasping the situation and relating it to President Franklin D. Roosevelt. However, Spearman felt that New Deal programs "didn't go far enough" and tended to save wealthy people, who rose to "the top of the economic power structure."[14]

In 1936, she married Eugene H. Spearman, who worked for the State Employment Service and the federal Rural Rehabilitation Program. They moved to his farm in Newberry, and when their only child, Eugene H. Spearman Jr. was born in 1937, her husband took over childcare duties so that she could continue in her position; despite the fact that both their jobs were partially funded by the state of South Carolina, under the Employment Act of 1932 both spouses could not continue to be employed by the federal government. She helped write political speeches for his Newberry County campaigns; he was twice elected supervisor. Their marriage was thus a partnership.[15]

Meanwhile, Alice Spearman's interests shifted toward human relations work. She had joined the South Carolina Commission on Interracial Cooperation in the 1930s and then was asked to serve on the executive committee in October 1942. Its moderately conservative leadership was exemplifed by chairman R. Beverley Herbert, a Columbia, South Carolina attorney, who believed that, despite their progress since emancipation, blacks lagged far behind whites in culture, education, and health standards. Spearman soon realized that while commission members might respond quickly as individuals to help African Americans, they had no desire for a mass movement. After the Commission on Interracial Cooperation was replaced by the Southern Regional Council (SRC) in August 1943, Spearman, Herbert, and others organized the South Carolina Division of the Southern Regional Council. It became the most inclusive and broad-based biracial civil rights organization in the state.[16]

14. ASW, interview by Hall, August 8, 1976; ASW, interview by Evans, July 3, 1981; ASW, interview by Hall, February 28, 1976; Alice B. Norwood, "Workers' Education," May 15, 1935, SCCHR, SCL.
15. Eugene H. Spearman Sr. attended Newberry College and served overseas in the army in World War I. Eugene H. Spearman Jr., interview by MGS, September 26, 1990, SCL; ASW, interview by Hall, August 8, 1976.
16. ASW, interview by Hall, August 8, 1976. J. M. Dabbs and ANS to "Dear Friend," June 13, 1947, SCCHR, SCL. Grantham, *Southern Progressivism*, 414; Link,

In 1951, family finances forced Spearman to seek full-time employment as executive secretary of the South Carolina Federation of Women's Clubs (SCFWC) and as associate editor of *Club Woman* magazine. During her three years as executive secretary, Spearman took as part of her salary living quarters for her family above the SCFWC's office.[17] The federation experience showed Spearman that women's feminine qualities—compassion, intuition, sensitivity to others, and "holistic" vision—could be a source of community building and reform. In October 1954, she eagerly seized the opportunity to become the first full-time, paid director of the South Carolina Council on Human Relations, the new name of this SRC affiliate. Her thirteen-year tenure as executive director of the South Carolina Council would be the longest of any state council executive director, man or woman.[18]

In the aftermath of the Supreme Court ruling in *Brown* v. *Board of Education*, Spearman's strategy was to reach out to various groups, among them white clubwomen, in an effort to encourage an honest discussion of the issues. First, as she put it, she tried to understand both the "feelings of fear and resentment" among whites and the "considerable disillusionment" of many blacks, who doubted that whites would help them gain their civil rights. Then she sought "to interpret the races to each other," as she networked behind the scenes with receptive whites and African Americans.[19]

Rather than issuing bold public statements, Spearman devoted her enthusiasm, personal warmth, and administrative skills to building up the membership and programs of the South Carolina Council. From

---

The Paradox of Southern Progressivism, 1880–1930, 257; Anne C. Loveland, *Lillian Smith, A Southerner Confronting the South: A Biography* (Baton Rouge: Louisiana State University Press, 1986), 57–60.

17. ASW, interview by MGS, July 11, 1983; "Introducing Mrs. Eugene Spearman," signed by Elise T. Spigner (Mrs. A. F.), Jessie H. Laurence (Mrs. C. F.), Eunice F. Stackhouse (Mrs. T. B.), Florence Olvey, *[South Carolina] Clubwoman* 7 (January 1951): 5, 22, in Alice Norwood Spearman Wright Personal Papers, SCL.

18. ASW, interview by Hall, August 8, 1976; ANS to Dick Foster, April 13, 1954, Minutes of the South Carolina Division of Southern Regional Council, Executive Board, Membership meeting, December 1, 1954, SCCHR, SCL. Dr. Leslie W. Dunbar, interview by MGS, November 19, 1994. Donovan, *Feminist Theory*, 31–32, 62; Julia Anne McDonough, "Men and Women of Good Will: A History of the Commission on Interracial Cooperation and the Southern Regional Council, 1919–1954" (Ph.D. diss., University of Virginia, 1993).

19. ANS to Rev. E. L. Byrd, January 10, 1955, SCCHR, SCL.

SCFWC files, she developed a database of potential donors. Spearman hoped that the federation would serve, along with the United Church Women, the Federation of Business and Professional Women, the League of Women Voters, and the YWCA, to help draw in the men's service clubs behind the *Brown* decision. But the tenuous coalition disintegrated when white clubwomen chose congeniality over social awareness and closed their minds to desegregation. For example, the program chair of the Rock Hill Women's Club told Spearman before she was to speak at their May 1956 meeting "that any mention of the Supreme Court's ruling or the present situation would 'break up' this fifty year old club!"[20]

The episode that most alienated the clubwomen and their friends centered on Federal District Judge J. Waties Waring, his twice-divorced second wife, and Mr. Marion A. Wright's tribute to the judge at a testimonial dinner sponsored by the South Carolina Conference of the National Association for the Advancement of Colored People. Waring, a ninth-generation Charlestonian, was despised by white South Carolinians for betraying his race and class through his judicial rulings, among them, *Elmore* v. *Rice* (1947) and *Brown* v. *Baskin* (1948), striking down South Carolina's all-white primary elections. The judge had also decided in favor of teacher salary equalization and in-state legal education for African Americans. Then he boldly attacked segregation in his dissent from the June 21, 1951, ruling of two colleagues that had upheld segregation in the Clarendon County public schools. Waring shocked white South Carolinians because prior to that time he had accepted their racial views—acting kindly toward one's African American servants but denying them their civil rights. Moreover, Waring had been a supporter of United States Senator Ellison DuRant ("Cotton Ed") Smith, who had waged a particularly racist reelection campaign in 1938. Although Waring did not necessarily share Smith's racist views, he was the beneficiary of the senator's influence in his

20. Mrs. Eugene H. Spearman to George S. Mitchell, October 19, 1954; Spearman to Mrs. Iola Jones, January 10, 1955; Spearman to Mrs. Joseph M. Perkins, February 14, 1955, SCCHR, SCL. ANS, executive director, SCCHR, October 1954 Report, Southern Regional Council microfilm, Reel 146; ASW, interview by Hall, August 8, 1976; Report of (Mrs.) ANS, April 1956, Southern Regional Council Archives Collection, Atlanta University Center Woodruff Library, Archives Division, Atlanta, Ga. (hereinafter SRCAC).

appointment in 1942 as federal judge of the Eastern District of South Carolina.[21]

Waring's judicial unpopularity had been preceded by social disapproval following his June 1945 divorce from Annie Gammell Waring, his wife of nearly thirty-two years. Eight days later, he remarried. His second wife was the recently divorced, Detroit-born Elizabeth Avery Mills Hoffman. She and her second husband had come from Litchfield, Connecticut, to Charleston as winter residents. Proper Charlestonians dubbed her "the witch of Meeting Street" and relished describing her in not-so-hushed terms as that "twice-divorced Yankee socialite." Although their condemnation may have been hypocritical, Charlestonians still frowned on divorce. They were outraged after Elizabeth Waring publicly castigated southern whites at the annual meeting of the African American Coming Street YWCA, on January 16, 1950, as "a sick, confused and decadent people . . . full of pride and complacency, introverted, morally weak, and low." To southern whites, she and Judge Waring were, she said, "like the atom bomb which they are afraid we will use to destroy their selfish and savage white supremacy way of life."[22]

Perhaps Elizabeth Waring wanted to shock white South Carolinians into speaking out against racial injustice. But her tone and strong words, reminiscent of nineteenth-century abolitionists, stunned whites into angry silence and shocked some African Americans, who feared that she and black civil rights activists might suffer reprisals. The next month, Elizabeth Waring broke tradition by hosting the city's first formal integrated luncheon for a visiting writer from *Collier's* magazine. The Warings were ostracized socially and harassed through obscene telephone calls, hate mail, and brick mortar thrown through the windows of their Meeting Street home. Having completed ten years as a federal district judge, Waring retired on full salary in February 1952 and moved with his wife to New York City. They did not return to

21. Tinsley E. Yarbrough, *A Passion for Justice: J. Waties Waring and Civil Rights* (New York: Oxford University Press, 1987), 12, 16–22, chap. 7.
22. Clipping, "Southern Whites 'Sick, Confused', U.S. Judge's Wife Says in Speech," *Charleston Evening Post*, January 17, 1950, in Albert Simons Papers, South Carolina Historical Society (hereinafter SCHS), Charleston; "Wife of Judge Waring Speaks at Annual Negro 'Y' Meeting," *Charleston News and Courier*, January 17, 1950, 8; Yarbrough, *Passion for Justice*, 130, chap. 6; William D. Smyth, "Segregation in Charleston in the 1950s: A Decade of Transition," *South Carolina Historical Magazine* 92 (April 1991): 102–4, 99–123.

Charleston until the state NAACP's testimonial dinner on November 6, 1954.[23]

Marion Wright, a past president of the South Carolina Division of the SRC and the incumbent president of the Southern Regional Council (1952–1958), was invited to speak at Waring's testimonial dinner. In urging Wright not to attend, R. Beverley Herbert, who had initially supported Waring's first ruling against the white primary, asserted a belief widespread among white South Carolinians that "the Judge has been given the cold shoulder . . . not because of his decision but because of the circumstances of his divorce." Wright dismissed the divorce issue, because the flood of "scurrilous and frequently anonymous letters" began after Waring decided the primary case. But Wright recognized that "public opinion in Charleston in recent years would have made it a chilling, if not hazardous, experience for Jesus Christ or Ghandhi [sic] to have lived in that community." Without hesitation, he gave the presentation address. The bronze plaque awarded to Waring recorded "that his dissenting opinion denouncing color segregation in the Clarendon County, South Carolina public schools became the unanimous decision of the highest court of this nation in striking down color segregation in American secondary schools."[24]

Spearman soon heard how greatly Wright's presentation had inflamed white Charlestonians. In a letter to Harriet Porcher Stoney Simons (1896–1971), she wrote that, while realizing "the value" of Wright's speech to blacks, she "deplored the fact that it no doubt placed an additional hurdle in our way as far as the white community is concerned."[25] Spearman admired Wright, but thought it unfortunate

23. Samuel Grafton, "Lonesomest Man in Town," *Collier's* 125 (April 29, 1950): 20–21; 49–50; As a result of the divorce, said Herbert, Annie Gammell Waring had "subsequently become demented." Yarbrough, *Passion for Justice*, 210–12, 226–29.

24. R. Beverley Herbert to Marion A. Wright, October 29, 1954, October 15–31, 1954; Wright to R. Beverley Herbert, December 13, 1954, December 10–30, 1954, Marion A. Wright Papers, Series I Southern Regional Council, SHC, UNC-CH. Presentation address of Marion A. Wright during a testimonial dinner given by the South Carolina Conference of the National Association for the Advancement of Colored People for the Honorable J. Waties Waring, Charleston, South Carolina, November 6, 1954, in Albert Simons Papers, SCHS; Program, Testimonial Dinner and Presentation of Bronze Plaque Commemorating the Historic Contribution of the Honorable J. Waties Waring, November 6, 1954, Arthur J. Clement Jr. Papers, Waring, J. Waties, SCL.

25. ASW, interview by MGS, July 10, 1983; Mrs. Eugene H. Spearman to Mrs. Albert Simons, January 10, 1955, and February 3, 1955, SCCHR, SCL.

that, as president of the Southern Regional Council, he had alienated Simons, the wife of Charleston architect, preservationist, educator, and author Albert Simons. Harriet Simons, a women's rights advocate and civic activist, had helped to organize the League of Women Voters of Charleston County in 1947 and had served as its first president. She then attained statewide influence as president of the South Carolina League of Women Voters (1951–1955). In 1947, Simons had gladly accepted service on the advisory committee of the South Carolina Division of the SRC, because she did not "know any work which requires the moral support of like minded people more than does this biracial problem."[26] Like Simons, Charleston novelist Josephine Pinckney (1895–1957) had been friendly to interracial cooperation during the 1940s. But after the Supreme Court's 1954 desegregation decision, both Simons and Pinckney began to separate from the South Carolina Council.[27] Although Spearman worked diplomatically to keep them within the South Carolina Council, she found that their attitudes had hardened against further participation.

As Harriet Simons explained to Spearman, she and other Charlestonians simply could not tolerate Judge Waring and his second wife. Charlestonians "who have known Judge Waring all his life," Simons wrote, in February 1955, "find it hard to accept his extraordinary conversion in later life," given his earlier "complete disregard . . . to the whole bi-racial problem." In addition to resenting Waring's divorce of his first wife and his second wife's speech at the African American YWCA, Charlestonians intensely disliked being "judged in their righteousness, their ability, their common decency by Judge Waring's

26. Mary L. Bryan, *Proud Heritage: A History of the League of Women Voters of South Carolina 1920–1976* ([Columbia, S.C.:] League of Women Voters of South Carolina, [1977]), 21–27, 29–42; Harriet P. Simons to Mary Frayser, April 9, 1947, Mary E. Frayser Papers, Interracial Cooperation Papers, Winthrop University Archives and Special Collections; Harriet P. Simons to ANS, February 18, 1948, and Spearman to Simons, April 10, 1948, SCCHR, SCL. Several years before the *Brown* decision, the Charleston League of Women Voters admitted black women to membership but did not allow them to attend the luncheons. Mrs. Albert Simons, comments, Minutes, August 18, 1954, League of Women Voters, Meeting of Presidents of Southern States Held in Atlanta, Georgia, July 27–28, 1954, Albert Simons Papers, SCHS.
27. ANS to Josephine Pinckney, May 18, 1948, SCCHR, SCL. See Pinckney's obituaries, October 6, 1957, *New York Times* and *Charleston News and Courier,* Josephine Lyons Scott Pinckney Papers, SCHS.

reports of us to the world at large and the New York Press in particular." The final affront was Wright's testimonial address honoring Waring. Although Simons accepted public school desegregation as "inevitable," she felt Wright was "going too fast for me personally." Lest it undermine the education of white pupils, she believed that integration "must come carefully, in counties or communities where the percentage of negro pupils to white is small" and should "be done on mental tests and IQs or some such programme."[28]

Having served with Wright on the Penn Community Services board, Spearman felt she could tell her friend Wright "in a sympathetic way" of Simons's criticisms. But Simons was not reassured. Given her feeling that SRC exercised too much control over the state affiliates, she would neither accept service on the South Carolina Council's Board of Directors nor join. With regret, Spearman acknowledged to SRC executive director George Mitchell, in May 1955, that "Mrs. Albert Simons can and will block our substantial progress" in Charleston; such obstruction was "principally her reaction to the Waring dinner" and to Wright's address.[29]

On May 31, 1955, the Supreme Court issued its decree to implement the 1954 *Brown* decision and remanded the five component cases to the federal district courts. Although specifying desegregation "with all deliberate speed," the Supreme Court recognized that "full implementation of these constitutional principles may require solution of varied local school problems." As a three-judge federal district court met in Columbia on July 15 to hear the Clarendon County case, whites adopted a policy of noncompliance and denounced the NAACP. Some white women who had previously been "mild in response to Supreme Court ruling were in high emotional state and expressed much fear of Negro men," Spearman noted. When African Americans began to petition for school integration, white citizens councils rapidly formed.[30]

28. Harriet P. Simons to the South Carolina Council on Human Relations, February 7, 1955, SCCHR, SCL.

29. Mrs. Eugene H. Spearman to Mrs. Albert Simons, March 10, 1956; Harriet P. Simons to Mrs. Eugene H. Spearman, April 3, 1955; ANS to George Mitchell, May 20, 1955; and Harriet P. Simons to Spearman, June 25, 1955, SCCHR, SCL; ANS, March 1955 Report, SRC microfilm, Reel 146.

30. Richard Kluger, *Simple Justice: The History of* Brown v Board of Education *and Black America's Struggle for Equality* (New York: Vintage Books, 1977), 744–

During that summer, Spearman undertook field trips from her Columbia office to Clarendon County, Charleston, and Georgetown to meet with both African Americans and whites. In Charleston, between July 25 and 27, 1955, she interviewed officials and community leaders and met with a group at the Charleston Public Library that included the librarian, Emily Sanders, Josephine Pinckney, and Harriet Simons. Spearman learned that the NAACP's recent petition to the Charleston School Board would be met with economic sanctions. In fact, nowhere in the state would she find a significant number of whites favoring school desegregation.[31]

Indeed, 68 percent of South Carolina voters had already approved, in a November 1952 referendum, an amendment repealing the section of the South Carolina Constitution of 1895 providing for "a liberal system of free public schools for all children between the ages of six and twenty-one years." The amendment had been requested by Governor James F. Byrnes (1951–1955) "as a preparedness measure" against a Supreme Court desegregation decree. However, it had also been attacked for being a political maneuver that would jeopardize American democracy by closing the public schools. The opponents included the South Carolina Conference of the NAACP and a number of civic and religious organizations, among them the public affairs committee of the YWCA, the executive committee of the Christian Action Council, an independent religious agency, and the state office and local chapters of the League of Women Voters. The principle of maintaining publicly supported, racially segregated schools was also endorsed by white public school teachers in the South Carolina Education Association. Ultimately, these groups exercised little influence over most voters, who accepted Governor Byrnes's arguments. On March 19, 1954, the South Carolina General Assembly ratified the amendment; the legislators' next step would be to repeal state statutes regarding the operation of public schools.[32]

45; Alice N. Spearman, September 1955 Report, SRC microfilm, Reel 146; William Bagwell, *School Desegregation in the Carolinas: Two Case Studies* (Columbia: University of South Carolina Press, 1972), 57–64, 148–53; Neil R. McMillan, *The Citizens' Council: Organized Resistance to the Second Reconstruction, 1954–1964* (Chicago: University of Chicago Press, 1971).

31. ANS, July 1955 Report, SCCHR, SCL.

32. Howard H. Quint, *Profile in Black and White: A Frank Portrait of South Carolina* (Washington, DC: Public Affairs Press, 1958), 15–17; Governor James F.

South Carolina found another way to avoid closing its public schools, however. A fifteen-member legislative committee, chaired by State Senator L. Marion Gressette, made legal counsel available to school districts facing lawsuits for the admission of African American children. In addition, black teachers faced dismissal for NAACP membership, and black farmers and small businessmen who initiated petition drives to enroll their children in white schools were denied credit, goods, and services. To blunt their protests, the state continued its school equalization program adopted during Byrnes's administration and funded by a 3–percent sales tax. As a result, special NAACP counsel Thurgood Marshall decided to delay an integration drive in South Carolina, because it would cause these new schools to be closed and their teachers fired. African American parents dropped their petitions, and the schools stayed open.[33]

The temper of many white South Carolinians was frankly revealed by Josephine Pinckney's August 1955 letter to Spearman. While Pinckney had "always wanted and worked for better schools, better economic opportunities and a better deal in the courts for Negroes," she recognized that "these recent school suits have forced the parents of white children in these districts to face what seem to me a very hard if not unanswerable question,—namely 'what effect will it have on my children to spend twelve formative years in a school where the attendance is heavily Negro?'" Pinckney also shared Simons's negative views of Marion Wright's leadership of the Southern Regional Council.[34]

In reply to Pinckney, Spearman asserted her "basic faith in our people both white and Negro" and flatly rejected "the fear which the

---

Byrnes, quoted in Howard G. McClain, "South Carolina's School Amendment," *New South* 8 (February 1953): 4; 1–5, 8; David G. Blick, "Beyond 'The Politics of Color': Opposition to South Carolina's 1952 Constitutional Amendment to Abolish the Public School System," in *Proceedings of the South Carolina Historical Association, 1995* (Columbia: South Carolina Historical Association, 1995), 20–30; Why the League of Women Voters Opposes the Proposed Constitutional Amendment to Remove State Responsibility for a System of Free Public Schools; Report of Conference with Governor Byrnes, May 28, 1952, Mrs. J. O. Erwin, Mrs. Martin Young, Mrs. Albert Simons, Albert Simons Papers, SCHS.

33. Marcia G. Synnott, "Desegregation in South Carolina, 1950–1963: Sometime 'Between "Now" and "Never,"'" in *Looking South: Chapters in the Story of An American Region*, ed. Winfred B. Moore Jr. and Joseph F. Tripp (New York: Greenwood Press, 1989), 57–58; 51–64.

34. Josephine Pinckney to ANS, August 30, 1955, SCCHR, SCL.

extremists of our race seem to be engendering in the minds of so many of our fine white citizens." She also expressed "shock" that Pinckney could not see where the South Carolina Council was heading: "If I did not have faith that there are persons like you and Mrs. Simons who are deeply committed to the human values to be conserved by communication between our races, I could not go on with this work in such strenuous times." By May of 1956, however, Spearman wrote George Mitchell that she had "temporarily given up working with Josephine Pinckney and Mrs. Albert Simons, though I realize that they do wield considerable influence and that we shall eventually need them."[35]

The explanations offered by Simons and Pinckney for their defection from the work of the South Carolina Council raised the question of which issue aroused them more: their intense disapproval of Judge Waring's divorce from his first wife or the threat of desegregation. Marion Wright, the Warings, and Spearman thought that, for the most part, the divorce issue influenced only "the elderly and primly correct social circle living 'below Broad Street,' a thoroughfare roughly dividing the echelons of Charleston society." But as Wright observed in an essay, "the mass desertion of the Warings came after and as a result of the primary case decisions."[36] Despite their general goodwill and concern for improving the status of African Americans, Simons and Pinckney were upper-class moderate conservatives, who felt that white South Carolinians, not federal judges, should control the degree and pace of change. While the judge's divorce offended their sense of social propriety, his decisions assaulted their beliefs on why racial change should be gradual and on how it should be implemented. Wright, Judge Waring, and Spearman belonged to that tiny minority of white southerners who had broken thoroughly with prevailing white racial attitudes and the philosophy of slow progress. In contrast, Pinckney, Simons, and R. Beverley Herbert, like most women and men of their social position, were unwilling to sweep away traditional patterns of white paternalism and expected black deference.

35. ANS to Josephine Pinckney, September 7, 1955; and ANS to Mrs. Albert Simons, November 17, 1955, SCCHR, SCL; ANS to George Mitchell, May 8, 1956, SRC microfilm.
36. Marion A. Wright, "South Carolina Vendetta," in *Human Rights Odyssey*, ed. Marion A. Wright and Arnold Shankman (Durham, N.C.: Moore Publishing Company, 1978), 89, 86–103.

Given the attitudes of white clubwomen, churchwomen, and civic leaders, Spearman found that African American women remained skeptical about receiving any sympathy from them. In the hope of increasing white understanding, she urged African American women to seek interracial contacts among churchwomen's groups. To prepare the women for such encounters, Spearman had them practice what they would say in interviews with white churchwomen; she directed them to rehearse in sociodramas with other members of their group. She was disappointed when those who took the role of white women portrayed them as unsympathetic to black women. Few interracial contacts resulted from her efforts.[37]

In July 1957, departing South Carolina Council president J. Claude Evans assessed what the council had been able to accomplish during its three years as an SRC affiliate: "I am not sure what progress we made. At least, we held things together when many all around us were going backwards." But Spearman and other council members had also shown white South Carolinians that there were African Americans of considerable ability, a fact that most whites were reluctant to recognize. Sustained by her commitment to the principle of equal rights for all persons and her belief that there was "fundamental decency" in South Carolinians, Spearman had forged on during the period of massive resistance.[38]

Despite South Carolina's prevailing climate of fear and confusion, she noted, in an optimistic report to the SRC in July 1957, that almost thirty groups—various chapters of the South Carolina Council, religious organizations, and social agencies—did work together biracially. Although "most of the positive forces in South Carolina today are frozen assets and respond slowly to thawing processes," she anticipated that "many whites will accommodate once it is definitely expected of them." The South Carolina Council's statewide membership of about seven hundred constituted a very small voice, but it spoke consistently for racial justice.[39]

37. Report of (Mrs.) Alice N. Spearman, November 1955, SRCAC.
38. J. Claude Evans to ANS, July 2, 1957, SCCHR, SCL; ASW, interview by MGS, July 10, 1983; Minutes of the Meeting of Board of Directors of the South Carolina Council, January 30, 1957, SCCHR, SCL.
39. ANS, SCCHR Report to the Southern Regional Council, Inc., Request for Financial Aid, July 12, 1957, SRCAC.

In 1959, Spearman achieved an important breakthrough with the state's African American community when she was asked to serve on an interorganizational steering committee to make arrangements for the Southern Christian Leadership Conference's semiannual meeting, held in Columbia from September 29 to October 1. The conference—and the Reverend Dr. Martin Luther King Jr.'s first publicly scheduled appearance in South Carolina—was to show "a united Negro front needed in the drive for first class citizenship." Spearman also accepted an invitation to join the January 1, 1960, Emancipation Proclamation Day pilgrimage to the Greenville airport to protest its discrimination against baseball star Jackie Robinson, when he had come to that city the previous October to address the annual meeting of the South Carolina Conference of NAACP Branches. She had been warned by the council's executive committee and president against participating because they feared negative press coverage would further discourage white membership in the council. But there were no disturbances, because of the cooperation of law enforcement officials. Indeed, with the November 1958 election of the thirty-six-year-old Ernest F. (Fritz) Hollings as governor, the white power structure increasingly had realized that improved race relations made both economic and political sense.[40]

Buoyed by a more favorable political climate, the council, under Spearman's leadership, launched several initiatives in the early 1960s. In addition to supporting the student sit-ins and lunch-counter demonstrations of the desegregation movement, the South Carolina Council founded in the fall of 1960 a biracial Student Council on Human Relations, advised by staff member Elizabeth C. Ledeen. The student council reached out to small groups of college students throughout the state and brought them to the Penn Center on St. Helena Island, one of the few places available for biracial conferences. When those students returned to their campuses, they encouraged

40. ASW, interview by Hall, August 8, 1976, 77–82; (Mrs.) Alice N. Spearman, Quarterly Report, June 1959–August 1959; Quarterly Report, September 1959–November 1959; and Quarterly Report, December 1959–February 1960, SCCHR, SCL; Jack Bass and Walter De Vries, *The Transformation of Southern Politics: Social Change and Political Consequence since 1945* (New York: New American Library, 1976).

other students to recognize that court-ordered integration was coming and that they should begin preparing for it.[41]

Although Clemson College would not admit Harvey Bernard Gantt to its School of Architecture without a federal court order (the Charleston black sought admission as a transfer student from Iowa State University), Governor Hollings, the president of Clemson College, and leading businessmen began to cooperate informally to neutralize the die-hard segregationists. Moreover, despite receiving letters that favored, by a five-to-one margin, Governor Ross Barnett's opposition to James Meredith's admission to the University of Mississippi on September 30, 1962, Hollings ignored the demands of segregationists that he lead a motorcade to Mississippi. Instead, he sent the chief of the South Carolina State Law Enforcement Division to Oxford, Mississippi, to learn how to prevent trouble.[42]

Ten days after the Ole Miss riot over Meredith's presence, Spearman wrote Hollings a politically perceptive letter and enclosed two South Carolina Council brochures. Complimenting his lack of political negativism, she suggested that with greater support from "people of tolerance and moderation," he would be enabled "as our state's executive to provide the level of leadership" required. The "rapidly growing sentiment for the preservation of law and order" and for the maintenance of public education demanded, Spearman said, "a statesmanlike accommodation to the spirit and the rulings of the

41. The Reverend Fred M. Reese Jr., interview by MGS, December 13, 1994, Columbia, S.C.; Minutes of the Executive Board of the South Carolina Council, March 6, 1960; (Mrs.) Alice N. Spearman, Quarterly Report, June 1960–August 1960; Mrs. T. J. Ledeen, Highlights: A Report of Program Activity, submitted with the Quarterly Report, December 1960–February 1961; and Spearman and other staff members, Quarterly Report, December 1962–February 1963, SCCHR, SCL.

42. *Gantt v Clemson Agricultural College of South Carolina*, 213 F. Supp. 103 (1962); George McMillan, "Integration with Dignity: The Inside Story of How South Carolina Kept the Peace," *Saturday Evening Post* 236 (March 16, 1963), 16–17; 15–21; John Hammond Moore, *Columbia and Richland County: A South Carolina Community, 1740–1990* (Columbia: University of South Carolina Press, 1993), 423; Marcia G. Synnott, "Federalism Vindicated: University Desegregation in South Carolina and Alabama, 1962–1963," *Journal of Policy History* 1 (July 1989): 292–318; Senator Ernest F. Hollings, interview by MGS, July 8, 1980, Modern Political Collections, SCL.

Supreme Court." She offered "to work constructively with you behind the scenes at any level where dedicated footwork may be needed."[43]

Spearman contributed proactively to the discourse on race relations by offering the council's point of view to political leaders like Hollings and by consistently talking to the public in a positive and courteous tone. She and the council also kept biracial communication alive so that when the political and business leadership finally accepted integration, there was more public support for it than the unyielding segregationists expected. At the same time, Spearman and the council worked to enlarge educational and economic opportunities for black South Carolinians. When Gantt entered Clemson on January 28, 1963, South Carolina became the last Deep South state to integrate a public college, but it did so peacefully. After a pro forma federal district court suit, the University of South Carolina also admitted without incident in September 1963 three African American students.[44] Although the Charleston County public schools began token integration the same month, most South Carolina school districts delayed integration until the late 1960s or early 1970s, when they were prodded by a possible loss of federal funds pursuant to Title VI of the 1964 Civil Rights Act. In 1968, moreover, the U.S. Supreme Court ruled that freedom-of-choice plans were unconstitutional if they perpetuated a dual school system and that the "deliberate speed" concept could not be used for further delay. By the mid 1960s, as formerly silent voices supported racial accommodation, moderation prevailed in South Carolina.[45]

43. ANS to Ernest F. Hollings, October 11, 1962, SCCHR, SCL.

44. Paul S. Lofton Jr., "Calm and Exemplary: Desegregation in Columbia, South Carolina," 71–72; 70–81; and Elizabeth Jacoway, "Introduction: Civil Rights and the Changing South," in *Southern Businessmen and Desegregation*, ed. Elizabeth Jacoway and David R. Colburn (Baton Rouge: Louisiana State University Press, 1982), 1–14; Margaret Edds, "Harvey Gantt: Against the Odds," in *Free at Last: What Really Happened When Civil Rights Came to Southern Politics* (Bethesda, Md.: Adler & Adler, 1987), 191–211; Harvey Bernard Gantt, interview by MGS, July 14, 1980.

45. Bagwell, *School Desegregation*, 162–84; Davis Rutledge Holland, "A History of the Desegregation Movement in the South Carolina Public Schools during the Period 1954–1976" (Ed.D. diss., Florida State University College of Education, 1978); Paul Brest, "Race Discrimination," in *The Burger Court: The Counter-Revolution That Wasn't*, ed. Vincent Blasi (New Haven: Yale University Press, 1983), 113–31, 256–59; John G. Sproat, " 'Firm Flexibility': Perspectives on Desegregation in South Carolina," in *New Perspectives on Race and Slavery in America: Essays*

Under Spearman's leadership, the South Carolina Council, chartered independently of the Southern Regional Council in 1963, joined the Voter Education Project (VEP) and participated in programs attacking illiteracy, lack of job skills, and poverty, particularly among rural South Carolinians. These programs were funded by the federal, state, and local governments and by philanthropic foundations. The council was ready for President Lyndon B. Johnson's Great Society. Given her New Deal experience, Spearman had the "know-how" to prepare within two days in 1965 the application for county Head Start programs. From June 1966 to June 1967, the South Carolina Council collaborated with its student council in launching the Student Program for Educational and Economic Development for Underprivileged People (SPEED-UP), under a demonstration grant funded by the Office of Economic Opportunity. Through this tutoring and community development program, students from twenty South Carolina colleges worked in the summer with economically disadvantaged children and adults to prepare them for further education. There were few areas of life that the South Carolina Council did not touch, whether it was fair housing or such welfare issues as food stamps, school lunches, and health care.[46]

Uniquely focused "upon the development of human resources and relationships," the council was, as Spearman asserted in her November 1966 quarterly report, "attracting more people of leadership potential," many of them "relatively young." Membership rose from 957 in late 1965 to 1,364 in December 1967. About a dozen local human relations councils were active. Spearman tempered her goals for the South Carolina Council, however, with a realistic assessment of the persistent lack of "adequate *citizen involvement*," which, in turn, inhibited momentum for positive change. Too few South Carolinians, she thought, as individuals or as members of student, ministerial, or women's groups, had developed within themselves her devotion to racial and

---

in Honor of Kenneth M. Stampp, ed. Robert H. Abzug and Stephen E. Maizlish (Lexington: University Press of Kentucky, 1986), 164–65, 181; 164–84.

46. ANS and other staff members, Quarterly Report, December 1962–February 1963; Elizabeth C. Ledeen, Report of Extension Director, June 1966–August 1966; Program Director's Report 1964–1969; and Report 1: South Carolina Council on Human Relations 1966–1967, SCCHR, SCL; ASW, interview by MGS, July 11, 1983; Bass, "South Carolinian," 8A.

social justice. By late 1966, she identified the staff's "biggest unmet needs" as "a strong office manager" and a new executive director.[47]

Many of the council's and Spearman's initiatives in the areas of welfare and criminal justice came to fruition under her successor, Paul Matthias, a Methodist minister, who served as executive director from October 1967 through June 1974. In 1969, the council redirected its efforts from assisting the economically disadvantaged to becoming an advocacy organization that sought to make governmental agencies publicly accountable. But both its membership and foundation funding plummeted in the recessionary 1970s. Then the South Carolina Council for Human Rights (its new name as of June 1973) faced internal divisions and a lawsuit in selecting its third executive director. By July 1975, less than eight years after Spearman's retirement, the board of directors decided that the council should dissolve itself.[48]

Through her years as executive director of the South Carolina Council on Human Relations, Alice Spearman ably exemplified the view, "Men Led, but Women Organized." In the Southern Regional Council and its state affiliates, white male leaders such as Marion Wright made their contributions through speeches and writings by defining issues and challenging the consciences of others. Using skills honed by a life of diverse experiences, Spearman forged consensus and elicited leadership from others by emphasizing task-sharing and equality, rather than domination and hierarchy. This unusual woman was "a visionary" who excelled as a developer of "a community of concern" and "a networker," said the Reverend Fred M. Reese, Jr., a former South Carolina Council president. Her "will to persevere was amazing," as she "coordinated groups" and "pulled people together with disparate views." Many of the South Carolina Council's achievements were due largely to Spearman's leadership and to the staff, officers, and members

47. ANS, Report, September 1966–November 1966; and Report I: South Carolina Council on Human Relations 1966–1967, SCCHR, SCL.

48. In 1974, South Carolina was one of only five states that still had a human relations council; the others were Alabama, Arkansas, Georgia, and Mississippi. "Black Group Protesting New SCCHR Director," Columbia Record, August 29, 1974; clipping, "Group Charged with Breach of Contract," Columbia State, October 2, 1974; "Civil Rights Group Feeling Financial Squeeze," Charlotte Observer, February 21, 1975. Thomas Koehler-Shepley, "The South Carolina Council on Human Relations 1967–1975" (History 858 graduate seminar paper, University of South Carolina, Columbia, 1992).

that she recruited. Thus, placing her executive directorship within the history of South Carolina's civil rights movement should encourage both a reexamination and a broadening of the existing histories. Such a reinterpretation would greatly modify the story of the civil rights movement and focus less on the roles of male leaders, white and black, while incorporating the actions of the less visible leaders and grassroots participants, a number of whom were women or students.[49]

Spearman was essentially a liberal feminist who shared some of the perspectives of both cultural and socialist feminists. She brought to her fight against racial discrimination and economic injustice a keen understanding of how white racial attitudes were reinforced by class structure and political power. Firmly committed to the New Deal and Great Society programs assisting the disadvantaged, she sought human rights for all: women and men, African Americans and whites. In 1970, three years after her retirement and eight years after Eugene H. Spearman died, she married Marion Wright with whom she had developed an enduring comradeship during the civil rights movement.[50]

49. The Reverend Fred M. Reese Jr., interview by MGS, December 13, 1994; Karen Sacks, "Gender and Grassroots Leadership" (paper, University of California at Los Angeles, n.d.), cited in Charles Payne, "Men Led, but Women Organized: Movement Participation of Women in the Mississippi Delta," in *Women in the Civil Rights Movement: Trailblazers and Torchbearers, 1941–1965,* ed. Vicki Crawford, Jacqueline Anne Rouse, and Barbara Woods (Brooklyn, N.Y.: Carlson Publishing Inc., 1990), 8–9; Kathryn L. Nasstrom, "Women, the Civil Rights Movement, and the Politics of Historical Memory in Atlanta, 1946–1973" (Ph.D. diss., University of North Carolina at Chapel Hill, 1993), 9–12. Howard H. Quint, *Profile in Black and White,* describes Spearman as a "sparkplug," 169.

50. Donovan, *Feminist Theory,* 25–26, 31–32, 62, 65–69, 72–76, 82–83, 85–89.

About the Authors and the Editors

Janet L. Coryell received her Ph.D. from the College of William and Mary and is associate professor of history at Western Michigan University. She is the author of *Neither Heroine Nor Fool: Anna Ella Carroll of Maryland* and has edited and written about numerous nineteenth-century topics. Her current research and presentations are on women active in antebellum partisan politics.

Kirsten Fischer received her doctoral degree from Duke University. She is assistant professor of history at the University of South Florida. Her essay " 'False, Feigned, and Scandalous Words': Sexual Slander and Racial Ideology among Whites in Colonial North Carolina," appears in *The Devil's Lane: Sex and Race in the Early South*, edited by Catherine Clinton and Michele Gillespie. She continues her research on the racial politics of illicit sex in colonial North Carolina.

Joanna Bowen Gillespie, who received her Ph.D. from New York University, is an independent scholar living in Vermont. Her book *Women Speak: of God, Congregations and Change* continues her work as co-founder of the Episcopal Women's History Project. She has been an NEH Senior Fellow of the Omohundro Institute of Early American Life and Culture and is currently researching the life of Martha Laurens Ramsay.

Anya Jabour is assistant professor of history at the University of Montana. Her articles on the Wirt family have been published in the *Virginia Magazine of History and Biography* and the *Journal of the Early Republic*. She is the author of the forthcoming book *Negotiating Marriage: Elizabeth and William Wirt in the Early Republic, 1802–1834*. She received her Ph.D. from Rice University.

Cynthia Lynn Lyerly received her Ph.D. from Rice University and is assistant professor of history at Boston College. Her articles have appeared in *Discovering the Women in Slavery*, edited by Patricia Morton, and *The Devil's Lane.* She is the author of the forthcoming book *Methodism and the Southern Mind.*

Norma Taylor Mitchell, who received her Ph.D. from Duke University, is professor of history at Troy State University, where she specializes in nineteenth- and twentieth-century women and religion. Her previous publications include "From Parsonage to Hospital: Louise Banscomb Becomes a Doctor," in *Stepping Out of the Shadows: Alabama Women, 1819–1990*, edited by Mary Martha Thomas, and "Women in Religion," in *Encyclopedia of Religion in the South*, edited by Samuel S. Hill.

Kimberly Schreck is a graduate student at the University of Missouri, Columbia. Her master's thesis, "Their Place in Freedom: African American Women in Transition from Slavery to Freedom, Cooper County, Missouri, 1865–1900," was completed in 1993.

Karen Manners Smith is assistant professor of history at Emporia State University in Kansas, where she teaches nineteenth-century U.S. women's history. She is the author of *New Paths to Power: American Women, 1890–1920*. She received her Ph.D. from the University of Massachusetts.

Susan L. Smith received her Ph.D. from the University of Wisconsin and is associate professor of history and women's studies at the University of Alberta, Canada. Her publications include *Sick and Tired of Being Sick and Tired: Black Women's Health Activism in America, 1890–1950*. She is currently researching the history of Japanese-American women and midwifery.

Martha H. Swain, Cornaro Professor of History Emerita at Texas Woman's University, now teaches at Mississippi State University. She is the author of *Pat Harrison: The New Deal Years* and *Ellen S. Woodward: New Deal Advocate for Women*. She has written and presented extensively on the Roosevelt and Truman period and southern women's history.

Marcia G. Synnott received her Ph.D. from the University of Massachusetts and is professor of history at the University of South Carolina. Since *The Half-Opened Door: Discrimination and Admissions at Harvard, Yale, and Princeton, 1900–1970*, she has written several articles on desegregation at southern state universities. She continues her work on Spearman and changing race relations in South Carolina between 1940 and 1990.

Sandra Gioia Treadway received her Ph.D. from the University of Virginia and is the deputy director of the Library of Virginia. Her publications on nineteenth- and twentieth-century southern women include *Women of Mark: A History of the Woman's Club of Richmond, Virginia, 1894–1994*. She co-edited (with Edward D. C. Campbell Jr.) *The Common Wealth: Treasures from the Collections of the Library of Virginia*.

Elizabeth Hayes Turner is associate professor of history at the University of Houston-Downtown. She specializes in southern history and women's history. She is currently visiting managing editor of the *Journal of Southern History*. She is the author of the forthcoming book *Women, Culture, and Community: Religion and Reform in Galveston, 1880–1920*.

Index

Abbott, Benjamin, 68
Abell, Elizabeth, 26–27
Abolitionism, 123
Adultery, 10–12, 16. *See also* Sexual
 misconduct
African Americans: and Alpha Kappa
 Alpha Mississippi Health Project,
 144–56; autonomy of freed slaves,
 112–16; as childcare givers, 33–34,
 165–66; and civil rights activity, 151,
 169–70, 176, 177, 184; and courtesy
 titles, 171–72; and Cuyler Children's
 Free Clinic, 142–43; and education,
 147, 150, 167, 184, 191–93,
 196–98, 203–4; emancipated
 slaves as servants, 99–118; and
 Episcopalians, 165–68, 170–78,
 180–82; extinction of, 140; and
 gender biases, 112–16; health care
 for, 6, 138–57; as informed readers,
 174; and interracial marriage,
 17–18; interracial sex, 17–19, 67,
 116; and Jim Crow legislation, 115,
 169; kin network of, 117–18; and
 legislation, 184, 193, 196–98, 204;
 literacy and, 86, 88, 93, 95, 97,
 150; lynching of, 116; and madness,
 59; and malnutrition, 138; and
 matrilineage, 17–18; as medical
 professionals, 141; mortality
 rates for, 139–40; and National

Negro Health Week, 141–42;
 and political power, 113–14; and
 poverty, 138–39, 145–47, 167; and
 preventive medicine, 141; and racial
 caste system, 112–15; racist attitudes
 toward, 113–16; and religious
 exclusiveness, 170; and school
 desegregation, 163, 170, 177–78,
 191–93, 196–99; and segregated
 travel, 148–49; and sexuality,
 112, 114, 115; as sharecroppers,
 139, 145–46, 149–51, 154; social
 boundaries of, 166–67; stereotype
 as servant, 168; and volunteer
 health work, 138–57; and white
 clubwomen, 7, 185, 192; and YMCA,
 162–63; and YWCA, 162–63, 185,
 189, 198. *See also* Slaves
AKA Mississippi Health Project. *See*
 Alpha Kappa Alpha Mississippi
 Health Project
AKA Non-Partisan Council on Public
 Affairs, 156
Alabama, 206n48
All-Asian Woman's Conference, 189
Allen, George, Doctor, 21
Alone (Terhune), 124, 126, 128
Alpha Kappa Alpha Mississippi Health
 Project, 6, 144–56
American Association of University
 Women, 185

American Council on Human Rights,
    156
*American Dilemma: The Negro Problem
    and Modern Democracy* (Myrdal),
    170
American Friends Service Committee,
    178
Americans for Democratic Action, 163
Anderson, Elizabeth, 62
Andover, Tom, 11, 12
Anglicanism, 56. *See also* Episcopalians
Anti-Semitism, 169, 170
Apprenticeship laws, 109
APVA. *See* Association for the
    Preservation of Virginia Antiquities
    (APVA)
Arkansas, 163, 206n48
Arrington, Hannah, 65
Arrington, Joel, 65
Association for the Preservation of
    Virginia Antiquities (APVA), 135
Auchincloss, Louis, 161
Authority: and daughters of Protestant
    Clergy, 172–73; of housekeepers,
    36–37, 48; moral authority of
    women, 54, 63, 70–72; women's
    religious leadership, 63

Bagby, George, 126
Bailey, William, 22
Baily, Rebekah, 24
Baptists, 55, 87–88, 189
Barker, William, 15
Barnett, Ross, Governor, 203
Beardsley, Edward, 157n
Beecher, Catharine, 31, 44–46, 123
Bible, 161
Bird, David, 91, 95–96
Blacks. *See* African Americans
Blancherd, Aaron, 20
Boonville Weekly Advertiser, 101, 114

Boyd, Norma, 156
Boyle, Sarah Patton: activism of,
    169–83; as author, 159–61; criticism
    of Episcopal church by, 180–82;
    death of, 183; and desegregation,
    6–7, 158–83; direct style of, 159n;
    divorce of, 182; and feminism,
    180–81; generic male language
    used by, 180–81; and Lost Cause
    mythology, 164–65; marriage
    of, 168; parentage of, 165–68;
    persecution of, 177–78; as racial
    activist, 161–62, 171–72, 186; racial
    reeducation of, 158–59, 166–67;
    religious education of, 161; and T. J.
    Sellers, 171, 174; and Lillian Smith,
    162–64, 173–74; and Southern
    Code, 161, 165–66, 169, 171, 173,
    179; and Southern White Myth,
    178; and Walsh, 168–69
Braden, Anne, 186
Braizer, Elizabeth, 15
Bright, Delaney, 18
Brontë, Charlotte, 125
Browder, Mary, 65
Brown, Roscoe C., Dr., 153
Brown v Baskin, 193
Brown v Board of Education of Topeka,
    184, 192, 197
Burkitt, Ed, 18
Burnham, Elizabeth, 16
Burnham, John, 16
Burrington, Governor, 13
Burwell, Mary, 86, 92
Byrd, William II, 135
Byrnes, James F., 198–99

Campbell, Arthur, 78
Campbell, David, 4–5, 74–98
Campbell, Frances, 89, 94
Campbell, John, 77–78, 94

Campbell, Joseph Francis Trigg, 97
Campbell, Margaret, 90, 93–94
Campbell, Mary, 4–5, 74–98
Campbell, Virginia Tabitha Jane, 4–5, 79, 84, 87, 93–95
Campbell, William, 78
Campbell, William Bowen, 79, 81, 93–94, 96, 97
Carter, Marion, 149
Cartwright, Ann, 16
Cartwright, Thomas, 16
Cash, W. J., 173
Children as slaves, 18, 109, 109n
Children's Bureau, 153
Christian Action Council, 198
Church of England, 55, 56
Churches. *See* specific denominations
Citizens' Councils, 184
Civil rights activities, 151, 169–70, 176, 177, 184. *See also* Desegration
Civil Rights Act of 1964, 204
Civil War, 95, 127–31, 134
Clay, Henry, 84
Clemson College, 203
Clenny, Mary, 16
Clinton, Catherine, 1n
Club Woman, 192
Colliers, 194
Colonel Floyd's Wards (Terhune), 128
Colonial America: sexual misconduct in, 3, 10–20
Columbia Teachers College, 146, 188
Commission on Interracial Cooperation, 163
Committee on Economic Security, 155
Common Sense in the Household (Terhune), 132
Converse College, 185, 187, 188, 189
Culpeper, Thomas, 13
Cumming, Hugh, 153
Cuyler Children's Free Clinic, 142

Daniel Hale Williams's Health Guild, 143
Daniels, Jonathan, 175
Daughters of the American Revolution, 136
Daughters of Pocahontas, 136
Davis, Hanah, 21, 27
Davis, Sam, 103
Deism, 62
Democratic-Leader, 116
Demonic possession, 56
Demsey, Amy, 18
Desegregated Heart (Boyle), 7, 159–61, 160n4, 167, 175, 177, 183
Desegregation: and Boyle, 6–7, 158–83; economics of, 178; and racial reeducation, 166–67; school desegregation, 163, 170, 177–78, 184–86, 192–204; in South Carolina, 191–204; and white clubwomen, 7, 185, 192; and Wright, 7, 184–85, 191–204
Dewey, John, 188
Dickens, Charles, 121, 125
Discrimination. *See* Desegregation; Segregation
Dixon, Jackson, 97
Domestic manuals, 132
Domestic servants. *See* Household servants
Douglass, Frederick, 156
Durr, Virginia, 186

Eastland, Sally, 70
Education: and African Americans, 147, 150, 167, 184, 191–93, 196–98, 203–4; and literacy, 86, 88, 93, 95, 97, 150, 205; Methodism and women's education, 95; racial reeducation, 158–59, 166–67; of women, 121–22, 167–68, 187–88

Eliot, Martha, Dr., 153
Elmore v Rice, 193
Emancipation, 99, 109
Emancipation of child slaves, 109
Emancipation Proclamation, 101
Emancipation Proclamation Day, 202
Embree, Frank, 116
Emergency Relief Administration
　(ERA), 190
Employment: of educated women,
　168n18; of housekeepers, 42–43;
　and poverty, 4, 37–38
Employment Act of 1932, 191
Enlightenment, 55–56
Enthusiasm: and women, 53–73; as
　women's weakness, 73
Episcopalian Advisory Committee on
　Intergroup Relations, 159
Episcopalians: and desegregation, 6–7,
　158–60, 163–68, 170–78, 180–82,
　183n41; individual nature of,
　178–80; as liberals, 176–6; Negro
　Episcopalians, 167; as racists, 173;
　as Southern aristocrats, 164–66;
　and Southern Cause, 161–62; and
　women's church role, 174–75
Episcopal Women's Auxiliary, 174
ERA. *See* Emergency Relief
　Administration (ERA)
Evangelicals, 55
Evans, Augusta, 126, 129
Evans, J. Claude, 201

Federation of Business and
　Professional Women, 193
Feminism, 180–81
Ferebee, Dorothy Boulding, 6, 147–53
Fornication. *See* Sexual misconduct
Fox-Genovese, Elizabeth, 1n
Francis, Saint, 172, 174
Freedman's Bureau, 144

Freedmen's Hospital, 147
Freedom: definition of, 100, 117–18
Fulton Bag and Cotton Mill, 188

Gale, Edmond, 26
Gamble, Catharine, 39
Gamble, Robert, 30
Gantt, Harvey Bernard, 203–4
Gender biases, and blacks, 112–16
Gender conventions: violation of,
　10–11, 21, 27, 54, 59–60, 62, 63,
　66–67, 70–71
Gentleman's Agreement (Hobson), 170
Georgia, 206n48
Gibson, James K., 93
Gilman, Caroline Howard, 126
Gilpin, Zenobia, Dr., 148
Glover, William, 24
Godey's Lady's Book, 124
Godwin, Martha, 15–16
Gone with the Wind (Mitchell), 1
Governesses, 33
Gray, Archie Lee, 155
Great Depression, 145
Great Society, 205, 207
Gressette, L. Marion, 199
Griffin, Jemima, 18

Hall, Jacquelyn Dowd, 186n3
Hamilton-News Graphic, 107
Harland, Marion. *See* Terhune, Mary
　Virginia Hawes
Harris, Barbara, 161
Hastings, Dorothy, 16
Hawes, Judith Anna Smith, 120–21
Hawes, Samuel Pierce, 120–23
Hawthorne, Nathaniel, 6
Head Start, 205
Health care: and African Americans,
　138–57; and Alpha Kappa Alpha
　Mississippi Health Project, 144–56;

and poverty, 6, 138–39, 145–47;
public health policy and black
women's volunteer work, 138–57;
and racial politics, 6, 140; as
socialism, 155; and socioeconomic
factors, 152; and South Carolina
Council on Human Relations, 205;
as women's work, 141
Hemphill, James, 63
Hentz, Caroline Lee, 126
Herbert, R. Beverley, 191, 195, 200
Hickam, Eda, 5, 99–118, 111n19
Hickam, James, 100–101, 104–6,
    110–11
Hickam, Joseph, 99, 106, 108, 110–11
Hickam, Squire, 102, 106–7
Hickam v Hickam, 99–118, 111n19
Hidden Path (Terhune), 124
Hinde, Mary, 53, 62
Hinde, Susanna, 53
Hinde, Thomas, Doctor, 53–55, 68, 72
Historic Virginia Homes and Churches
    (Lancaster), 96
Hobson, Laura Z., 170
Hoffman, Elizabeth Avery Mills.
    See Waring, Elizabeth Avery Mills
    Hoffman
Hoffman, Frederick L., 140
Hollamon, Samuel, 15–16
Holland, Otho, 21
Hollings, Ernest F. (Fritz), 202, 203
Household boundaries, 34, 74–76
Household servants: African American
    stereotype as, 168; degradation
    of, 31–32; emancipated slaves
    as, 5, 99–118; governesses as, 33;
    hierarchy of, 48–49; and household
    boundaries, 34; indentured servants,
    19–22; legal rights of, 5; livery
    requirement for, 31; nurses as,
    33; and racial hierarchy, 33–34,

45; sexual vulnerability of, 20–21;
shortage of, 38–39; social life of,
19–22, 46–47; in Wirt household,
28–52. *See also* Housekeepers
Housekeepers: authority of, 36–37,
48; as chaperones, 33; as childcare
givers, 33–34; degradation of, 31–32;
demand for, 38; employment terms,
42–43; and household boundaries,
34; overview of, 3–4; as property of
employer, 40; and racial hierarchy,
28–30, 33, 37, 45; references for,
38–39; responsibilities of, 28–29,
33; as "second mistress," 36–37;
segregation from slaves, 32; slaves
as, 84; social life of, 46–47; white
housekeepers, 28–52; of Elizabeth
Wirt, 28–52. *See also* Household
servants
Howard University, 145, 147
Hutchinson, Anne, 66

Illiteracy. *See* Education
Indentured servants, 19–22
India, 189
Indian Woman's Conference on
    Educational and Social Reform, 189
Insanity. *See* Madness
Institution for Pacific Relations
    Conference, 189
Interracial marriage, 17–18
Interracial relations. *See* Race relations
Interracial sex, 17–19, 26, 67, 116
Iowa State University, 203

Jack, Alexander, 16
Jackson, Ida Louise, 6, 146, 151–53,
    155
Jackson, Leathy, 79–80, 86–87, 95
Jane Eyre (Brontë), 125
Janson, Charles, 60

Jarvis, John Wesler, 75
Jefferson, Thomas, 78
Jeffries, Simon, Captain, 18
Jesus, 68, 177, 178
Jim Crow legislation. *See* Segregation
Johnson, Lyndon B., 205
Jones, Sister Sarah, 63–64
Jordan, Betsey, 40
Judith (Terhune), 133–34

Kentucky, 128
Killers of the Dream (Smith), 163
Kilpatrick, William Heard, 188
King, Martin Luther, Jr., 160, 202
Kingham, Margaret, 24
Kingham, Robert, 24
King's Mountain, Battle of, 78
Ku Klux Klan, 7, 17, 184

Lancaster, Robert A., 96
Lane, Mrs., 48–50
League of Women Voters, 185, 193,
   196, 196n26, 198
Ledeen, Elizabeth C., 202
Lee, Anne, Mother, 66
Leslie, Kent Anderson, 1n
*Letters to Persons Who Are Engaged in
   Domestic Service* (Beecher), 45–46
Lincoln, Abraham, 96, 106–8
Literacy. *See* Education
Little Rock desegregation crisis, 163
Lost Cause mythology, 164
Lumpkin, Katharine Du Pre, 186, 188
Lynching, 116

MacCarty, Margaret, 18
Madison, James, 63
Madness: and black Methodists,
   59; and Enlightenment, 55–56;
   "hereditary insanity" in Southern
   families, 128; as illness, 72; and

Methodism, 53–73; and satanic
   possession, 55–56; superstitious
   beliefs about, 58, 71; and witchcraft
   accusations, 58, 68, 71; and women,
   53–73
Mallory, Arenia C., 6, 146
Marriage: and indentured servants,
   19–20; interracial marriage, 17–18;
   and slaves, 17–18, 75, 87, 92; and
   social status, 21–22
Marshall, Thurgood, 199
Marston, Elizabeth, 25
Martha Washington College, 95
Martin, John, Major, 62
Maryland, 128
Massachusetts, 123, 147
Matrilineage, 17–18
Matthias, Paul, 206
McCormack, John, 21
McGowan, Bartholomew, 21
McIntosh, Maria, 126
Meacham, James, 69
Medical care. *See* Health care
Meredith, James, 203
Metcalf, Ann, 21
Methodism: and interracial sex,
   67; male conversion to, 71–72;
   opposition to, in the South,
   53–73, 69n37; overview of, 4; and
   persecution, 53–54, 58, 60, 65, 70;
   and prostitution, 65; and sexual
   license, 54; and slaves, 77, 82–83,
   86; and witchcraft accusations, 68;
   and women's education, 95; and
   women's madness, 53–73
Mexican War, 89
Michener, James, 170
Middleton, Isaac, 16
Midwifery, 155
Mississippi Health Project, 6, 144–56

Mississippi State Board of Health, 154–55
Missouri, 99–118
Mitchell, George, 197, 200
Moore, Lucy D., 108
Moss-Side (Terhune), 124–25, 128
Myrdal, Gunnar, 170

National Association for the Advancement of Colored People (NAACP), 156, 178, 193, 195, 197–98
National Association of Colored Women, 138
National Health Office, 155
National Negro Health Week, 141–44
Nemesis (Terhune), 124–26
New Deal, 6, 138, 145, 152, 190, 191, 205, 207
New Jersey, 127–28
New York City, 188, 194
New York Times, 163
New York University, 153
Nickens, Portia, 156
Norfolk Virginian-Pilot, 176
North Carolina: court prosecution in colonial North Carolina, 14; indentured servants in, 13–14, 19–22; interracial commerce in, 12, 23–24, 26; interracial marriage in, 17; interracial sex in, 18–19, 26; penalties for sexual misconduct in, 15–18; prostitution in, 24–27; sexual misconduct in, 10–27
Norwood, Albertine Buck, 186–87
Norwood, Alice Buck. *See* Wright, Alice Norwood Spearman
Norwood, Samuel Wilkins, 186–87
Nugent, Hannah, 22
Nurses: as household servants, 33

Odum, Elizabeth, 21
Office of Negro Health Work, 144, 153
Old Dominion. *See* Virginia
Olmsted, Frederick Law, 32
Our Continent, 133–34
Outlook, 119
Owen, John, 62
Owings, Deborah, 58

Page, Thomas Nelson, 130, 135
Pargeter, William, 57
Patrilineage, 17–18
Patton, George, General, 172
Paul, Apostle, 64
Penn Center, 202
Penn Community Services, 197
Perkins, Frances, 153
Perry, Ann, 28–31, 34, 35, 37, 40–41, 50
Persecution: of Boyle, 177–78; of Methodists, 53–54, 58, 60, 65, 70
Peterson, Thomas, 24
Pike, James, Doctor, 163
Pinckney, Josephine, 196, 198–200
Pollock, Thomas, 11
Porter, Nancy, 46, 50
Possession and women, 53–73
Poverty: and African Americans, 138–39, 145–47, 167; and employment for women, 4, 37–38; and health care, 6, 138–39, 145–47; and prostitution, 24–26; and sexual misconduct, 3
Presbyterians, 55, 82, 163
Preston, Francis, 63
Progressive Era, 7–8, 140
Prosser, Gabriel, 133
Prostitution, 24–27, 65. *See also* Sexual misconduct
Protestantism, 123, 128, 163. *See also* specific denominations

Public health. *See* Health care
Public Health Service, U.S., 144, 153
Puckett, Elizabeth, 18

Race relations: and economics, 202;
    emancipated slaves as servants,
    99–118; and Episcopalians, 165–68,
    170–78, 180–82; and household
    servants, 33–34, 45; interracial
    marriage, 17–18; interracial sex,
    17–19, 67; interracial socializing,
    23–24, 201; in postbellum period,
    5, 99–118; and prostitution, 26;
    and public health, 140; and race
    consciousness, 107–8; and racial
    reeducation, 158–59, 166–67; and
    religious exclusiveness, 170; school
    desegregation, 163, 170, 177–78,
    192–204; slave family in Virginia,
    74–98; and South Carolina Council
    on Human Relations, 191, 195–96,
    199, 202–3; and sports, 202;
    and Wright, 192–97; and YMCA,
    162–63; and YWCA, 162–63, 185,
    189, 198. *See also* African Americans;
    Slaves
Rankin, Adam, 64
Redin, Jane, 45, 50–51
Reese, Fred M. Jr., 206
Religion: and feminism, 180–81;
    and gender importance, 55;
    and madness, 53–73; as public
    forum for women, 61–62; and
    racial exclusiveness, 170; and
    self-expression for women, 54; and
    slaves, 77, 82–83, 86–88; and social
    class, 55; and witchcraft accusations,
    58, 68, 71; women as zealots,
    62–63; women supporting, 55; and
    women's sexuality, 54, 65, 66. *See
    also* specific denominations

Remer, Robert. *See* Terhune, Mary
    Virginia Hawes
Revolutionary War, 55
Richmond Enquirer, 78
Richmond Times-Dispatch, 176
Riddle, Estelle Massey, 155
Ritchie, Thomas, 78
Roads, Daniel, 16
Roads, Mary, 16
Robinson, Jackie, 170, 202
Rock Hill Women's Club, 193
Roosevelt, Eleanor, 153, 163, 191
Roosevelt, Franklin D., 155, 163, 191
Rose, Lurany, 16
Rural Rehabilitation Program, 191
Russell, Elizabeth, 63

Saints Industrial and Literary School,
    146, 149
Sanders, Emily, 198
Saturday Evening Post, 158, 176
Savannah Federation of Colored
    Women's Clubs, 142
Sawyer, Joseph, 16
Sawyer, Sarah, 16
SCFWC. *See* South Carolina Federation
    of Women's Clubs (SCFWC)
Scott, Anne Firor, 1n
Scott, Ruth A., 151–52
Segregation, 6–7, 113–15, 169,
    196n26. *See also* Desegregation
Sellers, T. J., 171, 174
Servants. *See* Household servants;
    Housekeepers
Sexuality: and African Americans, 112,
    114, 115; and household servants'
    vulnerability, 20–21; interracial
    sex, 17–19, 67, 116; religion and
    women's sexuality, 54, 65, 66
Sexual misconduct: adultery as, 10–12,
    16; in colonial America, 3, 10–20;

fornication as, 16; of indentured servants, 20–22; interracial sex as, 17–19, 67; and Methodism, 54, 65; overview of, 3; prostitution, 24–27; punishment for, 11, 15, 17–19, 22–23, 26–27; and supernatural influences, 66

Shakespeare, William, 121, 125

Sharecroppers, 139, 145–46, 149–51, 154

Shelton, Virginia Campbell. *See* Campbell, Virginia Tabitha Jane

Shelton, William, 90

Sherwin, Dorothy, 23

Sikes, Ben, 16

Sikes, Joseph, 16

Sikes, William, 16

Simkins, Modjeska, 186n3

Simmons College, 147

Simons, Albert, 196

Simons, Harriet Porcher Stoney, 195–96, 198–200

"Sin of Racism," 183

Slaves: abolition of slavery, 99, 109; adoptive kin of, 80; and apprenticeship laws, 109; autonomy of, 77, 84, 86, 93–95, 97–98; and census, 105; child slaves, 18, 109, 109n; as childcare givers, 33–34; and crime, 11–12, 89–90, 92, 95, 97; definition of slavery, 100, 117–18; degradation of, 31–32; duties of, 80–82, 89, 102; education of, 4–5; emancipated slaves as servants, 5, 99–118; faithfulness of, 90–91; hierarchy with other servants, 3–4; and household boundaries, 34, 74–76; and interracial marriage, 17–18; and interracial sex, 17–19, 67; kin of, 80, 102–3, 117–18; legal rights of, 5, 99, 113; and literacy,

86, 88, 93, 95, 97; living quarters, 74–76; marriage of, 17–18, 75, 87, 92; and Methodism, 77, 82–83, 86, 88; mistress-slave relationships, 28–52; negative experiences of, 98; and owners' death, 93–97; in postbellum period, 5, 99–118; and public health policy, 140; relationship with owners, 79, 83, 89, 91, 97–98, 103–4; and religion, 77, 82–83, 86–88; runaway slaves, 12, 12n; segregation from household, 32, 74–76; and tuberculosis, 90; unlicensed trade with, 11–12; Virginia slave family, 74–98; as wet-nurses, 81

Smith, Alfred Edgar, 153

Smith, Ellison DuRant ("Cotton Ed"), United States Senator, 193

Smith, Judith Anna. *See* Hawes, Judith Anna Smith

Smith, Lillian, 162–64, 173–74, 176, 186

Snell, Roger, 10–11

Snelling, Paula, 186

Social hierarchy: challenges to, 10–12

Socialism, 155, 189–91

Social Security Act, 153, 155

Sons of Temperance, 86

South Carolina: Battle of King's Mountain, 78; desegregation in, 184–86, 192–204; literacy in, 205; rural resettlement program in, 190–91

South Carolina Commission on Interracial Cooperation, 191

South Carolina Conference of the NAACP, 193, 198, 202

South Carolina Council for Human Rights, 206

South Carolina Council on Human

Relations, 7, 185, 189, 192, 200–201, 203, 206n48
South Carolina Department of Education, 190
South Carolina Federation of Women's Clubs (SCFWC), 185, 189, 192
South Carolina General Assembly, 198
South Carolina League of Women Voters, 196
South Carolina State Employment Service, 191
South Carolina State Law Enforcement Division, 203
Southeast Settlement House, 148
Southern Association for Women Historians, 2
Southern Cause, 7
Southern Christian Leadership Conference, 160, 202
Southern Code, 161, 165–66, 169, 171, 173, 179
Southern Conferences on Women's History, 2, 7
Southern Literary Messenger, 126
Southern Regional Council (SRC), 163, 184, 191, 195–96, 199, 205–6
Southern White Myth, 178
Southern women. *See* Women
Soviet Union, 187
Spearman, Alice Norwood. *See* Wright, Alice Norwood Spearman
Spearman, Eugene H., 191, 207
Spearman, Eugene H. Jr., 191
SPEED-UP, 205
Spellman, John, 10–11
Spruill, Julia Cherry, 1n
SRC. *See* Southern Regional Council (SRC) States' Rights Leagues, 184
Steel, Dorothy, 10–11, 27
Steel, William, 10–11
Stowe, Harriet Beecher, 169

Strange Fruit (Smith), 163
Student Council on Human Relations, 202
Student Program for Educational and Economic Development for Underprivileged People (SPEED-UP), 205
Sunnybank (Terhune), 129–31, 134
Swanson, Gregory, 169, 170–71
Sweden, 189
Symons, Damaris, 18–19

Tales of the South Pacific (Michener), 170
Taylor, William R., 130n22
Tennessee, 78, 79, 81–82, 85, 88, 90, 92–93, 97
Terhune, Albert Payson, 136–37
Terhune, Edward Payson, 127
Terhune, Mary Virginia Hawes: abolitionist views of, 123; biography of, 5–6; Civil War as literary topic for, 128–31, 134; during Civil War years, 127–28; domestic manuals written by, 132; education of, 121–22; English ancestry of, 131; literary career of and books by, 119–20, 124–27, 129–35; parentage of, 120–21; pseudonyms of, 124, 124n10; social prejudices of, 123; southern identity in writing of, 119–37; view of African Americans, 133; women's club affiliations of, 136
Thirteenth Amendment, 96
Thompson, John R., 125
Tice, Jacob, 20
Tillet, Ann, 18
Tillet, Ruth, 18
Tool, Frances, 22
Tourgee, Albion, 133–34

Tribune, 171
Trotter, James, 25
True as Steel (Terhune), 125
Tucker, Henry St. George, 79
Tufts Medical College, 147
Turner, Nat, 133
Tuskegee Institute, 149

Underwood, Felix J., Doctor, 154
Union Theological Seminary, 188
Unitarianism, 123
United Church Women, 193
United Daughters of the Confederacy, 136
University of California at Berkeley, 146
University of Mississippi, 203
University of South Carolina, 204
University of Virginia, 168, 169
Urmston, Reverend, 15

Vail, Jeremiah, 22
Valentine, Hannah: autonomy of, 86; as caregiver for elderly, 90; emancipation of, 97–98; relationship with other slaves, 80–81; relationship with owners, 76–78; and religion, 81–82; sale of family members, 91–92, 94–95, 97
Valentine, Michael, 80, 82, 84, 88, 94–95
Vardaman, James K., 114
Villette (Brontë), 125
Vina, Elizabeth, 10–11
Virginia: birthplace of Dorothy Boulding Ferebee, 147; as "church," 164; interracial marriage in, 17; in literature, 126, 129, 133; as "Old Dominion," 135; politics in antebellum Virginia, 78, 83–85, 89–90; race relations in,
165–68, 170–78, 180–82; school desegregation in, 177; sexual misconduct in, 14; slave family in, 74–98
Virginia Council on Human Relations, 178
Virginia Gazette, 57–58
Virginia Historical Society, 135
Virginia Military Institute, 85
Virgin Mary, 66
Volunteerism, 138–57, 174

Wallace, Elizabeth, 23
Wallace, Mary, 23
Walsh, Chad, Reverend, 168
Waltham, William, 24
Ward, Thomas, 21
Waring, Annie Gammell, 194
Waring, Elizabeth Avery Mills Hoffman, 194
Waring, J. Waties, 193–97, 200
Waring, Mary Fitzbutler, 138
Warren, Jane, 20
Washington, Booker T., 141
Washington, George, 34n11, 135
Washington, Martha, 34n11, 35
Washington, Mary Ball, 135
Washington Post, 177
Wells, George, 69
Wesley, John, 56, 58
Western Insane Asylum of Virginia, 85
Wheeler, Marjorie Spruill, 2n1
Whigs, 127
White housekeepers. *See* Housekeepers
Wilde, Oscar, 1
Williams, Mary E., 149
Williamson, Sarah, 18
Wirt, Elizabeth, 3, 28–52
Wirt, William, 3, 28–52
Witches, 58, 66, 68, 71
"Witness of a Lone Layman," 159, 180

Wolfe, Margaret Ripley, 2n1
Women: and African American health
    care, 138–57; church as public
    forum for, 61–62; control of, 53–55,
    64; and demonic possession, 53–73;
    education of, 121–22, 167–68,
    187–88; and enthusiasm, 53–73;
    gender convention violation of, 54,
    59–60, 62, 63, 66–67, 70–71; image
    of Southern lady, 1; interracial sex
    and white women, 17, 67; and
    madness, 53–73; moral authority
    of, 54, 63, 70–72; and poverty,
    4, 24–25, 37–38; and "privileged
    subordination," 174–75; and
    prostitution, 24–27; and racial caste
    system, 112; as racists, 185; religious
    leadership of, 63, 174; religious
    rebellion of, 4; as religious zealots,
    62–63; and self-expression through
    religion, 54; sexual vulnerability
    of female servants, 20–21; and
    volunteerism, 141–57, 174; and

    witchcraft accusations, 58, 68,
    71. *See also* Household servants;
    Housekeepers; and specific women
Women's Meeting of the Pasquotank
    Society of Friends, 18
Women's rights movement, 123
Workers' Education, 190–91
Works Progress Administration (WPA),
    153, 190
Wright, Alice Norwood Spearman: and
    desegregation, 7, 184–85, 191–204;
    education of, 187–88; as feminist,
    186–87, 207; and literacy programs,
    205; marriage of, 191; parentage of,
    186–87; personality of, 186n3; as
    socialist, 189–91
Wright, Benjamin, 181
Wright, Marion A., 193, 197, 199–200,
    206, 207
Wright, Mary C., Doctor, 151

YMCA, 162–63
YWCA, 162–63, 185, 187–89, 193,
    198